Public Health Law

Public health activity, and the state's public health responsibilities to assure the conditions in which people can be healthy, can only be achieved through different means of social coordination. This places law and regulation at the heart of public health. They are fundamental both to methods of achieving public health goals and to constraints that may be put on public health activity. As such, trainees, practitioners, and leaders in public health need to understand the breadth and nature of wide-ranging legal and regulatory approaches and the place of ethics in public health.

Public Health Law, written by three leading scholars in the field, defines and examines this crucial area of study and practice. It advances an agenda whose scope extends far beyond that covered in traditional medical law and health care law texts. The authors provide an account of the scale of contemporary public health policy and practice and explain its philosophical depths and implications and its long legislative and regulatory history. They advance a definition of the field and explore how different legal approaches may serve and advance or constrain and delimit public health agendas.

This ground-breaking book presents the field of public health ethics and law and goes on to examine the impact within the UK of private law, criminal law, public law, EU and international law, and 'softer' regulatory approaches. It is a primary point of reference for scholars, practitioners, and leaders working in public health, particularly those with an interest in law, policy, and ethics.

John Coggon is Professor of Law at Bristol University, UK, and an Honorary Member of the UK's Faculty of Public Health.

Keith Syrett is Professor of Public Health Law at Cardiff University, UK.

A. M. Viens is Associate Professor in Law at the University of Southampton, UK.

'This book is a seminal addition to the field of public health law. Through ten thoroughly readable chapters, the book provides an invaluable exploration of the nature of public health and its philosophical underpinnings, and the central importance of law to public health policy and practice. The book – a tour de force in its concise and intellectual presentation – will leave those studying and working in public health in no doubt as to the vital place of public health law in their thinking.'

Professor Anthony Kessel, Director of Global Public Health, Public Health England;
Honorary Professor, London School of Hygiene & Tropical Medicine

'Trainees and practitioners will benefit significantly from this accessible introduction to the field of public health law, broadly conceived and clearly explained. It explains how ethics impacts on public health practice, the history of public health regulation in the UK, and the many different ways that contemporary laws can both serve and constrain public health. After thirty years in public health I thought I had heard all this, argued about it, considered it a talk shop subject. But this book brought it alive and new and fresh to me. Public health ethics and law is live, vital and kicking! I commend this book to everyone in public health – young and old, specialist practitioner or interested enthusiast. The public needs to be interested and concerned about public health ethics and law. This is a good place to start.'

Professor John Middleton, President, UK Faculty of Public Health

'This excellent book has now filled the gap by providing the necessary tools for the development of public health law courses, and provides the knowledge behind the use of public health law as a public health tool. It is to be hoped that this volume will prompt an understanding of the importance of law in the practice of public health. I highly recommend it to anyone involved in the study or practice of issues of public health.'

Professor Robyn Martin, Emeritus Professor of Public Health Law,
Centre for Research in Primary and Community Care, University of Hertfordshire

Public Health Law

Ethics, Governance, and Regulation

John Coggon, Keith Syrett, and A. M. Viens

Routledge
Taylor & Francis Group

LONDON AND NEW YORK

First published 2017
by Routledge
2 Park Square, Milton Park, Abingdon, Oxon OX14 4RN

and by Routledge
711 Third Avenue, New York, NY 10017

Routledge is an imprint of the Taylor & Francis Group, an informa business

British Library Cataloguing in Publication Data
A catalogue record for this book is available from the British Library

Library of Congress Cataloging in Publication Data
Names: Coggon, John, 1980– author. | Syrett, Keith, author. | Viens, A. M. (Adrian M.),
    author.
Title: Public health law : ethics, governance, and regulation / John Coggon, Keith
    Syrett, A. M. Viens.
Description: Abingdon, Oxon ; New York, NY : Routledge, 2017. | Includes
    bibliographical references.
Identifiers: LCCN 2016043156 | ISBN 9781138790759 (hbk.) | ISBN 9781138790780 (pbk.) |
    ISBN 9781315764023 (ebook)
Subjects: | MESH: Public Health—legislation & jurisprudence | Legislation as Topic |
    Europe
Classification: LCC RA393 | NLM W 33 GA1 | DDC 362.1—dc23
LC record available at https://lccn.loc.gov/2016043156

ISBN: 978-1-138-79075-9 (hbk)
ISBN: 978-1-138-79078-0 (pbk)
ISBN: 978-1-315-76402-3 (ebk)

Typeset in Joanna MT
by Apex CoVantage, LLC

MIX
Paper from
responsible sources
FSC FSC® C013056
www.fsc.org

Printed and bound in Great Britain by
TJ International Ltd, Padstow, Cornwall

Contents

Acknowledgments   vii
Introduction   ix

PART I
Foundations   1

1   Public health   3

2   Public health, philosophy, and ethics   19

3   The evolution of public health legislation and regulation   37

PART II
The field of public health law   63

4   Defining the scope of public health law   65

5   Private law and public health   77

6   Criminal law and public health   101

7   Public law and public health   117

8   European Union law, international law, and public health   139

9   Policy, self-regulation, and governance for public health   161

PART III
Concluding reflections   181

10   Law and public health: future directions   183

Index   191

Acknowledgments

In the production of this work, we have accumulated various debts of gratitude. It is a work that has developed in parallel with our own teaching and research agendas, and we owe thanks to students and collaborators for their invaluable support in helping our ideas and understandings to evolve. We should particularly like to thank Angus Dawson, Larry Gostin, and Robyn Martin for the inspiration and support they have offered us over several years. We have also very gratefully received comments on earlier drafts of various chapters of the work and owe particular thanks to David Coggon, Paula Giliker, Sheelagh McGuinness, Elen Stokes, and Caroline Vass. We are also very grateful to the editorial and production teams at Routledge for all of their encouragement and assistance.

Introduction

Few questions are of greater importance, socially or ethically, than how governments assure the conditions in which people can be healthy. In examining such questions, there is a clear need for understanding of laws and other modes of social coordination. The past fifteen years have seen a surge in interest in public health ethics and law, both in teaching and research agendas. However, whilst there is a wealth of textbooks on the legal regulation of medicine and health care, relatively little attention has been given to producing similar works on the field of *Public Health Law*, particularly in the UK. It is in response to the problem of this deficit that we have developed the current book. Our aim in developing a book-length presentation of the subject has been to produce a specialist text that will be accessible to students, practitioners, and policy-makers from a range of disciplinary backgrounds, explaining and examining how legal and regulatory approaches do and can serve to advance, or constrain, public health agendas.

Our primary focus is the law of the jurisdiction of England and Wales, although we do also engage broader legal perspectives. Our hope is that the book might serve as a core text on degree level (primarily postgraduate) and professional training courses in public health ethics and law, or on degrees and courses with a strong public health law and policy component. As a resource, we aim that it should serve as a primary point of reference for scholars, practitioners, and policy-makers working in public health and allied health professions and fields.

Our approach is designed to explain the essence of the field of public health law, characterised as:

> A field of study and practice that concerns those aspects of law, policy, and regulation that advance or place constraints upon the protection and promotion of health (howsoever understood) within, between, and across populations.

In order to do this, the book is divided into three parts. Part I comprises three foundational chapters. These first explain how we understand the idea of public health itself, which we take to be a broad field of practice. We then explore the role of philosophy – and especially ethics – in relation to public health activity, and finally present a history of public health legislation and regulation in the UK.

Part II of the book then engages in detail with the contemporary field of public health law. This entails, in Chapter 4, an explanation and rationale for our definition of the field, followed by five chapters that aim to demonstrate the relationships between public health and different areas of law. Such an approach may be contrasted with a problem-based approach (e.g. a text that focuses on specific public health issues such as tobacco regulation). Our aim, instead, has been to provide a clear understanding of how the law 'works' to advance or limit public health agendas. This entails chapters respectively on private law, criminal law, public law, EU and international law, and 'softer' modes of governance. Rather than present a comprehensive picture of every law that might be relevant to public health (a task that would not be possible in a single book), we explain different areas of law and exemplify their pertinence through discussion of case studies.

Part III of the book comprises a short, concluding chapter. This allows some closing reflections on how public health law, as a field of study and of practice, might develop over time. Overall, our project aims to maximise the explanatory potential and utility that might be gained in a single book on this subject, for as wide an audience as possible. Our hope is that the work will provide a useful reference point and a foundation for advances in study and practice in the field.

We have sought to present the law as it stands up to 1 November 2016.

Part I

Foundations

Chapter 1

Public health

1.1 Why public health and law?

This book defines and explores the field of public health law, examining its foundations, its scope and limits, and its many and varied facets. It explains how legal and other regulatory measures can both serve and restrict the pursuit of agendas in public health. Our aim is that it should provide an introduction for practitioners, policy-makers, students, scholars, and general readers who are interested in public health ethics and law and who want to understand how they impinge on different aspects of public health policy and practice. Contemporary understandings of public health conceive a field whose breadth extends across political divides and transcends social and jurisdictional boundaries. Conceptually, public health is not limited to one sector or discipline. Rather it pervades governmental activities and social responsibilities, drawing on expertise in the humanities and social and natural sciences, as well as clinical medicine. It entails responding to and preventing disease, assuring a sound infrastructure to provide a sanitary environment, and understanding and addressing the social determinants of ill health.[1]

In addressing this vast agenda, various approaches may be adopted, ranging from self-regulation, through different private and policy interventions that might 'nudge' or 'push' people and organisations in particular directions, to hard legal provisions that more forcefully direct conduct and behaviour. An understanding is needed, therefore, of how public health practice may both be facilitated by legislation as well as constrained by legal, political, and social standards that prioritise competing values, such as individual or economic liberty. This book considers the importance of different modes of governance to public health activity; their intrinsic limitations; and the constraints that legal and political rules, principles, and norms can impose on the advancement of public health agendas.

It is striking that there are not already more legal textbooks in this area.[2] Textbooks on health care ethics and law abound, yet there is a remarkable dearth of similar works with a focus on public health.[3] The ethical provision of health care is clearly a crucial component of the state's responsibility for health, and it is therefore proper that health care law should

---

1 See also Lawrence Gostin and Lindsay Wiley, *Public Health Law: Power, Duty Restraint* (3rd edn., Berkeley: University of California Press 2016).
2 The leading text is Gostin and Wiley's book, which focuses primarily on US law: ibid.
3 See Keith Syrett and Oliver Quick, 'Pedagogical Promise and Problems: Teaching Public Health Law' (2009) 123 *Public Health* 222. In the UK, there are some book-length works, most notably Robin Martyn and Linda Johnson (eds), *Law and the Public Dimension of Health* (London: Routledge-Cavendish 2001).

be the subject of so much attention. But, within the ethico-legal literature, there are equally important, yet much less comprehensively addressed, questions both about the provision of a sound public health infrastructure, and concerning the basis and scope of a defensible political response to the social determinants of health.[4] Notwithstanding that textbooks on health care law often include a limited discussion of public health,[5] it is particularly surprising that there are few dedicated public health law texts because there are especially strong and important roles for governance in the sphere of public health. Throughout this work, we relate our discussion of public health law to three spheres of public health responsibility: systems of health care, the public health infrastructure, and the wider social determinants of health. In brief, we understand these core public health functions respectively as:

● *Systems of health care*: government has a core responsibility to ensure that people have access to a health care system, in particular to respond to conditions of ill health. In the context of English law,[6] this is explicit in the overarching responsibility of the Secretary of State for Health to promote a comprehensive health service that will improve people's physical and mental health through prevention, diagnosis, and treatment of illness.[7]
● *Public health infrastructure*: government has a core responsibility to provide wider infrastructural conditions that are necessary for good health – for example, in assuring a sanitary environment (e.g. with good sewerage systems, provision for proper waste disposal). In the context of English law, such matters fall within the purview of various sectors and levels of government, with roles for different departments in both central and local administration.[8]
● *The social determinants of health*: government has a core responsibility, through understandings generated in social epidemiology and related disciplines, to consider and respond to insights into the health impacts of our social environments. In the context of English law, this might be related in part to obligations to reduce health inequalities[9] and in part to wider concerns about the discharge of public health duties in light of concerns for social justice.[10]

Beyond governmental responsibilities, the advancement of 'public health' has been taken to embrace also the activities and responsibilities of private actors. Thus, without clarification, there is a risk of misunderstanding when people use the term 'public health'.[11] In this book, we adopt a broad understanding of public health activity, and in the sections that follow, we

---

4 Lawrence Gostin, Foreword, in John Coggon, *What Makes Health Public? A Critical Evaluation of Moral, Legal, and Political Claims in Public Health* (Cambridge: Cambridge University Press 2012); Lawrence Gostin, *Global Health Law* (Cambridge, MA: Harvard University Press 2014), chapter 14.
5 See e.g. J.K. Mason and Graeme Laurie, *Mason and McCall Smith's Law and Medical Ethics* (7th edn., Oxford: Oxford University Press 2013); Jonathan Herring, *Medical Law and Ethics* (5th edn., Oxford: Oxford University Press 2014).
6 Note that the term 'English law' refers to the law extant in the jurisdiction of England and Wales, albeit that (as discussed in Chapters 3 and 7) legislative powers, including those relating to health, have been devolved to Wales since 1998. There are distinct systems of law in Scotland and Northern Ireland. These will not be the primary focus of this text, although they will be referenced on occasion.
7 See National Health Service Act 2006, s. 1 (as amended); Health and Social Care Act 2012, s. 1. Note that, in the context of this textbook, we focus less on this first component of public health responsibility given the range of existing works that already address the laws that govern the health care system.
8 See National Health Service Act 2006, ss. 2A ("Secretary of State's duty as to protection of public health"), 2B ("Functions of local authorities and Secretary of State as to improvement of public health"); and further the discussion in Chapter 7.
9 See ibid, s. 1C.
10 E.g. in the exercise of the powers and obligations under ibid, ss. 2A and 2B.
11 See Coggon (n 4), chapter 3.

set out how we conceive the field, and why. It will become apparent that the collective activity of public health requires the sorts of coordination that necessarily invite different forms of state intervention or oversight.[12] In other words, an understanding of public health ethics and law is essential to a full understanding of public health.

We will describe, furthermore, how a great deal of potential public health activity sits in the shadow of the 'prevention paradox', outlined by Geoffrey Rose.[13] This includes the observation that much of the collective burden of disease in the general population is borne by people who, before the onset of their illness, would be classed as having relatively low risk. Despite being at low risk individually, they contribute substantially to overall incidence because they are much larger in number than the minority who are at high risk. This may make it hard to achieve major gains by incentivising individuals towards 'healthier living', since, amongst the 'low-risk' people who generate the majority of cases, individual benefits will be minimal.

The prevention paradox presents a particular challenge to governance for population health. Reduction of salt intake, for example, has demonstrable health benefits if followed across a low-risk population, but it will not obviously benefit any individual member of that population. So how (if it all) do we establish that, as a matter of public policy, consumption of salt should be reduced and, from there, develop viable regulatory measures to achieve that goal? Throughout this book, we will explore in depth the sorts of issues that these two questions raise but note immediately the logical importance of having means of effecting changes in behaviour where individuals acting alone may not be motivated to alter their lifestyle. Coordinating mechanisms peculiar to law, and to governance more widely, stand centre stage.

To come to a definition of public health that is pertinent to our study, we first consider two preliminary questions. In section 1.2, we explain how the goals of public health might be *approached*. In doing this, we highlight the particular insights that can be achieved by studying populations, and the distinctive reasons for targeting health measures at populations. Then, in section 1.3, we outline approaches to understanding of the field from the perspective of public health ethics and law. Next, we come to a definition of public health, setting it in the context of those offered by three authoritative sources: the Faculty of Public Health (FPH), the UK Government (with particular reference to Public Health England [PHE]), and the World Health Organization (WHO). In section 1.5, we contextualise our broad definition of public health within critical discussions of the field, and in section 1.6, we emphasise key areas of focus, key approaches, and key stakeholders, all of which fall under our spotlight throughout the book.

1.2 Public health approaches: populations and institutions

Our route to characterising public health as a broad endeavour is founded on an analysis of the *concerns* that motivate contemporary interest in the field.[14] We do not suggest that there is

---

12 cf Mark Rothstein, 'Rethinking the Meaning of Public Health' (2002) 30 *Journal of Law, Medicine and Ethics* 144.
13 Geoffrey Rose, 'Sick Individuals and Sick Populations' (1985) 14 *International Journal of Epidemiology* 32.
14 See the characterisations outlined in section 1.4, below. Contrast also the concerns of authors regarding public health law and policy, such as Gostin and Wiley (n 1); Wendy Parmet, *Populations, Public Health, and the Law* (Washington: Georgetown University Press 2009); Lindsay Wiley, 'Rethinking the New Public Health' (2012) 69 *Washington and Lee Law Review* 207.

a universal consensus amongst practitioners, researchers, policy-makers, and theorists on the exact scope of public health.[15] But there is a general recognition that *populations* stand at the centre of public health, and this is especially so in two important ways. First, public health research builds on understandings derived by reference to health within and across different populations; the focus is on groups of people, rather than just individuals.[16] Second, public health policies and interventions generally operate through collective measures, which target populations. That is to say, when it comes to implementation, public health is about shared responsibility for health and about aiming to improve health through collectively organised means.[17] A corollary of this latter point is that, as well as identifying 'populations' as a core interest, there is a strong focus on the roles and legitimacy of legal, political, and social institutions. Because public health practice requires collective interventions, we need to understand how institutions might effect different measures and how to assess the legitimacy of their doing so.

To flesh out this point, it is useful to begin by considering Geoffrey Rose's analysis in his celebrated paper 'Sick Individuals and Sick Populations'.[18] In that work, Rose outlines how epidemiological research – research that examines how health compares within and across different populations and that aims to understand causes and effects of population health phenomena – affords insights distinct from those offered by clinical medicine and those available when only individuals or a single population are studied. In beginning to explain how and why these insights contrast, Rose says:

> If everyone smoked 20 cigarettes a day, then clinical, case-control and cohort studies alike would lead us to conclude that lung cancer was a genetic disease; and in one sense that would be true, since if everyone is exposed to the necessary agent, then the distribution of cases is wholly determined by individual susceptibility.[19]

In other words, to reach our current understanding of the health impacts of smoking tobacco, an approach was required that could compare two populations – smokers and non-smokers. It was only by that method that we could move towards a proof that smoking tobacco causes disease.[20]

Drawing out his point, Rose emphasises the importance of looking, not just for the causes of individual cases of disease, but also for reasons why the frequency of disease varies between different populations. Here, his concern takes us beyond asking why certain individuals suffer ill health, to looking at why one entire population exhibits a higher rate of a particular disease than another entire population. An example that Rose uses to demonstrate the difference between the population and individual perspective concerns levels of serum cholesterol.[21] If we look only at determinants of differences in cholesterol levels within a population, he argues, we can observe individual characteristics (e.g. genetic constitution) that

---

15 Note that some authors do elicit commonalities from across a range of definitions of public health: see e.g. Parmet ibid; Marcel Verweij and Angus Dawson, 'The Meaning of "Public" in "Public Health"' in Angus Dawson and Marcel Verweij (eds), *Ethics, Prevention, and Public Health* (Oxford: Oxford University Press 2007) 13–29.
16 For an introduction, see David Coggon, Geoffrey Rose and David Barker, *Epidemiology for the Uninitiated* (5th edn., London: BMJ Books 2003).
17 See Charles Guest, Walter Ricciardi, Ichiro Kawachi, and Iain Lang (eds), *Oxford Handbook of Public Health Practice* (3rd edn., Oxford: Oxford University Press 2013).
18 Rose (n 13).
19 ibid, 32.
20 Richard Doll and A Bradford Hill, 'The Mortality of Doctors in Relation to Their Smoking Habits' (1954) 1 (4877) *British Medical Journal* 1451.
21 Rose (n 12), 34.

explain variation. But these do not necessarily explain why one whole population – say, men in Finland – has higher average levels of serum cholesterol than another – say, men in Japan.

Rose demonstrates how, by studying populations, we may find otherwise inaccessible explanations of why there is an unusually high or low occurrence of a particular disease in a community. In this way, public health research has, over time, afforded valuable insights into the *associations* of health status with particular behaviours and environmental conditions. And it has also allowed elucidation of causal mechanisms, enabling scientists to predict health outcomes given the different circumstances of different groups. This work of epidemiologists has led notably to a large and growing literature on the *social determinants of health*, advanced by scholars such as Michael Marmot.[22] Public health research allows an understanding of how variations in our physical and social environments, and our ways of living and working, correlate with, and in some cases cause, specific good or poor health outcomes.

As well as speaking to the unique insights afforded by public health research, Rose goes on to discuss practical responses that might be advanced in response to what is learned through epidemiological analysis. If we understand (probable) causes of the incidence of ill health within a population, we may also understand how to stop it occurring. It is in particular at this stage that we may appreciate the importance of understanding public health law. The point is well explained if we take a step back and consider what we might label a *governmental perspective* on health. At the heart of health policy and practice, Rose suggests, there are two sorts of approach. First, we can focus on treatment of individuals who have developed disease (cases): here, we aim to remediate existing disease and illness, focussing on individual patients and attempting to effect a cure, or at least to mitigate their impact. Second, we can develop *preventive measures*, which aim either to stop a disease arising altogether, or more modestly to reduce its incidence, prevalence, or severity in a community. In this case, the focus is on populations and their social and physical environment.

An example of a health care intervention would be treatment of a patient who is a smoker and presents to her GP complaining of certain symptoms: she is coughing up blood, and on further inquiry, additional symptoms emerge. Following clinical analysis, she is found to have lung cancer, for which treatment is attempted through chemo- and radiotherapy. An example of a preventive approach, by contrast, would be smoking cessation programmes, which aim to reduce the overall incidence of lung cancer (and other respiratory disease) in the target population. Through coordinated measures that reduce rates of smoking in a population – amongst both those who would, and those who would not, go on to suffer respiratory disease – overall rates of disease are lowered.

Most of what we have said so far will be familiar to readers who research or work in public health. The groundwork presented in this section leads into the definitions of public health from which we draw. However, before outlining those definitions, one more piece of background analysis is needed. The different ways of considering populations – in terms of research and in terms of approaches to health protection – lead, in legal and regulatory spheres, to questions about our understanding of how the world *is* and how we think it *should be*. In the jargon of lawyers and philosophers, it moves us to considerations of the relationships between the *descriptive* and the *normative*. An understanding of these terms, and their distinctions and relationships, is crucial to public health practice and public health law.

---

22 See e.g. Michael Marmot, *Status Syndrome: How Your Social Standing Directly Affects Your Health and Life Expectancy* (London: Bloomsbury 2004); Michael Marmot, *The Health Gap: The Challenge of An Unequal World* (London: Bloomsbury 2015).

1.3 The descriptive and the normative in public health

Following directly from the ideas presented in section 1.2, we can say that those interested in public health have an interest in *both* descriptive and normative concepts. When we speak of descriptive concepts, we mean matters that are points of (e.g. scientific) fact. For example, a consideration of descriptive studies might show that health status is worse in a population whose constituent members consume over 14 units of alcohol per week as compared with a population whose members consume 14 or fewer units per week.[23] In this instance, we have a scientific observation: an account of, and potentially an explanation for, a particular fact about the world. Although this descriptive side of public health may be seen as neutral, because it relates itself to science, it should be noted that controversy can arise both in regard to the soundness of the methods used in conducting the research and the 'objective' data that establish the relative health of populations.[24] However, for present purposes, we would emphasise that descriptive claims do not, of themselves, imply prescriptive measures. Knowledge about the health impacts of alcohol consumption does not equate to an understanding of whether, and if so how, alcohol should be regulated. So, in its descriptive sense, public health research simply, and non-directively, tells us about the world: we use it to understand, for example, that alcohol consumption heightens the risks of heart disease, cancer, liver disease, and epilepsy.

When we speak of normative concepts, by contrast, we are suggesting that a particular course of action (or inaction) is *prescribed*, rather than merely *described*. To continue the example given in the previous paragraph: scientists have shown that heavier drinking causes poorer health outcomes. As we move into normative territory – into offering an *evaluation* and a 'prescription' – we say that, on the basis of what our research has shown, particular governmental responses are due. So we might move from the descriptive evidence that alcohol causes population-level health harms to the normative assertion that this is a problem to which government should respond through measures such as, for example, the imposition of minimum pricing on alcoholic drinks.

In regard to normative ideas, it will always, in some sense, be overtly controversial to come to the view that we should act on a particular health concern in any given way. First, people will reasonably disagree on what specific matters are rightly considered to be other people's business and, thus, the proper subject of law and policy. For example, some will say that a person's drinking habits are no-one else's concern and not a matter that is properly impacted by public policy.[25] In crude terms, they will say, 'It is none of *your* business what I choose to drink. And, less still, the business of the government and meddling professionals!' Others will disagree and advance arguments for why health concerns are shared concerns.[26]

At another level, people may agree that a health-affecting matter – say, alcohol consumption – is a shared concern but will reasonably disagree about what constitutes an appropriate means of intervention, or why an intervention might be justified. For example, some will say that public information campaigns are acceptable, whilst coercive measures to

---

23 See Department of Health, *Alcohol Guidelines Review – Report from the Guidelines Development Group to the UK Chief Medical Officers* (London: Department of Health 2016).

24 Sam Harper, Nicholas King, Stephen Meersman, Marsha Reichman, Nancy Breen, and John Lynch, 'Implicit Value Judgments in the Measurement of Health Inequalities' (2010) 88 *Milbank Quarterly* 4.

25 cf Richard Epstein, 'In Defense of the "Old" Public Health' (2004) 69 *Brooklyn Law Review* 1421.

26 cf Lawrence Gostin and Gregg Bloche, 'The Politics of Public Health: A Response to Epstein' (2003) 46 *Perspectives in Biology and Medicine* S160.

regulate what we drink cannot be justified. Here, the focus of argument is on what justifies particular practical responses to public health problems. In the next chapter, we explore the nature of ethical argument in regard to public health and then go on to look at how law and regulation might serve or limit public health activity. We now move, in section 1.4, to give an overview and analysis of influential positions on how the scope of public health should be defined. When considering these positions, it is important to examine both their descriptive and their normative components, to understand the 'jurisdiction' that they claim, and to reflect on how they give rise to scientific understanding, social missions, and political controls and coordination.

1.4 Key definitions of public health

Within the literature on public health, wide-ranging conceptual and analytical claims are advanced to support different definitions of its scope. That is to say, different authors find themselves motivated by different concerns about how it makes sense to define the field. Whilst in this chapter we will not attempt anything approaching a full survey of the various definitions that have been proposed,[27] we present in this section some of the most influential – and broad – definitions of public health. We will then go on in section 1.5 to note some of the critical discussion of adopting a broad understanding of the field and explain our rationale for adopting such an understanding. It will become evident that advocates for wide definitions are driven to find comprehensive means of assuring good health across the population as a whole. A broad definition looks both to 'upstream issues' – to means of pre-empting the occurrence of ill health in different populations – and to responsive means of addressing immediate health needs. Similarly to public health law scholars such as Lawrence Gostin, we apply our legal analysis to an understanding of public health as operating within the three arenas as outlined in section 1.1: responsibilities to provide a health care system, responsibilities to ensure there is a sound public health infrastructure, and responsibilities to understand and influence the social determinants of health and respond to problems of health inequalities.

Our starting point for an analysis of the concept of public health, which leads to this comprehensive approach, is Charles-Edward Winslow's celebrated characterisation of the field:

> Public health is the science and the art of preventing disease, prolonging life, and promoting physical health and efficiency through organized community efforts for the sanitation of the environment, the control of community infections, the education of the individual in principles of personal hygiene, the organization of medical and nursing service for the early diagnosis and preventive treatment of disease, and the development of the social machinery which will ensure to every individual in the community a standard of living adequate for the maintenance of health.
>
> Public health conceived in these terms will be something vastly different from the exercise of the purely police power which has been its principal manifestation in the past.[28]

Winslow's definition of public health, now almost a hundred years old, is clearly echoed in many contemporary characterisations.[29] For present purposes, we will refer to three definitions

---

27 For a deeper analysis of different characterisations of public health, see Coggon (n 4), chapter 3.
28 Charles-Edward Winslow, 'The Untilled Fields of Public Health' (1920) 51 (1306) *Science* 23, 30.
29 See Verweij and Dawson (n 15).

that are particularly pertinent in the context of public health law in England: those respectively of the Faculty of Public Health (FPH), Public Health England (PHE), and the World Health Organization (WHO).

1.4.1 The Faculty of Public Health

FPH describes itself as 'the standard setting body for specialists in public health in the United Kingdom'.[30] It is a joint faculty of the Royal Colleges of Physicians, with a membership drawn from various professional backgrounds and working in a range of areas. It works towards its strategic goals through collaborative engagement with other organisations and by aiming to shape the profession of public health.[31] The Faculty characterises public health as:

> The science and art of promoting and protecting health and well-being, preventing ill-health and prolonging life through the organised efforts of society.

In explaining what this means, FPH presents its 'Public Health Approach':

The Faculty's approach is that public health

- is population based;
- emphasises collective responsibility for health, its protection and disease prevention;
- recognises the key role of the state, linked to a concern for the underlying socio-economic and wider determinants of health, as well as disease;
- emphasises partnerships with all those who contribute to the health of the population.[32]

The Faculty outlines 'three key domains of public health practice' and 'nine key areas for public health practice'. The three domains are health improvement, improving services, and health protection. These are broken up under various headings. Health improvement, FPH says, focuses on inequalities, education, housing, employment, family/community, lifestyles, and surveillance and monitoring of specific diseases and risk factors. Improving services focuses on clinical effectiveness, efficiency, service planning, audit and evaluation, clinical governance, and equity. Health protection focuses on infectious diseases, chemicals and poisons, radiation, emergency response, and environmental health hazards.[33]

When explaining its areas of practice, FPH notes six 'core values':

The Faculty's core values are that public health practice should be

- equitable;
- empowering;
- effective;
- evidence-based;

---

30 Faculty of Public Health, <www.fph.org.uk/what_is_public_health> accessed 5 April 2016.
31 ibid.
32 ibid.
33 ibid.

- fair;
- inclusive.[34]

The Faculty then advances nine 'key areas' of practice:

- Surveillance and assessment of the population's health and wellbeing;
- Assessing the evidence of effectiveness of health and healthcare interventions, programmes and services;
- Policy and strategy development and implementation;
- Strategic leadership and collaborative working for health;
- Health Improvement;
- Health Protection;
- Health and Social Service Quality;
- Public Health Intelligence;
- Academic Public Health.[35]

1.4.2 The UK Government

The UK Government defines public health as follows:

> Public health is about helping people to stay healthy, and protecting them from threats to their health. The government wants everyone to be able to make healthier choices, regardless of their circumstances, and to minimise the risk and impact of illness.[36]

As part of the radical reforms to health policy in England that were introduced by then Secretary of State for Health Andrew Lansley, under the Conservative-led Coalition Government, PHE was established in April 2013, as an executive agency of the Department of Health, to administer public health services within England (see further: Chapters 3 and 7).[37] It serves to assure that the Secretary of State meets his statutory duty to take appropriate steps 'for the purpose of protecting the public in England from disease or other dangers to health'.[38] PHE says, 'We protect and improve the nation's health and wellbeing, and reduce health inequalities',[39] and outlines its responsibilities as follows:

- making the public healthier by encouraging discussions, advising government and supporting action by local government, the NHS and other people and organisations;
- supporting the public so they can protect and improve their own health;
- protecting the nation's health through the national health protection service, and preparing for public health emergencies;
- sharing our information and expertise with local authorities, industry and the NHS, to help them make improvements in the public's health;

---

34 ibid.
35 ibid.
36 UK Government, <www.gov.uk/government/topics/public-health> accessed 5 April 2016.
37 See HM Government, *Healthy Lives, Healthy People: Our Strategy for Public Health in England* (CM 7985 2010).
38 See National Health Service Act 2006, s. 2A.
39 Public Health England, <www.gov.uk/government/organisations/public-health-england/about> accessed 5 April 2016.

- researching, collecting and analysing data to improve our understanding of health and come up with answers to public health problems;
- reporting on improvements in the public's health so everyone can understand the challenge and the next steps;
- helping local authorities and the NHS to develop the public health system and its specialist workforce.[40]

1.4.3 The World Health Organization

The WHO defines public health in the following way:

> Public health refers to all organized measures (whether public or private) to prevent disease, promote health, and prolong life among the population as a whole. Its activities aim to provide conditions in which people can be healthy and focus on entire populations, not on individual patients or diseases. Thus, public health is concerned with the total system and not only the eradication of a particular disease. The three main public health functions are:
>
> - The assessment and monitoring of the health of communities and populations at risk to identify health problems and priorities.
> - The formulation of public policies designed to solve identified local and national health problems and priorities.
> - To assure that all populations have access to appropriate and cost-effective care, including health promotion and disease prevention services.[41]

WHO goes on to illustrate the breadth of its understanding of public health by reference to a list of public health campaigns:

- Vaccination and control of infectious diseases;
- Motor-vehicle safety;
- Safer workplaces;
- Safer and healthier foods;
- Safe drinking water;
- Healthier mothers and babies and access to family planning;
- Decline in deaths from coronary heart disease and stroke;
- Recognition of tobacco use as a health hazard.[42]

1.4.4 Shared themes and emphases

Readers will observe that there are a number of substantive differences between the above definitions, as well as distinctions in emphasis. However, all three share important qualities in common, and we suggest that each owes a great deal to Winslow's foundational ideas. In particular, it is useful to carry forward the following themes and points:

- The definitions give a focus to protection of health through preventive measures and health promotion. With references to health and wellbeing, and remembering the WHO's

---

40 ibid.
41 WHO, <www.who.int/trade/glossary/story076/en/> accessed 5 April 2016.
42 ibid.

famous characterisation of health as a 'complete state of physical, mental, and social well-being and not merely the absence of disease or infirmity',[43] we would note that Winslow's reference to 'physical health' may be updated now to include also mental health.

- The definitions highlight that public health is concerned with the application of measures to populations. Furthermore, such measures are to be applied through organised means. Organisation here suggests a clear, coordinating role for public health practitioners and is not limited to organisation by political actors.
- It is clear that public health involves a range of sectors and professions: there is a role for health care professionals, but for others too.
- The characterisations of public health all focus on widespread determinants of health status, and suggest broad means of effecting change so that people may enjoy better health.
- Although protection of health in times of emergency is mentioned, public health activity and responsibility is not reducible to coercive measures (or the use of 'police powers').
- Finally, and relatedly, we might say that the different definitions offer visions of a social mission. There is significant potential for variation here. For example, the Faculty presents a commitment to equality and social justice, whilst the politically right-of-centre UK Government's definition seems to emphasise individual responsibility and freedom, and the WHO emphasises the centrality of public health across sectors.

Before moving in section 1.5 to a theoretical academic explanation and justification for our broad understanding of public health, we close the current discussion by making a practical point about public health governance in England. Whilst PHE is an agency of the Department of Health, governmental responsibility for public health in England is devolved to local authorities.[44] Following amendments introduced in section 12 of the Health and Social Care Act 2012, section 2B(1) of the National Health Service Act 2006 provides that: 'Each local authority must take such steps as it considers appropriate for improving the health of the people in its area'. PHE has a legal duty to support this function and, furthermore, formally has a role 'providing government, local government, the NHS, Parliament and MPs, industry, public health professionals and the public with evidence-based, scientific and delivery expertise and advice'.[45] Given this, and the wider, multidisciplinary and cross-sector functions of PHE,[46] public health can be seen as a wide-reaching field, in a way that underscores the concerns claimed by FPH and WHO. It nevertheless is worth considering the academic coherence of taking this sort of broad approach: a point to which we now turn.

1.5 The scope of public health: critical views and the rationale for adopting a broad understanding

We would argue that it is best to define the scope of public health by reference to the current, most dominant, thinking, as outlined above. The activities that these institutions identify as relevant include, but extend markedly beyond, what may be characterised as the standard

43 United Nations, Preamble to the Constitution of the World Health Organization, entered into force 7 April 1948, 14 UNTS 185.
44 See further the discussion of devolution in Chapter 3.
45 Department of Health/Public Health England, *Framework Agreement between the Department of Health and Public Health England* (London: Public Health England 2013), 4.
46 ibid.

practical focus of mainstream bioethics and health care law.[47] Whilst the latter fields are centrally concerned with interactions, rights, and obligations within the health sector, our interest is with much wider questions. Practitioners and scholars in public health law, driven by a mission to understand shared responsibility for health, do indeed focus on health care and its proper provision. But, as we have emphasised, public health practice looks also to political responsibilities for assuring the public health infrastructure and responding to the social determinants of health. Access to medical attention is worth relatively little in the absence of a sanitary environment; clean water, proper sewerage, availability of safe foods, and so on are vital to sound health. Moreover, there is growing acceptance that our social environment impacts directly on our health.[48] There is clear and consistent evidence that social status, both currently and across the lifespan, determines health status.[49] And, even amongst people of similar social status, social interactions can importantly influence health-related beliefs and behaviours, thereby modifying the occurrence of illness and disability. For these reasons, public health activity as characterised in the previous section has a legitimate interest in the whole natural and social environment, its impact on health, and its potential for adaptation to improve health.

Of necessity, and as explained above, broad definitions of public health therefore embrace actors, practices, and approaches from across society. They are not limited to the work of a single governmental department or agency or the practice of any one group of professionals. Within the literature on public health ethics and law, a broad view of the scope of public health has greatly influenced the understanding and work of various scholars, including lawyers such as Lawrence Gostin[50] and Wendy Parmet[51] and philosophers such as Marcel Verweij and Angus Dawson.[52] However, there is also a critical philosophical and legal literature, which suggests that we should be wary of expansive definitions of public health. One of us has discussed elsewhere how there are two particularly prominent concerns about broad definitions of public health: the first may be labelled the libertarian critique and the second the jurisdictional critique.[53] It is useful here to consider briefly each in turn.

The libertarian critique is well demonstrated in the work of Richard Epstein.[54] We explore different philosophical approaches within public health ethics in Chapter 2. Suffice to say here that libertarianism, understood in a general sense, may be defined by two features. The first is an ethical concern that the state only has limited authority to force people to behave in particular ways; in other words, there are stringent limits on the extent to which governmental power can be exercised legitimately to coerce citizens. As noted in the Nuffield Council on Bioethics' report on public health ethics, this authority has classically been restricted to state coercion that is needed to protect life, liberty, and property.[55] Thus, we can say that when libertarians make claims about the limits of governments' authority to engage in public health activity, they are advancing a normative basis for the argument that public health should only be narrowly conceived. Libertarian public health lawyers accept that the government might legitimately exercise its police powers, for example, to contain an

---

47 Compare also the discussion in Gostin and Wiley (n 1), chapter 1.
48 Gostin (n 4), chapter 14. Irene H. Yen and S. Leonard Syme, 'The Social Environment and Health: A Discussion of the Epidemiologic Literature' (1999) 20 *Annual Review of Public Health* 287.
49 See Marmot, *Status Syndrome* (n 22).
50 Gostin and Wiley (n 1).
51 Parmet (n 14).
52 Angus Dawson and Marcel Verweij, 'Public Health Ethics: A Manifesto' (2008) 1 *Public Health Ethics* 1.
53 See Coggon (n 4), 52–59.
54 See Epstein (n 25).
55 Nuffield Council on Bioethics, *Public Health: Ethical Issues* (London: Nuffield Council on Bioethics 2007).

outbreak of a contagious disease such as Ebola in the context of a public health emergency. Such lawyers do not, however, accept that coercive laws can be justified to control 'lifestyle diseases'. Thus, for example, libertarians such as Epstein have criticised the term 'obesity epidemic', arguing that the phrase wrongly implies that the state has a legitimate role in coercing people into lifestyles that will reduce obesity. They believe that a conception of public health that includes state activity directed at matters such as social determinants of health is unacceptably wide because it relies on an indefensible role for the state. In more colloquial terms, it creates a 'nanny state' and ignores individuals' rights and responsibilities to assume whatever risks they might choose.

To complement this form of normative critique, libertarians may also advance descriptive (i.e. empirical) arguments against a broad scope for public health. Formally, these are distinct from the normative arguments, although they may feed into justifications for adopting a libertarian position. The idea in this instance, however, is not directly about moral rights to life, liberty, and property. Rather, it relates to a rejection of claims about the social determinants of health and of arguments about efficiency and efficacy in regulation. The following passage, from one of Epstein's works, exemplifies how empirical claims may be advanced to bolster normative arguments:

> [T]he indisputable evidence shows that more people, both adult and infants, are overweight than before and that changes in diet and increases in exercise could go a long way to prevent obesity from undermining a solely individual problem. But the use of the term "epidemic" is just the *wrong* way to think about this issue. There are no non-communicable epidemics.[56]

Epstein continues:

> [D]esignating obesity as a public health epidemic is designed to signal that state coercion is appropriate when it is not. Education and persuasion, yes; but private institutions and foundations can supply these things without government coercion and even without government guidance and warnings over what personal health targets should be and how they are best achieved.[57]

Here, we see in Epstein's argument an acceptance of growing rates of obesity but a denial about the soundness of referring to an 'obesity epidemic'. Furthermore, he suggests that incentives to maintain a healthier weight are greater with less public interference rather than more: public welfare, on this view, provides an incentive to live unhealthily because there is a 'safety net'. And Epstein suggests that, anyway, private actors will do a better job than public authorities: 'Indeed, here as elsewhere, there is good reason to fear that the increased levels of guaranteed health care works to undermine overall health levels'.[58]

In slightly different senses, the libertarian critiques against a broad public health rest on principled grounds: normative arguments are advanced against the legitimacy of allowing public health activity a wide remit. What we are labelling here 'the jurisdictional critique', by contrast, advances an alternative, *pragmatic* rationale for working only with a

---

56 Epstein (n 25), 1462.
57 ibid, 1462–1463.
58 ibid, 1463.

narrow concept of public health. The most notable proponent of the jurisdictional critique
is Mark Rothstein, especially in his paper 'Rethinking the Meaning of Public Health'.[59]
Rothstein argues that we should limit our understanding of public health actors – and
thus of public health – to a narrow band of specifically designated governmental actors.
His argument is essentially that a wider understanding of public health cannot be soundly
contained: if it extends across governmental and social sectors, it demands too much. For
public health ethics and law to be viable areas of study, they should not, on this view, have
too wide a practical concern. We might say that sheer manageability means we should not
go with an expansive understanding of public health. Furthermore, whilst he does not
believe that public health interventions are necessarily coercive, he considers that they will
always be steeped in some sort of controversy. As such, for public acceptance, they must not
be too widely conceived: popular acceptance of public health measures will be undermined
if public health interventions claim too great a scope. Rothstein's view is that: 'The term
public health is a legal term of art, and it refers to specifically delineated powers, duties,
rights, and responsibilities'.[60]

We are not persuaded that Rothstein's position makes a compelling case for a narrow
definition of public health. Primary amongst our reasons is that, as we have shown, the
most relevant public health actors work with broad understandings. If we were to follow
Rothstein's reasoning, the obvious governmental agencies to consider, at least in England,
would be PHE and local authorities, to whom public health responsibilities are delegated.[61]
But we have already seen that PHE reaches across levels and sectors of government and
engages many stakeholders. Even if a public health theorist were to think it wrong that PHE
should be structured as it is, in studying its functions we must take account of its wide
remit if we are to develop understandings of public health law that are pertinent to current
practice in England.

Beyond this practical concern, there are further reasons to adopt a broad conception of
public health. These stand in response to positions such as the libertarian critique, if that is
seen as a route to closing down inquiry before it is undertaken. As a scholarly enterprise, the
study of public health law cannot limit itself to the field as idealised by normative libertarians. A textbook on public health law needs to account for other perspectives too, allowing
the libertarian voice to be heard, but not insisting that it preclude the alternative perspectives. Similarly, it would be a mistake to disregard arguments about social determinants of
health without considering them.

Finally, regardless of how things are currently formulated in English public health law,
there is significant merit in examining how different modes of regulation are relevant to
understanding both how population health outcomes occur and how they may be improved.
We therefore propose in this book to work with the broad accounts, inspired by Winslow
and discussed in the previous section. Readers do not have to be convinced of the normative
value of these definitions (see further: Chapter 2) to find utility in the chapters that follow.
The real prize is not in finding the 'true' definition of public health but in understanding
how health is impacted by our social and physical environments, and the implications of this
understanding for different forms of governance and their legitimacy.

---

59 Rothstein (n 12).
60 ibid.
61 National Health Service Act 2006, s. 2B; Health and Social Care Act 2012, s. 12. See further: Chapters 3, 7, and 9.

1.6 From contemporary public health approaches to a definition of public health law

The preceding sections have explained how and why public health should be understood as a broad field of study and practice. We have seen that it is founded on knowledge derived from the study of populations. We have also seen that public health activity is identifiable by a general commitment to socially coordinated interventions. Returning to Winslow, public health agendas relate to 'preventing disease, prolonging life, and promoting physical [and now we would add mental] health and efficiency through organized community efforts'.[62] With reference to the definitions of FPH, PHE, and WHO, we have introduced a field with enormous scope and depth. In particular, we would stress again WHO's emphasis of the idea that public health *activities aim to provide conditions in which people can be healthy and focus on entire populations, not on individual patients or diseases*'.[63]

This book seeks to apply legal analysis to this broad area of inquiry and practice. We will see how public health laws can be used – rightly or wrongly – to pursue ends that libertarian theorists such as Epstein argue to be incoherent or illegitimate. And we will see that the field of public health law encompasses actors – public and private – whom Rothstein would consider should not be part of public health governance and practice. In short, our study is of how law and governance might be employed to help engender the conditions in which people can be healthy and also how legal, political, ethical, and social limitations might limit potential public health agendas.

In Part II of this book we advance and explain our definition of the field of *public health law* (see Chapter 4) and then provide an explication through studies of private law, criminal law, public law, European Union and international law and policy, self-regulation, and governance for public health (in Chapters 5 to 9, respectively). Before that, two further pieces of groundwork are covered in Part I of this book. In Chapter 2, we examine the field of public health ethics. Given its highly political and contested contexts and content, normative arguments feature significantly in debates regarding public health law and practice. Doctrinally, contemporary public health law could be studied without regard to public health ethics. But we consider any such dissociation to miss an essential aspect of the field. Equally, we would argue an historical awareness of the field is crucial to an understanding of modern public health law. Accordingly, in Chapter 3, we provide an account of how this area of law has evolved in the United Kingdom over time.

This groundwork will bring us to the following definition of public health law:

> *Public health law is a field of study and practice that concerns those aspects of law, policy, and regulation that advance or place constraints upon the protection and promotion of health (howsoever understood) within, between, and across populations.*[64]

From the ideas presented in the current chapter, it should already be clear why we choose to work with this wide-reaching characterisation. Readers of this book should recall throughout that, in considering the provision of conditions in which people can be healthy, regard

---

62 Winslow (n 28), 30.
63 WHO (n 41).
64 Contrast Coggon (n 4), 90–91.

is needed for systems of health care, public health infrastructure, and the social determinants of health. Each of these is necessarily captured within our definition of public health law. Both legal and political responsibilities underpin the governmental responsibilities to attend to these concerns. Within them, we find activity that involves public and private actors, and which aims to overcome disease when it arises, to prevent the incidence of disease in the first place, and to improve the social environment in response to social determinants of ill health. Each of the authors of this book has advanced arguments in public health ethics. And, whilst we share the view that the practice of public health law entails ethical agendas, we do not in this book commit to, or advocate, any specific position. Rather, we take the above understandings of what is involved in public health and examine how those matters relate to hard laws and to softer modes of governance.

Chapter 1: Summary

- Public health activity encompasses a broad agenda, including governmental and social responsibilities to assure access to a health care system, to provide a public health infrastructure, and to attend to social determinants of ill health.
- Public health research focuses on populations, and public health interventions generally focus on measures that will effect change at a population rather than an individual level.
- Given these points of focus, public health activity of necessity incorporates legal and other forms of social coordination.
- When considering the implementation of public health law and policy, it is essential to consider both descriptive and normative questions:

  o Descriptive questions relate to matters of fact (e.g. the evidence-based claim that smoking tobacco causes disease).

  o Normative questions relate to matters of evaluation (e.g. a claim that it is bad that people might choose to smoke) and action-guiding claims (e.g. a claim that it is right that the government should act to eradicate smoking).

- To help explore these points, this book explores and explains public health law defined as:

  A field of study and practice that concerns those aspects of law, policy, and regulation that advance or place constraints upon the protection and promotion of health (howsoever understood) within, between, and across populations.

1.7 Further readings

John Coggon, *What Makes Health Public? A Critical Evaluation of Moral, Legal, and Political Claims in Public Health* (Cambridge: Cambridge University Press 2012).

Richard Epstein, 'Let the Shoemaker Stick to His Last: A Defence of the "Old" Public Health' (2003) 46 *Perspectives in Biology and Medicine* S138.

Lawrence Gostin and Gregg Bloche, 'The Politics of Public Health: A Response to Epstein' (2003) 46 *Perspectives in Biology and Medicine* S160.

Wendy Parmet, *Populations, Public Health, and the Law* (Washington: Georgetown University Press 2009).

Geoffrey Rose, 'Sick Individuals and Sick Populations' (1985) 14 *International Journal of Epidemiology* 32.

Chapter 2

Public health, philosophy, and ethics

2.1 The significance of philosophy in public health law and practice

Philosophy has significant relevance to public health policy, practice, and research. There is a growing number of philosophers and philosophically-minded lawyers who are interested in the philosophical questions underpinning and raised by public health. Nevertheless, since most public health practitioners and policy-makers have not received exposure to philosophy as part of their education or training, there can be some reluctance or uncertainty about how to apply philosophy to the context of public health. As we have seen in the first chapter, even trying to define what constitutes 'public health' is itself a philosophical enterprise. As we have also seen, how this conceptual question is answered will have direct practical implications for what areas public health activity is concerned with, who has public health obligations, and which methods it would be appropriate to use to promote and protect public health.

At its core, bringing philosophical reflection and analysis to questions of public health involves bringing a critical evaluation of questions concerning possible, actual, and proposed public health policies and measures.[1] This critical evaluation can help us to expose particular presuppositions; identify essential claims and distinctions; and reason through how various moral, political, and legal considerations should impact upon different public health activities. Further, greater familiarity with philosophical theories, definitions, and concepts can also help by providing us with a useful vocabulary and basis of analysis for public health and public health ethics and law.

This chapter explores philosophy's relevance to public health – especially in the context of the ethical issues raised by public health and central aspects of public health ethics that seek to respond to these issues. It begins with an elucidation of normative considerations and the different ways in which they can be relevant for public health. When the mission and aims of public health law and practice are examined, we can see that normative considerations either implicitly or explicitly play a significant role in shaping different public health activities. In particular, we often see how different moral and political values underpin public health policies. The chapter goes on to examine the different ways in which philosophy's task

---

1 John Coggon, *What Makes Health Public? A Critical Evaluation of Moral, Legal, and Political Claims in Public Health* (Cambridge: Cambridge University Press 2012) 93.

of clarifying, critiquing, integrating, and reassessing these values can be useful in our critical evaluation of public health. We then proceed to outline the different ways in which ethical considerations and values bear on questions of professional ethics, ethical guidance, and the appropriate social role for public health authorities. Finally, focussing primarily on ethical guidance and ethical regulation, the chapter concludes with different approaches to public health ethics that can be used to reflect on the ethical dimensions of public health enterprise, guide public heath practice, and develop public health policy.

2.2 Philosophy and public health

Public health raises numerous philosophical questions that demand serious consideration. This is true both in that they are interesting and important questions in themselves, but also because of the ways in which they can illuminate various aspects of public health policy, practice, and research. The primary focus of this chapter is on questions regarding public health ethics. However, it should be understood that ethics is not the only branch of philosophy that impacts on public health. For example, public health raises metaphysical or ontological questions; that is to say, questions about how the world is and what things exist in the world, such as what health or disease are,[2] what constitutes a population,[3] or how we should understand the nature of causation.[4] Public health also raises epistemological questions; that is questions about what we know or are justified in believing.[5] Equally, it raises questions within logic and the philosophy of science about critical reasoning and how we should collect and analyse evidence used to decide on public health policy and action. These include concerns about why statistical tests or forms of inference are warranted in a study, or why particular methods of data collection should be used, or what standards of evidence are required before we are justified asserting that, for example, smoking causes lung cancer.[6] All such philosophical questions contribute to grounding the conditions of what makes something true or false, objective or subjective, rational or irrational. Attention to these matters is important because it makes scientific practice more methodologically rigorous and less prone to bias or error.

When people think of public health, it is often as an objective enterprise concerned with scientific investigation and statistical evaluation – and developing policies in line with such scientific inquiry. Public health activity seeks to be informed by the best information available and the action taken is led by what the scientific evidence tells us would promote or protect the health of a population.[7] For this reason, public health is often thought of as being primarily a descriptive enterprise; it can tell us what makes a population or group healthy

---

2 Christopher Boorse, 'Health as a Theoretical Concept' (1977) 44 Philosophy of Science 542; Ian Kennedy, The Unmasking of Medicine (London: Allen and Unwin 1983); K. Codell Carter, The Rise of Causal Theories of Disease (Aldershot: Ashgate 2003).
3 Nancy Krieger, 'Who and What Is a "Population"? Historical Debates, Current Controversies, and Implications for Understanding "Population Health" and Rectifying Health Inequities' (2012) 90 The Millbank Quarterly 634.
4 Kenneth Rothman and Sander Greenland, 'Causation and Causal Inference in Epidemiology' (2005) 95 American Journal of Public Health S144; Alex Broadbent, Philosophy of Epidemiology (London: Palgrave 2013).
5 Stephen John, 'Expert Testimony and Epistemological Free-Riding: The MMR Controversy?' (2011) 61 The Philosophical Quarterly 496.
6 Sam Harper, Nicholas King, Stephen Meersman, Marsha Reichman, Nancy Breen, and John Lynch, 'Implicit Value Judgments in the Measurement of Health Inequalities' (2010) 88 The Milbank Quarterly 4.
7 Michael McGinnis and Deborah Maiese, 'Defining Mission, Goals, and Objectives' in F. Douglas Scutchfield and C. William Keck (eds), Principles of Public Health Practice (Albany, NY: Delmar 1997) 131; Hebe Gouda and John Powles, 'The Science of Epidemiology and the Methods Needed for Public Health Assessments: A Review of Epidemiology Textbooks' (2014) 14 BMC Public Health 139.

or unhealthy and which interventions could be used to affect different health statuses. It would be wrong, however, to think that activities such as epidemiological research or policy development are merely descriptive in nature or neutral to particular normative commitments. Different normative perspectives or values frame and shape what questions are asked, what forms of evidence are accepted, which processes will be adopted, and what outcomes will be judged as successes. We outlined this important distinction between descriptive and normative claims in Chapter 1 and will now explain it in further depth.

When we make *descriptive claims*, we are concerned with empirical considerations that express an understanding about how something is or how it might be. We can contrast this with *normative claims*. Normative claims are expressions of how things should be or why possible alternatives might be better. Public health is both a descriptive and normative enterprise. For this reason, it is important to be able to better understand how attention to the normative aspects of public health can impact on policy and practice. In particular, it is crucial to establish properly how we should move from descriptive claims about population health itself to normative claims about what kinds of public health activity should result. As Daniel Goldberg has noted:

> The notion that epidemiologic evidence 'speaks for itself' in generating policy implications is dubious. Moving directly from the descriptive to the normative perpetrates the naturalistic fallacy; the mere fact that the world is a certain way does not as such demonstrate the way the world ought to be.[8]

Much of the work of public health ethics is concerned with establishing how we might go about demonstrating why particular public health policies should, or should not, be in place or why we would be justified, or not, in using particular public health measures to advance these policies.

2.2.1 Normativity

Many of the questions that we are concerned with in this book are normative in nature. These are areas primarily covered by the areas of moral, political, and legal philosophy. When philosophers are interested in normative questions or normativity, they are largely concerned with what we have reasons to do in a particular circumstance. There are two aspects to normativity: the *deontic* (from the Greek *deon*, meaning that which is binding) and the *evaluative* (from the Latin *valores*, meaning that which has worth).[9]

When normative claims are made, we often see familiar terms that seek to guide prospective action or render a judgment on actions that have already been taken. Some normative terms are *deontic* – for instance, when we say that an action is right, wrong, just, unjust, required, prohibited, obligatory, or permissible or that it ought or ought not be done. Deontic norms – such as the claim that someone has a right to health or that someone has an obligation not to infect others with an infectious disease – relate to requirements, prohibitions, or permissions that express imperatives for action. Some normative terms are also *evaluative* – for instance, an action is good, bad, better, worse, best, evil, blameworthy,

8 Daniel Goldberg, 'Social Justice, Health Inequalities and Methodological Individualism in US Health Promotion', (2012) 5 *Public Health Ethics* 104, 106–107.
9 Christine Tappolet, 'Evaluative vs. Deontic Concepts' in Hugh Lafollette (ed), *International Encyclopedia of Ethics* (Oxford: Wiley-Blackwell 2013) 1791–1799.

praiseworthy, rewardable, punishable. Evaluative norms – such as the claim that it would be a happier society if everyone had a guaranteed right to health or that infecting someone with an infectious disease is thoughtless and rude behaviour – relate to the assessment of significance or worth of particular activities or states of affairs.

While both categories are normative, we need to be careful in how we understand the relationship between the deontic and the evaluative. In particular, we need to understand how deontic and evaluative claims underpin arguments for developing or revising some public health policy or justify enacting some public health intervention. Consider the evaluative claim, 'Too much sugar in your diet is bad for your health'. Even if we all agree with this evaluative claim, what should be the deontic implications that follow? It would be morally wrong for you to eat too much sugar? We have an obligation to encourage people to consume less sugar? We have a right to ban food products with too much sugar from being sold? It cannot be taken for granted that just because some evaluation is true that a deontic imperative for action necessarily follows from it. Any of those potential deontic responses to the evaluative sugar claim would require further support and argumentation in order to be legitimate.

There are substantive theoretical questions about whether one category of normativity is more fundamental than the other or whether we should understand one normative category in terms of the other. These questions need not be settled here. Nevertheless, being aware of how different normative categories can interact will be an issue that frequently arises for public health policy and practice. It is often the case that public health advocacy presents apparently firm deontic conclusions, when an author has only raised a presumptive evaluative claim. Part of the work of public health ethics, which leads directly into public health practice and public health law, is in establishing what should or should not be done in the name of public health.

Take, for example, the question of whether health inequalities are bad and whether this inequality is unfair. (Recall that Chapter 1 shows how public health bodies claim a mandate to address health inequalities.) There might be different ways we could go about seeking to explain the unfairness of health inequalities. Some moral theories will appeal to evaluative facts in order to explain deontic facts. For instance, classical utilitarianism claims that what makes an act wrongful is explained by the badness of its consequences. For the utilitarian, what makes the badness of health inequalities unfair is that such inequalities result in a greater overall poor health. According to such theories, the evaluative has conceptual priority over the deontic – all moral claims are fundamentally evaluative claims about why some act or policy would be good, bad, better, or worse for someone's health, wellbeing, etc. Consider, for instance, the right to health. According to utilitarians, since we should understand rightness or wrongness in terms of consequences, we should only have a right to health if its existence would bring about higher levels of health. If the overall aggregate consequences of having a right to health would not bring morally good consequences, then we should not think there is a right to health (or that, if this right exists, it can be overridden if there are better consequences to be obtained).

Other moral theories will appeal to deontic facts in order to explain evaluative facts. For instance, classical deontology claims that what makes an act wrongful is explained by whether someone's rights or duties have been violated. For the deontologist, what makes health inequalities unfair is not the badness that results from them but how such inequalities violate someone's rights to be treated as an equal (e.g. to have equal access to health care). According to these theories, the deontic has conceptual priority over the evaluative – all moral claims should be based in claims about why some act or policy would protect or promote deontic concepts, such as duties or rights. Returning again to the example of a right to health: according to deontologists, since we should understand rightness or wrongness independent of consequences, the existence of a right to health is predicated on its role in, for example, protecting human dignity or capabilities. On this view, people have a right to health whether or not this right itself leads to higher levels of health.

It is important to recognise that all moral theories make both deontic and evaluative claims. Thus, even though 'deontic' and 'deontology' share the same terminological root, it would be a mistake to simply think utilitarianism is an evaluative view and deontology is a deontic view. Both theories are concerned with what makes an action or policy right or wrong, just or unjust. As we noted above, however, we see that different theories will give priority to one normative concept over the other – even going as far to explain one concept in relation to the other. When making a moral argument, we need to keep in mind whether we are appealing to deontic or evaluative facts and how these facts relate to each other – as well as how different moral theories disagree about these matters in advancing a justification about public health policy or action. This theoretical disagreement not only makes a difference in terms of how we justify some policy or action but, depending on which justification we endorse, could result in one public health intervention being chosen over another. Imagine, for example, that a public health policy could bring about only one of the following two outcomes, in which the figures below represent the health status of different populations – each population and the two groups within the populations are the same size:[10]

Group 1	Group 2
50	50

Outcome 1. Equality

Group 1	Group 2
90	20

Outcome 2. Inequality

All of the individuals in Equality will have equally healthy lives, while those in Inequality will fare differently with some living much healthier lives than others. When choosing a public health policy, and given two different possible outcomes, which one should we select? Utilitarianism would advise us to enact the second policy (Inequality) because it provides the greatest amount of health, ignoring how health is distributed between the groups. According to utilitarianism, public health is in the business of maximising the health of the population, and this second policy ensures more health overall.[11] Recall, for utilitarianism, since it defines the morally right course of action in terms of what provides the best consequences, it takes this evaluative fact (i.e. best consequences would be those that provided more health overall) to be what determines the deontic fact (i.e. it would be right to enact the second policy, Inequality).

Deontology would advise us to enact the first policy (Equality) because it provides equal respect to the health needs of everyone – even knowing the health of individuals in group 1 would be lower than it could otherwise be under the second policy. According to deontology, the loss of the freedoms or capabilities that result from ill health suffered by group 2 in Inequality cannot be made right by the fact that group 1 enjoys better health or that there is more overall health in Inequality compared to Equality. Again recall, for deontology, the morally right course of action is determined in relation to how actions conform to moral norms, such as rules, obligations, and rights. It is the deontic fact (i.e. the moral norm that people

---

10 The example is borrowed from Roger Crisp, *Mill on Utilitarianism* (London: Routledge 1997) 169.
11 Marc Roberts and Michael Reich, 'Ethical Analysis in Public Health' (2002) 359 *Lancet* 1055.

should be given equal respect is best satisfied by enacting the first policy, Equality) that deter-mines the evaluative fact (i.e. it would be best for everyone to enjoy equal health outcomes).

Such an example also illustrates that we often appeal to different values when seeking to justify why we should undertake some public health policy or action. Someone might appeal to the value of efficacy and efficiency as reasons why we should choose an intervention. Indeed, we frequently hear appeals to the fact that some public health intervention, for example, will reduce mortality and morbidity as the justification for why we ought to do something. Con-sider, for example, recent suggestions that we should institute a tax or levy on high-sugar foods and drinks as a public health intervention aimed at reducing sugar intake and its association with being overweight or obese, which are risk factors for several health conditions, including diabetes, cardiovascular disease, and some cancers.[12] Someone might also appeal to the value of fairness as a reason why we should choose one intervention over another. It is becoming more common, for instance, to hear appeals within public health concerning the importance of taking into account health inequalities or inequities as the reason for undertaking particular activities.[13] In either case, whether the values relied upon appeal to evaluative or deontic facts, what matters is understanding the nature of these facts and how they can relate to each other. Different moral theories, such as utilitarianism and deontology, provide us with a systematic way of thinking about the nature and relation of these different normative concepts.

While the choice between the equality versus inequality policy above is a simplistic exam-ple, it is easy to see how similar issues arise in real-world contexts. For example, consider how policies that have a net effect of reducing tobacco use may be endorsed from a utilitarian per-spective, yet may be criticised from a deontological perspective where they widen inequalities in the proportionate numbers of smokers respectively in wealthier and poorer socio-economic groups.[14] What is useful about this example is that it demonstrates that, not only do ethical values underpin our selection of public health policy and action, but also how the values we select play a central role in how we justify these public health activities – and may even deter-mine which activities we will ultimately select. It is for this reason that it is important to further examine the role of moral and political values in our deliberation and justification of public health policy and action, as well as how these values underpin debates within public health ethics and feature in wider debates within moral, political, and legal philosophy.

2.2.2 Values and the task of philosophy

As we have begun to see, another way in which philosophy is vital to public health – as well as public health law – is the way it can be used to better understand the nature of public health; the values that are relevant to public health; and how public health agendas might be strengthened or limited through interrogating the concepts, principles, perspectives, and practices that constitute public health activity. One of the best definitions of philosophy comes from philosopher John Campbell, who maintains that:

> Philosophy is thinking in slow motion. It breaks down, describes and assesses moves we ordinarily make at great speed – to do with our natural motivations and beliefs. It then becomes evident that alternatives are possible.[15]

---

12 Public Heath England, *Sugar Reduction: The Evidence for Action* (London: Public Health England 2015). A 'sugar tax' was announced by the Chancellor of the Exchequer in the Budget of 2016; see further: Chapter 7.
13 See, for instance, Jennifer Prah Ruger, *Health and Social Justice* (Oxford: Oxford University Press 2012).
14 Kristin Voigt, 'Smoking and Social Justice' (2010) 3 *Public Health Ethics* 91.
15 Quoted in Steve Pyke, *Philosophers* (Manchester: Cornerhouse 1993).

Thinking philosophically about public health invites us to be sceptical. In being sceptical – in raising questions, analysing presuppositions, and demanding that claims be resistant to counterarguments and recalcitrant evidence – the examination of alternative possibilities is not necessarily about rejecting those values or approaches that currently constitute public health practice and policy. It is fundamentally about taking a critical stance, which allows us to be better placed to understand whether and why the values we use to justify particular public health policy or action are ultimately defensible. In taking a critical attitude, there are different tasks that can be undertaken – a better awareness of which will make it easier to appreciate the different modes of analysis that can be used when examining ethical and legal issues that arise in the context of public health.

One task is *value clarification*. This task concerns being able to identify all of the relevant values in the circumstance and investigate the nature, strength, and scope of these values. For example, imagine a policy that would limit the sales of 'junk food' near to schools. What are the values underpinning why such a public health intervention or policy is being advanced? Is it to promote the wellbeing of the entire population? Is it to reduce relative health inequalities – perhaps to the benefit of those who are the least advantaged in society? Is it to demonstrate solidarity? Perhaps, and indeed often, it is some combination of these and other values. We can also ask are the different values intrinsic (i.e. valuable in themselves) or instrumental (i.e. valuable for the sake of something else)?

This task is about elucidation and interpretation. Ethical analysis involving value clarification in the context of public health need not be prescriptive in nature. Merely endorsing the set of relevant values need not entail that any particular outcome must be brought about. It is possible, for example, to argue that alcohol-related harms are especially ethically problematic if they are distributed unequally across different socio-economic groups. However, to endorse this claim does not, in itself, serve to justify measures to address the problem, such as the introduction of a minimum-pricing regime. Policy or action prescriptions will require further argumentation, explaining how these values interact and how they should be balanced against each other, as part of a substantive defence of why a specific policy or action should be undertaken. These arguments help us to understand whether values should have a particular ranking in terms of priority or strength and what we should do when conflicts between values make reconciliation difficult. Nevertheless, in clarifying the multiple and frequently conflicting values within public health, we should heed Jennings's warning not to fall into the trap of imagining:

> values as self-contained as far as their proper interpretation is concerned . . . as if they were colliding and jockeying for position like billiard balls. Practical ethical discourse is complex and contextualized because it brings many ethical concepts together in ways that affect and delimit the reasonable interpretation of each of them.[16]

As such, attending to the ethical issues that arise in relation to public health should not be thought to be simply a matter of finding some candidate theory or set of principles and mechanistically applying them to the problems at hand. We need to question and be critical: what is appropriate in one situation might not be so in a different situation. For instance, while liberty is an important value, it need not win out in all, or perhaps even most, situations.[17]

---

16 Bruce Jennings, 'Relational Liberty Revisited: Membership, Solidarity and a Public Health Ethics of Place' (2015) 8 *Public Health Ethics* 7, 9.

17 Consider, for example, the discussions of the Rampton Smokers' case, in Chapter 5, and *Enhorn v Sweden*, in Chapters 6 and 7.

It is for this reason that we also need to attend to another task: *value critique*. Once we are clear about the relevant values at stake in analysing or justifying some public health activity, we need to examine whether those are the correct values and if those values have been taken into account in the correct way. This task, as Jeremy Garrett maintains, seeks:

> to unmask, interrogate, and challenge the presuppositions that underlie . . . discourse. . . . These largely unarticulated premises establish the boundaries within which problems can be conceptualized and solutions can be imagined. The function of fundamental critique, then, is not merely to clarify these premises but to challenge them and the boundaries they define. Only then will we be able to imagine new solutions.[18]

In carrying forward this critical approach, it is then necessary to do more than merely articulate possible interpretations or options that one could take from critiquing the values involved. The value critique should be understood as a deliberative task that seeks to inquire into what might arise from challenging premises and boundaries or exploring new solutions to an ethical issue. This is accomplished through the task of *value integration*. This task, again clarified by Garrett, seeks:

> [t]o "honor" and unify what is right in competing values. . . . The function of integration, then, is to envision actions or policies that not only resolve conflicts, but that do so by jointly realizing many genuine values in deep and compelling ways.[19]

This need not presuppose that all values are comparable or commensurable or even that integration is always possible. Nevertheless, in seeking to integrate relevant values, it compels us to go beyond a simple balancing exercise – for instance, asking with respect to a particular intervention whether liberty is more important than the common good and, if liberty is more important, thinking the intervention can be automatically justified. Asking questions and providing answers to public health ethics issues requires a more nuanced and sensitive analysis of the complexity and contextualised interaction of values.

The final task is *value reassessment*. Ethical inquiry as a critical process should continuously seek to evaluate and re-evaluate its premises and conclusions. New facts can come to light, our knowledge improves, our values can become more or less robust. Often, when particular ethical arguments or positions become popular, it can be easy to fall back on received wisdom or past assessments. In taking this critical stance, we are also asking, for instance, if the values selected have been chosen based on personal preference, whether the values confer advantage to particular individuals or groups, or whether the values that have worked for similar situations in the past need to be re-evaluated. The implications for such a task suggests, as Bruce Jennings has put the point:

> That important ethical concepts and categories, such as "liberty" or "solidarity" do not have a stable, prior meaning that is simply imported into policy and practice discourse concerning public health. . . . Ethical concepts are not overlaid on public health discourse as a whole, put there to insert their independent moral significance and authority. Instead, when discussion of ethical concepts and values arises in the setting of

---

18 Jeremy Garrett, 'Two Agendas for Bioethics: Critique and Integration' (2015) 29 *Bioethics* 440, 443.
19 ibid, 444.

public health issues and problems, the meaning of these concepts is transformed and contextualized or localized.[20]

While these tasks are philosophical in nature, this is not to imply that public health ethics is solely the domain of philosophers. In order to ensure a robust and comprehensive ethical inquiry, there is a need for public health ethics to be interdisciplinary and informed by issues faced by public health practitioners and policy-makers.

2.3 Ethics of, in, and for public health: professional standards, applied ethics, and public health advocacy

We have begun to see some of the various ways in which public health ethics seeks to engage in critical analysis and evaluation of the enterprise of public health. In particular, philosophical perspectives underline the importance of elucidating and examining the normative considerations relating to the policies and activities of public health professionals and agencies. With greater philosophical interest in, and exploration of, public health, it becomes evident that the philosophical, and especially ethical, issues that arise in this context are special and distinct from those in areas such as clinical medicine. With a focus on populations and public interests, and the different ethical issues that arise as a result, it is now very clear that attempts to translate ideas, principles, and concepts from medical ethics and bioethics to public health ethics are insufficient.[21] With both the relevant questions and the methods by which we seek to answer those questions being markedly different, there have been increasing attempts to develop an independent public health ethics.[22] Efforts to develop and expand public health ethics as a distinct area of scholarly and practical inquiry have revealed that there are different ways in which ethics can contribute to public health professionalism, policy, and activities. Lawrence Gostin has adopted a tripartite categorization that provides a useful way of framing some of these major contributions.[23]

First, there is ethics of public health, which is 'concerned with the ethical dimensions of professionalism and the moral trust that society bestows on public health professionals to act for the common welfare'.[24] When concerned with the ethics of public health, we can think about its mission and overarching objectives and the role this plays in how public health frames and analyses the issues it seeks to confront. Take, for instance, Public Health England (PHE)'s mission statement, noted in Chapter 1, that it exists 'to protect and improve

---

20 Jennings (n 16), 8–9.
21 See e.g. Ronald Bayer, Lawrence Gostin, Bruce Jennings, and Bonnie Steinbock, 'Introduction: Ethical Theory and Public Health' in Ronald Bayer, Lawrence Gostin, Bruce Jennings, and Bonnie Steinbock (eds), *Public Health Ethics – Theory, Policy, and Practice* (Oxford: Oxford University Press 2006) 3–25; Angus Dawson, 'The Future of Bioethics: Three Dogmas and a Cup of Hemlock' (2010) 3 *Bioethics* 218.
22 See, for instance, Madison Powers and Ruth Faden, *Social Justice: The Moral Foundations of Public Health and Health Policy* (Oxford: Oxford University Press 2006); Angus Dawson and Marcel Verweij (eds), *Ethics, Prevention, and Public Health* (Oxford: Oxford University Press 2009); Sridhar Venkatapuram, *Health Justice: An Argument from the Capabilities Approach* (Cambridge: Polity Press 2011); John Coggon, *What Makes Health Public? A Critical Evaluation of Moral, Legal, and Political Claims in Public Health* (Cambridge: Cambridge University Press 2012).
23 Lawrence Gostin, 'Public Health, Ethics, and Human Rights: A Tribute to the Late Jonathan Mann' (2001) 29 *Journal of Law, Medicine and Ethics* 121.
24 ibid, 124.

the nation's health and wellbeing, and reduce health inequalities'.[25] We find an articulation of the primary moral values – i.e. health, wellbeing, equality – that will act as standards to shape and guide PHE's professional policies and activities.[26] We also find how these values underpin an ethos that provides society with a basis for trusting and investing power and resources to such professionals in order to act for the common good. Attention to considerations of the ethics of public health is especially important for how these contribute to legitimising why government bodies, such as PHE, are justified in taking action in intervening in our lives to promote public health. Indeed, one of the most important questions tackled by the ethics of public health concerns "what makes health public?" – that is to say, on what basis can we justifiably establish the role of the state, through its agencies and officials, in endorsing or encouraging compliance with health-related imperatives, and the means it should use in advancing these imperatives?[27]

Second, there is ethics in public health, which is:

> concerned not so much with the character of professionals as with the ethical dimensions of the public health enterprise itself. Here, scholars study the philosophical knowledge and analytical reasoning necessary for careful thinking and decision-making in creating and implementing public health policy.[28]

When concerned with ethics in public health, we can think about an area of applied ethics that is concerned with analysing and providing guidance to practitioners and policy-makers about specific ethical issues that arise in the context of public health. This may take the form of generalised guidance through an account of the values pertinent to public health or ethical decision-making criteria, as well as directive, issue-led guidance within specific areas. Take, for instance, the ethical issues that arise during a pandemic. Attention to considerations of the ethics in public health will focus on providing substantive answers to questions such as when we would be justified in placing individuals in quarantine or isolation, which professional duties health care workers have in putting themselves at greater risk of infection, to whom we should give priority in allocating scarce vaccines or anti-viral medications, and whether waivers of consent should be provided for pandemic-related research.[29] In engaging with these questions through applied ethics, we do not ask what public health professionals would, perhaps, endorse; rather, we examine basic moral and political theories or principles and explain philosophically what would, or would not, be justified.

Third, Gostin explains how there is ethics for public health, which is concerned with articulating 'an "advocacy" ethics informed by the single overriding value of the health community. Under this rationale, public health authorities posit what they think is socially

---

25 Public Health England, <www.gov.uk/government/organisations/public-health-england/about> accessed 5 April 2016.

26 When understanding public health ethics as a form of professional ethics, Callahan and Jennings maintain that it concerns 'the values and standards that have been developed by the practitioners and leaders of a given profession over a long period of time, and . . . those values most salient and inherent in the profession itself': Daniel Callahan and Bruce Jennings, 'Ethics and Public Health: Forging a Strong Relationship' (2002) 92 American Journal of Public Health 169, 172. Of course, as Jennings also argues, we can question whether public health really is a single, unified profession and whether all public health practitioners can be said unproblematically to hold the same values and standards. See Bruce Jennings, 'Frameworks for Ethics in Public Health' (2003) 9 Acta Bioethica 165.

27 Coggon (n 1), chapter 12.

28 Gostin (n 23), 125.

29 See, for example, Lawrence Gostin, 'Public Health Strategies for Pandemic Influenza: Ethics and the Law' (2006) 295 Journal of the American Medical Association 1700.

appropriate, and their function is to advocate for that social goal'.[30] When concerned with ethics for public health, we can think about the various ways in which public health activity can and should go beyond the impartial and scientific enterprise of describing the health of populations towards taking active means to represent and advocate for the (health) inter-ests of populations – especially populations that are suffering deprivation, oppression, and inequalities. Attention to considerations of the ethics for public health focuses on the appro-priateness of public health as a force that can use its pragmatic and political power in order to influence a particular health agenda. Nevertheless, as Jennings is careful to warn, a form of public health ethics as advocacy ethics 'has little to calm and reassure those outside the field who may question the legitimacy of public health's use of its governmental or social power'.[31] While advocacy is seen by many public health practitioners as a component of their work, the extent and approaches to advocacy used within public health raise important ethical questions. Is health really the most important and overriding value that should always dictate our activities? In advocating for more interventionist policies or adopting adversarial tactics – especially in areas such as alcohol, tobacco, and food where there are powerful lob-bying efforts by industry that may need to be countered – to what extent does the public health profession risk being seen as just another interest or pressure group?

In examining these categorisations of areas where ethics raises central questions for public health policy and practice, it quickly becomes evident that we also need to identify the understanding, knowledge, and skills necessary to begin seeking answers to the ques-tions raised by these different areas. In order to work towards greater clarity on what public health professional standards should be, how we ought to answer public health ethics ques-tions, and how far public health professionals should go in enforcing health-related impera-tives, we need a wider appreciation of different approaches to ethical guidance and ethical regulation.

2.4 Ethical guidance and regulation

We began this chapter by examining the relevance of normative considerations for public health and the manner in which moral and political values play a central role, not only in justifying public health activity, but also in determining which policies and interven-tions are ultimately selected. In elucidating the importance of ethics to public health, we also saw the various ways in which addressing ethical questions raised by public health requires attention to professional standards, applied ethics, and public health advocacy. The final component of a public health ethics involves identifying perspectives and approaches from which to provide answers to these questions. The two most prevalent means by which public health ethics seeks to do this work are through the provision of ethical guidance and through ethical regulation. While we do not endorse any particular account of public health ethics here, it is useful to broadly outline different ways in which public health ethics questions can be approached.

Public health practitioners and policy-makers frequently report facing ethical chal-lenges and recognise the importance of their actions and policies being ethically justified.[32]

---

30 Gostin (n 23), 126.
31 Jennings (n 16), 173.
32 See, e.g. Barry Pakes, *Ethical Analysis in Public Health Practice: Heterogeny, Discensus and the Man-on-the-Clapham Omnibus* (PhD thesis, University of Toronto 2014).

Sometimes it can be difficult or uncertain how to best integrate ethics into their activities or apply ethics to a particular policy question. Through the use of ethical guidance and ethical regulation, practitioners and policy-makers can better understand the different ways in which they can help ensure they are acting ethically. Much of the ethics guidance seeks to identify the ways in which individuals or even small groups can help direct themselves and their colleagues in ways that are ethical. Thus, ethics guidance tends to be internally directed – individuals using different ethics tools to help themselves act in ways that would be justifiable. It is also important, however, to consider ethics regulation as a further component of public health ethics. Ethics regulation is externally imposed; it is an institution-based method of formulating policy and guiding collective actions through identified authorities who are charged with enforcing it (e.g. identifying who counts as a professional, giving permissions, punishing non-compliance). As such, there are many aspects of ethics regulation that will have a closer proximity to law and governance than to philosophy. Perhaps one of the most familiar modes of ethics regulation is in the form of research ethics committees. Ethics guidance and ethics regulation, however, can take many forms and involve using different tools aimed at achieving different ends. It is important that individuals and institutions choose the appropriate form of guidance or regulation depending on the task at hand.

The first approach focuses on increasing *ethical awareness*. These forms of guidance or regulation are designed to act as a prompt, as a way of getting users to slow down or expand their thinking beyond scientific or technical issues and explore whether there might be some relevant ethical issues involved. For example, a pandemic preparedness and response plan might prompt users to recognise that the distribution of scarce resources is not merely a technical problem to be solved but also involves ethical questions about how such resources should be fairly distributed.

The second approach focuses on providing *ethical action guidance*. These forms of guidance or regulation are designed to tell people how to act when faced with particular ethical situation types or cases. Such an approach may be selected in contexts where individuals have no prior specialist ethics education or training, or in order to ensure everyone is following the same rules for reasons of consistency. For instance, a pandemic preparedness and response plan might require us to give priority to vulnerable patients in the distribution of scare resources as a matter of course.

The third approach focuses on facilitating *ethical deliberation*. These forms are designed to act as either an *aide-mémoire*, re-enforcing already existing ethical knowledge through prior education or training, or providing more directive instructions leading individuals through the process of ethical decision-making. The focus of such deliberative guidance often centres on providing an overall approach to working through the identification and resolution of ethical issues through the use of values or principles, or a checklist of ethically relevant questions. For example, a pandemic preparedness and response plan might provide different values or ways of reasoning that can be used to determine which of two patients should receive the last ventilated ICU bed when both clinically identical patients are vulnerable.

The fourth approach focuses on explaining *ethical justification*, providing a generalised account of what kinds of institutions, policies, or actions are ethical. For example, a pandemic preparedness and response plan might explain why all the right decisions and policies involve seeking to save as many lives as possible during a pandemic, whether they are vulnerable or not.

Of course, some forms of ethical guidance and regulation seek to accomplish more than one of these approaches. Nevertheless, once we are clear as to what form of ethical guidance or regulation would be appropriate, there is still a matter of selecting which type of different possible guidance or regulation we should use to address the ethical issue. In some respects, it might be useful to think about types of ethical guidance or regulation as tools. Whether it is analysing a public health problem, formulating a public health policy, or a public health practitioner deciding what to do in the moment, the right tool has to be chosen for the right job. As with all tools, each has its advantages and disadvantages, and proper selection of the appropriate tool is essential for getting the best results. Ultimately, we should try to select public health ethics tools that reflect both the practical realities of the situation (i.e. being empirically informed and account for the nature of the issue/problem of concern), as well possessing normative validity (i.e. being comprehensive, determinate, and justified).

2.4.1 Theories

Normative theories, such as moral and political theories, are concerned with explaining what we morally should do – individually or as a society. They provide a generalised and abstract account of, for instance, what makes an institution, policy, or action right or wrong, virtuous or vicious, just or unjust. Examples could include moral theories, such as consequentialism, deontology, and egalitarianism, and political theories, such as liberalism, communitarianism, and libertarianism. Within the literature, scholars have developed theories of public health ethics predicated on these various moral and political theories, such as liberalism,[33] libertarianism,[34] civic republicanism,[35] sufficientarianism,[36] human rights approaches,[37] and the capabilities approach.[38]

Normative theories can take two forms: ideal and non-ideal. Ideal theories are utopian or idealistic in nature, focussing on fundamental questions such as: if we were constructing a just society today, what it should look like? In order to be sufficiently abstract and comprehensive, they often make simplifying presuppositions, such as that all relevant individuals comply with the normative standards of the theory and that natural and historical considerations are favourable enough to realise such full compliance with these standards. Non-ideal theories, on the other hand, aim to be more realistic in theorising about the world as we find it – including its complexities, vagaries, and injustices – in order to develop an account of how we can, for instance, set out rules and develop institutions that can help make society more just from our current situation. Both forms of theory have their advantages and disadvantages, and it remains a persistent debate as to whether a worked-out and defended ideal theory is a necessary precursor to establishing what our non-ideal theory should look like.[39]

Theories are primarily concerned with ethical justification, though some argue that they can play a useful role in ethical deliberation as well. While a great deal of progress has been made in the development of moral and political theories, there remains persistent disagreement between theorists as to which moral or political theories are correct. While it is difficult, if not impossible, to find a theory that will satisfy all people, this lack of unanimity

---

33 See Coggon (n 1).
34 Richard Epstein, 'Let the Shoemaker Stick to His Last: A Defense of the "Old" Public Health' (2003) 46 *Perspectives in Biology and Medicine* S138.
35 Bruce Jennings, 'Public Health and Civic Republicanism: Toward an Alternative Framework for Public Health Ethics' in Angus Dawson and Marcel Verweij (eds), *Ethics, Prevention, and Public Health* (Oxford: Oxford University Press 2009) 30–58.
36 See Powers and Faden (n 22).
37 Lawrence Gostin and Zita Lazzarini, *Human Rights and Public Health in the AIDS Pandemic* (Oxford: Oxford University Press 1997); Jonathan Mann, Sophia Gruskin and Michael Grodin (eds), *Health and Human Rights: A Reader* (London: Routledge 1999).
38 See Ruger (n 13); Venkatapuram (n 22).
39 For a discussion, see Coggon (n 1), especially chapter 8.

does not mean that moral and political theorising is necessarily a subjective enterprise or doomed to relativism. Concomitantly, even if there is wide agreement on some moral or political theory, it need not mean such a theory will always provide the best answer for all questions or in all contexts. For this reason, one should not just blindly select and apply one theory to analyse public health. Different moral and political theories bring to light important concepts, values, and distinctions that are worthwhile and worthy of consideration in the determination of what can justify particular public health policy or action. Nevertheless, one should equally not unthinkingly 'pick and mix' components of disparate theories in one's analysis or reasoning.

2.4.2 Frameworks

Frameworks designate a set of substantive and/or procedural standards that should be followed in order to work through an ethical issue. The standards within a framework can include a set of values or principles articulating ethically defensible views or can reflect generally accepted precepts. Noteworthy examples include principlist frameworks by Upshur,[40] Childress et al,[41] Public Health Leadership Society,[42] the Nuffield Council on Bioethics,[43] and Public Health Ontario.[44] The standards can also take the form of a checklist, designed to help users identify whether ethical considerations are relevant in the situation and which ethical considerations should be taken into account in moving forward. Noteworthy examples include checklist frameworks by Kass[45] and Grill and Dawson.[46] Not all frameworks, however, involve articulating principles or a checklist – or a mixture of both.[47] Some also incorporate case-based approaches, such as casuistry.[48]

Frameworks are primarily concerned with ethical deliberation and ethical action guidance, depending on how they are structured. As a result, as Dawson notes:

> It makes no sense to criticise any framework for failing to contain well-worked out substantive theoretically-justified answers to deep normative questions. If they focus on such things, they cease to be a framework and adopt more of a theoretical role, as their primary intent becomes one of offering a justified account for the answers provided.[49]

Frameworks can either be general in nature (e.g. applying to all public health issues, including issues that may not have been foreseen) or designed to address a specific public health issue (e.g. pandemic preparedness and response). Frameworks can be developed by public health

---

40 Ross Upshur, 'Principles for the Justification of Public Health Intervention' (2002) 93 *Canadian Journal of Public Health* 101.

41 James Childress, Ruth Faden, Ruth Gaare, Lawrence Gostin, Jeffrey Kahn, Richard Bonnie, Nancy Kass, Anna Mastroianni, Jonathan Moreno, and Phillip Nieburg, 'Public Health Ethics: Mapping the Terrain' (2002) 30 *Journal of Law, Medicine and Ethics* 170.

42 Public Health Leadership Society, *Principles of the Ethical Practice of Public Health* (New Orleans: Public Health Leadership Society 2002).

43 Nuffield Council on Bioethics, *Public Health: Ethical Issues* (London: Nuffield 2007).

44 Public Health Ontario, *A Framework for the Ethical Conduct of Public Health Initiatives* (Toronto: Public Health Ontario 2012).

45 Nancy Kass, 'An Ethics Framework for Public Health' (2001) 91 *American Journal of Public Health* 1776.

46 Kalle Grill and Angus Dawson, 'Ethical Frameworks in Public Health Decision-Making: Defending a Value-Based and Pluralist Approach' (forthcoming) *Health Care Analysis*.

47 Andrew Tannahill, 'Beyond Evidence—To Ethics: A Decision-Making Framework for Health Promotion, Public Health and Health Improvement' (2008) 23 *Health Promotion International* 380.

48 Albert Jonsen and Stephen Toulmin, *The Abuse of Casuistry: A History of Moral Reasoning* (Berkeley: University of California Press 1988); Steven Coughlin, *Case Studies in Public Health Ethics* (Washington: American Public Health Association 2009).

49 Angus Dawson, 'Theory and Practice in Public Health Ethics: A Complex Relationship' in Stephen Peckham and Alison Hann (eds), *Public Health Ethics and Practice* (London: Policy Press 2009) 191.

ethics scholars and by organisations with an interest or mandate to formulate regulatory policy on public health. Sometimes, development of frameworks also involves engagement with the wider community, reflecting a commitment to respecting community values or issues – and, according to some, providing them with greater legitimacy.

2.4.3 Models

Models are designed to provide a simplified way of dealing with an ethical issue. They may take the form of diagram or algorithm or perhaps even a metaphor as a means of structuring the restricted perspective from which one should approach the issue. Models do not seek to justify or help us work through an ethical problem – they are used to remind us of something of ethical relevance. Models are typically focussed on raising ethical awareness or providing a means of structuring ethical options – for example, in a flowchart that identifies the different inputs relevant to an issue (in which case one of the arrows includes an ethically relevant consideration) or a figure illustrating different levels of moral coercion a public health intervention can possess (see next section).

2.4.4 Illustrating the differences between theories, frameworks, and models in public health ethics

Theories, frameworks, and models are different ways in which ethical guidance and regulation can be approached in public health ethics. They each involve different aims and different corresponding tools. Which approach is selected will depend upon the task at hand and the nature of the ethical questions involved. Nevertheless, it can be useful to see an example of these approaches as a means of elucidating the different ways and different levels at which one can approach questions in public health ethics. As a result of its familiarity within UK public health practice and policy, it is convenient to use the Nuffield Council on Bioethics' 2007 report on public health ethics as an illustrative example of these different approaches, how they differ in terms of their aims and level of analysis, and the manner in which there can be connections between the approaches.[50] The Nuffield Council's approach involves a theory, a framework, and a model. It envisions an overall approach in which all of these components are coherently grounded and related to each other. This is not to say this will always be the case with different theories, frameworks, and models – indeed, they often operate independently.

The Nuffield Council's approach begins by endorsing liberal theory as its overarching theoretical framework – in particular, John Stuart Mill's liberalism and harm principle. As a theory primarily concerned with ethical and political justification, it maintains that 'it is the state's business to uphold and defend certain fundamental individual rights, it is also the state's responsibility to care for the welfare of all citizens'.[51] This extends to public health activity – while it is the state's business to promote values such as autonomy and liberty, it is also justified in using coercive, liberty-infringing state interventions if it is to prevent harm to others.[52]

As a theory, there is a level of generality and abstraction in this position that does not always make it easy to apply to specific public health issues. For this reason, the Nuffield

---

50 Nuffield Council on Bioethics (n 43).
51 ibid, 14.
52 ibid, 16.

Council suggests that there is a corresponding *stewardship framework* that has its basis in this liberal theory. Stewardship is intended to be more illuminating in determining what degree of intervention it would be morally justifiable for the state to use in order to protect or promote public health in any given instance. According to the report:

> The concept of 'stewardship' is intended to convey that liberal states have a duty to look after important needs of people individually and collectively. It emphasises the obligation of states to provide conditions that allow people to be healthy and, in particular, to take measures to reduce health inequalities. The stewardship-guided state recognises that a primary asset of a nation is its health: higher levels of health are associated with greater overall wellbeing and productivity.[53]

As a framework, the stewardship approach provides more specific action guidance on particular goals, as well as elucidating different substantive values that should be used to guide our selection of public health policy and activity – such as liberty, autonomy, needs, health equality, health, wellbeing, and productivity. This framework can therefore provide public health policy-makers and practitioners with a basis on which to develop justifiable ethical guidance and ethical regulation.

The Nuffield Council also includes a model – what it calls the intervention ladder – which outlines different possible public health intervention types, from the least intrusive to the most intrusive in terms of personal choice and behaviour regulation. As a model, it helps to remind us that different levels of intervention involve different ethical considerations and will require different levels of ethical stringency to be rendered acceptable. However, the ladder does not help us deliberate through which level of intervention is most appropriate, nor does it recommend or justify any particular policy or action – that work is done through the stewardship framework and liberal theory. (Note that the ladder is discussed further in Chapters 3 and 9):

The intervention ladder

The ladder of possible government actions is as follows:

- Eliminate choice. Regulate in such a way as to entirely eliminate choice, for example through compulsory isolation of patients with infectious diseases.
- Restrict choice. Regulate in such a way as to restrict the options available to people with the aim of protecting them, for example removing unhealthy ingredients from foods, or unhealthy foods from shops or restaurants.
- Guide choice through disincentives. Fiscal and other disincentives can be put in place to influence people not to pursue certain activities, for example through taxes on cigarettes, or by discouraging the use of cars in inner cities through charging schemes or limitations of parking spaces.
- Guide choices through incentives. Regulations can be offered that guide choices by fiscal and other incentives, for example offering tax-breaks for the purchase of bicycles that are used as a means of travelling to work.
- Guide choices through changing the default policy. For example, in a restaurant, instead of providing chips as a standard side dish (with healthier options available),

---

53 ibid, xvi–xvii.

menus could be changed to provide a more healthy option as standard (with chips as an option available).

- Enable choice. Enable individuals to change their behaviours, for example by offering participation in a NHS 'stop smoking' programme, building cycle lanes, or providing free fruit in schools.
- Provide information. Inform and educate the public, for example as part of campaigns to encourage people to walk more or eat five portions of fruit and vegetables per day.
- Do nothing or simply monitor the current situation.[54]

In elucidating the theory, framework, and model (as we have characterised them) in the Nuffield Council's approach to public health ethics, we can appreciate how each component is concerned with different ethical tasks and is to be used for different ethical purposes. When selecting or endorsing different public health ethics theories, frameworks, or models, it is important not only to be clear what kinds of questions each approach seeks to answer but also the extent to which the approaches themselves are ultimately defensible. The quality and reach of the critical evaluation that public health ethics can bring to bear on public health policy and activities will depend on how these tools of ethical reflection and analysis are selected and applied.

Chapter 2: Summary

- Philosophy has significance for all areas of public health policy, practice, and research – especially moral philosophy and political philosophy.
- Moral philosophy and political philosophy are concerned with examining, analysing, and understanding normative concepts – the concepts that we use to justify and evaluate actions, institutions, and policies.
- Many normative concepts are expressed or underpinned by moral values – clarifying, critiquing, integrating, and reassessing values through ethical analysis is a crucial task for public health ethics.
- Public health ethics is concerned with professional standards, applied ethics, and public health advocacy. Two ways in which public health ethics seeks to contribute to these areas are through the provision of ethical guidance and ethical regulation.
- Ethical guidance and ethical regulation can take different forms: theories, frameworks, and models.

2.7 Further readings

Sudhir Anand, Fabienne Peter, and Amartya Sen (eds), *Public Health, Ethics, and Equity* (Oxford: Oxford University Press 2006).
Ronald Bayer, Lawrence Gostin, Bruce Jennings, and Bonnie Steinbock (eds), *Public Health Ethics: Theory, Policy, and Practice* (Oxford: Oxford University Press 2006).
Dan Beauchamp and Bonnie Steinbock (eds), *New Ethics for the Public's Health* (Oxford: Oxford University Press 1999).

---

54 ibid (cross-references within the report omitted).

Ruth Gaare Bernheim, James Childress, Alan Melnick, and Richard Bonnie (eds), *Essentials of Public Health Ethics* (Burlington: Jones and Bartlett Publishers 2014).

John Coggon, *What Makes Health Public? A Critical Evaluation of Moral, Legal, and Political Claims in Public Health* (Cambridge: Cambridge University Press 2012).

Angus Dawson and Marcel Verweij (eds), *Ethics, Prevention, and Public Health* (Oxford: Oxford University Press 2009).

Angus Dawson (ed), *Public Health Ethics: Key Concepts and Issues in Policy and Practice* (Cambridge: Cambridge University Press 2011).

Lawrence Gostin (ed), *Public Health Law and Ethics: A Reader, Revised and Updated* (Berkeley: University of California Press 2010).

Also, generally, see the journal *Public Health Ethics*, published by Oxford University Press http://phe.oxfordjournals.org.

Chapter 3

The evolution of public health legislation and regulation

3.1 The history of public health legislation

3.1.1 Origins

Notwithstanding the relative lack of academic attention accorded to public health law, which we noted in Chapter 1, the roots of public health law are both deep and long. The earliest forms of public health regulation were sanitary laws, such as those to be found in the Bible, which distinguished between 'clean' and 'unclean' animals. These differentiated ruminants (grazing animals such as sheep and deer) from carnivores and scavengers (such as pigs), the former being less likely to transmit zoonoses, although the extent of knowledge of food hygiene at the time – and thus its role as a rationale for these provisions – remains a matter for speculation.[1] Such laws provided justification for state regulation of population health as late as the second half of the nineteenth century.[2]

Sewers, a product of the advances in sanitary engineering pioneered by the Romans, who also instituted governmental supervision of public baths, street cleaning, water supplies, and the sale of spoiled food, were the first object of what might now be regarded as legislation on public health in England. An Act regulating the repair of sewers was passed in 1225, as was further legislation controlling nuisances.[3] Later in the same century, a Regulation of the City of London forbade permitting pigs to wander in the streets, while in 1309 a further Regulation prohibited the casting of filth from houses into the streets and lanes of the City; instead, persons 'ought to have it carried to the Thames or elsewhere out of the city'.[4]

Although steps had been taken to isolate lepers from the wider community from the pre-Christian period onward, it was the bubonic plague (or 'Black Death') 'which stimulated the earliest direct involvement of civil government in the control and prevention of epidemic disease'.[5] Especially in the Italian city-states, a sophisticated civic public health administration began to emerge, which had the twofold aims of controlling the spread of

1 See Thomas Key and Robert Allen, 'The Levitical Dietary Laws in the Light of Modern Science' (1974) 26 *Journal of the American Scientific Affiliation* 61.
2 See Report of the Special Committee . . . to consider the expediency of establishing a State Board of Health, *Massachusetts Senate Documents* 340 (22 May 1869), stating that 'all governments since the time of Moses are established to protect the life and health of their people'.
3 9 Hen. III, c.15&16 and 9 Hen. III, c.23 & 25 respectively.
4 See Michael Warren, *A Chronology of State Medicine, Public Health, Welfare and Related Services in Britain 1066–1999* (London: Faculty of Public Health Medicine 2000).
5 Diana Porter, *Health, Civilization and the State* (London: Routledge 1999) 45.

disease and of maintaining the political *status quo*. This entailed the quarantining of vessels, posting of watchmen at city gates to inspect travellers, isolation of affected individuals, intelligence and surveillance measures, and the establishment of permanent health boards administered by political authorities with the power to issue licences to visitors or for merchandise. In short, 'plague founded public health as a function of the modern state, aimed at the management of the relationship between disease and social disorder'.[6] This approach, which relied largely upon deployment of 'police powers' to maintain stability in the face of a threat originating from beyond the community in question, underpins the traditional paradigm of public health law as a means of protecting the public from dangers, usually externally generated.

England, which lacked the urban political infrastructure of Italian and other continental European city-states, developed measures more slowly and haphazardly. Porter notes that, prior to 1518, there were no fixed regulations relating to plague.[7] However, the emergence of a strong centralised political administration in the Tudor and Stuart period facilitated a regulatory response. In 1578, Elizabeth I's chief minister, William Cecil, issued orders of the Privy Council based upon northern European control methods; just over a quarter of a century later, the first national statute, 'an Act for the charitable relief and ordering of persons with the plague' was enacted.[8] This allowed for the appointment of 'searchers, watchmen, examiners, keepers and buriers' by state authorities and prescribed criminal punishment for an infected person who failed to 'keep to his house'. Such measures were, of course, ineffective to prevent the 'Great Plague' of London in 1665–66, which has been estimated to have killed up to 100,000 people, or approximately one-quarter of the city's population.[9]

Regulatory interventions were shaped by the prevailing theories and understandings of the manner in which diseases were spread. Quarantine and isolation were premised upon the belief that disease was spread by contagion, whether by direct contact between individuals, or through some atmospheric means. Conditions that were especially prevalent from ancient to early modern times, such as leprosy and plague, tended to reinforce the validity of such beliefs. But it is important to note that adherence to a particular theory of disease had implications that went beyond the merely 'scientific' and instead connected to conceptions of the appropriate role for the state (and, hence, to the function of law as a mode of state intervention). Ackerknecht expresses the matter well:

> Contagionism was not a mere theoretical or even medical problem. Contagionism had found its material expression in the quarantines and their bureaucracy, and the whole discussion was thus never a discussion on contagion alone, but *always on contagion and quarantines*. Quarantines meant, to the rapidly growing class of merchants and industrialists, a source of losses, a limitation to expansion, a weapon of bureaucratic control that it was no longer willing to tolerate. . . . Contagionism would, through its associations with the old bureaucratic powers, be suspect to all liberals, trying to reduce state interference to a minimum.[10]

---

6 ibid, 62.
7 ibid, 57.
8 1 Jac. I, c. 31 (1604).
9 See Harvard University Library Open Collections Program, <http://ocp.hul.harvard.edu/contagion/plague.html> accessed 5 April 2016.
10 Erwin Ackerknecht, 'Anticontagionism between 1821 and 1867' (2009) 38 *International Journal of Epidemiology* 7, 9 (emphasis in original).

3.1.2 The Victorian era: foundations of modern public health legislation

The spirit of rationalism and critical scientific inquiry that emerged in the eighteenth century prompted a re-evaluation of the contagionist theory. This understanding of the spread of disease was 'held. . . up to ridicule as a kind of futile mythology from the dark ages of medicine' by some;[11] for such critics, 'this was a fight for science, against outdated authorities and medieval mysticism; for observation and research against systems and speculation'.[12] As in the preceding centuries, changing patterns of epidemic disease were influential in this process of rethinking. In particular, cholera, estimated to have killed nearly 75,000 people in England and Wales during two pandemic episodes in 1831–32 and 1848–49,[13] had a significant impact upon nineteenth-century mentality. The disease appeared not to be contained by those quarantine or isolation measures which had been more or less efficacious to deal with plague, although such measures were initially employed to contain its spread. Further incentive to reconceptualise the mode of protection was afforded by the social unrest that frequently followed in the wake of outbreaks of the disease. The use of 'police powers' to enforce quarantine and cordons sanitaires generated suspicion and opposition within a populace that, in light of the rise of popular democratic movements, was less inclined to passivity than previous generations.

While there had been theories concerning the role of foul contaminated air in causing diseases since the ancient Greek era, 'miasmatism', which held that epidemics were caused by inanimate particles produced from decaying organic matter that combined to form a poisonous vapour, gained particular currency in the West in the early nineteenth century. Thus, Thomas Southwood Smith, one of the leading English proponents of the theory (and the man to whom Jeremy Bentham willed his body for dissection), argued that:

> To assume the method of propagation by touch, whether by the person or of infected articles, and to overlook that by the corruption of the air, is at once to increase the real danger, from exposure to noxious effluvia, and to divert attention from the true means of remedy and prevention. . . . If the great practical truth, taught by modern investigation and experience, be, that the only real security against any degree and kind of epidemic disease is an abundant and constant supply of pure air, the prevention of overcrowding, and the dispersion of the sick; and if, as is generally agreed, confinement in a foul atmosphere can convert common fever into pestilence, and ventilation and dispersion can dissipate any contagion, then quarantine must not only be useless but pernicious . . . the only means of preventing the origin and spread of epidemic disease is the adoption of sanitary measures. Substitution of sanitary measures for quarantine restrictions would render the importation of any disease from one country into another in the highest degree improbable.[14]

The 'sanitary movement', led by Edwin Chadwick, a lawyer, regarded the removal of 'filth' as the means of eliminating disease, such disease being causative of poverty (and hence, instability and unrest). This suggested an entirely different form of regulatory intervention

---

11 Porter (n 5), 104.
12 Ackerknecht (n 10), 9.
13 Stephanie Snow, 'Commentary: Sutherland, Snow and Water: The Transmission of Cholera in the Nineteenth Century' (2002) 31 International Journal of Epidemiology 908, 908.
14 T Baker (ed), The Common Nature of Epidemics, and Their Relation to Climate and Civilisation: Also Remarks on Contagion and Quarantine: From Writings and Official Reports by Southwood Smith, M.D. (Philadelphia: J.B. Lippincott & Co. 1866) 68–69, 74, 75.

by the state, one that focussed upon environmental improvement rather than quarantining and isolation. In fact, the sanitary idea rested upon an engineering rather than a medical model, whereby construction of efficient sewage and drainage systems, the provision of clean water, and the widening of streets would reduce 'filth' and thus disease. While this approach might seem limited, it had considerable political and legislative purchase, and it might be viewed as the forerunner of modern approaches that focus on the social determinants of health.

At his own expense, Chadwick compiled and published *The Sanitary Condition of the Labouring Population of Great Britain* in 1842. This recommended establishment of a central public health authority that would require local boards, headed in this regard by a Medical Officer of Health and assisted by an inspector of nuisances, to provide 'drainage, the removal of all refuse of habitations, streets and roads, and the improvement of the supplies of water',[15] in addition to cleansing; paving; and regulation of dwellings, nuisances, and offensive trades. Chadwick's ideas were given impetus by the establishment of a Health of Towns Association in 1844, which sought to place pressure on government to adopt his recommendations, and by the report of Royal Commission on the Health of Towns published in 1845.[16] Following local implementation of the proposals in Liverpool in 1846, the first national Public Health Act was enacted in 1848. This created a central department, the General Board of Health, but in other respects, implementation was largely left to the discretion of local authorities. Town councils or corporations became local boards of health in metropolitan areas, whereas elsewhere these took the form of special boards elected by ratepayers; however, the institutional framework was permissive, not mandatory – one-tenth of the ratepayers in a locality could petition the General Board for adoption of the Act.[17] The local bodies were empowered to appoint officials, including a surveyor, an inspector of nuisances, and an officer of health, who must be a qualified medical practitioner. They were responsible for cleansing of sewers; regulation of cellar dwellings and houses unfit for human habitation; supervision of lodging houses; regulation of offensive trades; supervision of drainage, water, and gas supplies; maintenance of pavements; and provision of burial grounds, public parks, and baths.

The Act was far from an unqualified success. While 284 districts applied to adopt it between 1848 and 1853, and it was established in 103 towns in the same period,[18]

> vigour varied between sanitary authorities. Some failed to make any improvements to mains drainage or to implement the Board's engineering schemes. In other districts, the same insanitary conditions persisted whether they adopted the Act or not. Some authorities, however, took up their new responsibilities with a vengeance and instituted model reforms under the direction of the Board's inspectors.[19]

In large part, ideological antipathy to state intervention underpinned opposition to this legislation; the *Herald* newspaper remarked that 'a little dirt and freedom, may after all, be more

15 *Report from the Poor Law Commissioners on an Inquiry into the Sanitary Conditions of the Labouring Population of Great Britain* (London: HMSO 1842) 369–372.

16 *Second Report of the Commissioners for Inquiring into the State of Large Towns and Populous Districts*, 602 (1845) XVIII.

17 Note, however, that it was obligatory to establish Boards where the death rate in a locality was greater than 23 in 1,000 persons.

18 The Act did not apply to London; see Metropolitan Commission of Sewers Act 1848.

19 Porter (n 5), 150.

desirable than no dirt at all and slavery'.[20] The General Board was dissolved by the Public Health Act 1858, and its functions transferred to the Privy Council, which was empowered to make enquiries into any aspect of public health in any area. However, this certainly did not amount to the death knell for public health law in England; indeed, 'the legislative base of public health expanded dramatically after 1848'.[21] Statutes that were enacted in the field in the quarter century after the 1848 Act included the Nuisances Removal and Diseases Prevention Acts 1848 and 1849; the Vaccination Acts 1853, 1867, and 1871; the Diseases Prevention Act 1855; the Sanitary Acts 1866 and 1868; and the Public Health Act 1872, to name but a few. However, this haphazard and piecemeal approach was 'so chaotic that even enthusiastic local authorities found it too bewildering to implement'.[22] The eventual response was the enactment of consolidating legislation, the Public Health Act 1875, which has been described as 'the Magna Carta of public health until 1936'.[23] Significantly, this statute – which amounted in effect, to a code of sanitary law[24] – required local authorities to undertake public health responsibilities and to constitute local boards of health and appoint a local Medical Officer of Health. The Act therefore represented something of a watershed between the more permissive early Victorian era and the late nineteenth-century state, which functioned – at least in the context of public health – in an increasingly bureaucratic and 'command and control' manner.

The 1875 Act marked a turning point in the history of public health law in an additional respect. Section 84 obliged a 'keeper of a common lodging-house' in which a person was residing who was 'ill with fever or any infectious disease' to 'give immediate notice thereof to the medical officer of the local authority'; subsequent provisions made access to such premises mandatory and imposed penalties for failure to comply.[25] This represented the introduction of statutory notification, a regulatory measure that was repeated and expanded on a number of occasions in the remaining quarter of the nineteenth century, initially through local Acts in particular areas,[26] then in 1889 nationally on a permissive basis,[27] and finally on a mandatory basis in 1899.[28] The diseases that were listed as notifiable, under section 6 of the 1889 Act, were 'smallpox, cholera, diphtheria, membranous croup, erysipelas, the disease known as scarlatina or scarlet fever, and the fevers known by the following names, typhus, typhoid, enteric, relapsing, continued, or puerperal'.

Notification provisions, and the attendant isolation of the infected, were indicative of a further emergent understanding of the spread of disease: the bacteriological model, or 'germ theory'. Especially influential in developing this approach in England was John Snow, regarded as the 'father of modern epidemiology',[29] whose famous investigations of the cholera outbreak in Soho, London, led to the removal of the handle of the public water pump in Broad Street. The germ theory did not gain significant purchase until the 1860s, but

20 Quoted in David Roberts, *Paternalism in Early Victorian England* (London: Croom Helm 1979) 200.
21 Porter (n 5), 156.
22 ibid, 158.
23 Warren (n 4).
24 See Part 3 of the Act.
25 ss. 85, 86.
26 For example, Bolton in 1877 and Edinburgh in 1879.
27 Infectious Diseases Notification Act 1889. The Act made notification mandatory in London.
28 Infectious Diseases Notification (Extension) Act 1899.
29 See e.g. Francis Chappelle, *Wellsprings: The History of Bottled Spring Waters* (New Brunswick: Rutgers University Press 2005) 82; Renaud Piarroux and Benoît Faucher, 'Cholera Epidemics in 2010: Respective Roles of Environment, Strain Changes and Human-Driven Dissemination' (2012) 18 *Clinical Microbiology and Infection* 231, 237; and, for a slightly more sceptical view, which still acknowledges Snow as 'unquestionably an essential link in the causal chain that led epidemiology to what it is now', see Cesar Victoria, 'The Causes of Epidemiology' (2013) 381 (9874) *Lancet* 1302, 1302.

thereafter, it was increasingly reflected in regulatory measures that sought to provide means to identify the sources of outbreaks of communicable disease and to interrupt transmission through segregation and isolation.[30]

Another legislative reflection both of the bacteriological approach and of the increasing tendency of the Victorian state to adopt a 'command and control' mode of regulation, was the initiation of compulsory schemes of vaccination against smallpox. The Vaccination Act 1853 had begun this policy,[31] applying to all infants up to the age of three months (four months in the case of children in orphanages), but with ineffectual sanctions for failure to comply. Further legislation was enacted in 1867 (which provided for continuous and cumulative penalties for defaulting parents), 1871, 1873, and 1898; and in Scotland, in 1863.

This legislation provoked significant resistance. Riots occurred in several towns in response to the 1853 legislation. Organised movements emerged in opposition to the laws, notably the Anti-Vaccination League (established in 1853) and the Anti-Compulsory Vaccination League (1867). Some parents repeatedly flouted the law, either choosing to pay the fine on each occasion, or accepting imprisonment.[32] A particular locus of resistance was the city of Leicester; here, the number of prosecutions rose from 2 in 1869 to 1154 in 1881;[33] by 1885, nearly 3000 parents were awaiting prosecution,[34] and a demonstration that took place there that year attracted 80,000–100,000 people.[35] The long-term consequence of such resistance was the establishment of a Royal Commission to investigate grievances against vaccination. Reporting in 1896,[36] it concluded that vaccination was effective but also that cumulative penalties should be abolished and that a conscientious objection clause be inserted, both of which proposals were given effect in the 1898 Act.

Motives for opposition to compulsory vaccination were, of course, varied: they might include fear of the impact upon children, religious belief, or distrust of the medical profession. However, a significant strand was ideological: hostility towards state interventionism in private family life, exacerbated by the fact that such measures were being visited upon otherwise healthy children. For example, William Hume-Rothery, later President of the Anti-Compulsory Vaccination League, argued that:

> it is only by the voluntary and judicious exercise of their own powers that the people can progress; it is clear so far as the State does for them . . . the duties which are within their own sphere and competence, to that extent it limits and retards their development . . . if even vaccination were the greatest blessing in existence it would not be the duty of the State to enforce it.[37]

30 In addition to the Acts noted in nn.27–28 above, see also Contagious and Infectious Diseases (Animals) Act 1878; Diseases of Animals Act 1894; Contagious Diseases Act 1864–1869.

31 Note, however, that the Vaccination Act 1840 had first made free vaccination available as a charge on the poor rates, this therefore constituting 'the first free health service provided through legislation on a national scale and available to all': Warren (n 4).

32 Stanley Williamson, 'Anti-Vaccination Leagues' (1984) 59 Archives of Disease in Childhood 1195, 1195.

33 Dale Ross, 'Leicester and the Anti-Vaccination Movement 1853–1889' (1967–68) 43 Transactions – The Leicestershire Archaeological and Historical Society 35, 37.

34 Stuart Fraser, 'Leicester and Smallpox: The Leicester Method' (1980) 24 Medical History 315, 330.

35 Nadja Durbach, 'They Might as Well Brand Us: Working-Class Resistance to Compulsory Vaccination in Victorian England' (2000) 13 Social History of Medicine 45, 57.

36 Final Report of the Royal Commission Appointed to Inquire into the Subject of Vaccination, C-8270 (1896).

37 William Hume-Rothery, Vaccination and the Vaccination Laws: A Physical Curse and a Class Tyranny (Manchester: Tulley 1872).

Similarly, speaking in debates upon the Bill which became the 1898 Act, the MP for Chester-field, Thomas Bayley, noted that there were:

> people who believe that they have control of their own bodies and of their children, and that they should not allow the State or anybody else to tell them what they should do with their bodies or with their children. It is a question of the freedom of parents, to do what they think right with their children.[38]

In conclusion, enactment and application of laws relating to public health became a significant activity of the British state during the Victorian era. This might seem somewhat paradoxical, given the pervasiveness of liberal individualism as a political ideology during the period, and, indeed, widespread opposition to certain of the laws was reflective of popular concern with the 'growth of authoritarian, paternalist power of central government on the one hand and the growth of the despotic influence of a particular profession – the medical profession, on the other'.[39] However, when we consider that the consequences of ill health amongst the urban poor were inevitably negative for the free market economy favoured by the Victorian political elite, and that utilitarianism prescribed that the state should do the greatest good for the greatest number, the contradiction appears less profound than it might appear at first sight.

We have noted, also, the evolution of regulatory measures in line with changing understandings of the nature of contagious disease. Of course, it is important not to overstate the abruptness of the shift from contagionism, to miasmatism, to bacteriology; vestiges of previous approaches continued for some time after the new theories emerged, and time lags also inevitably occurred before legislation was enacted:

> On closer inspection, these phases [of intervention] are . . . not so clear-cut, different models co-existing in the same time period. It is therefore more appropriate to view each phase as being subjected to different influences, with one particular model having a stronger influence over public health policy and practice, but co-existing with others exerting less influence.[40]

Nonetheless, one might argue that modes of regulation broadly kept pace with the 'science' of public health in Britain during the nineteenth century. This was far from the case during the twentieth century, as will next be examined.

3.1.3 The twentieth century: the marginalisation of public health legislation?

> British public health through much of the twentieth century has been hard to characterise. The maturation of the welfare state and the great changes in health policy that came with it did not transform public health in Britain; it remained an ill-unified amalgam of programmes and institutions, central and local, influenced by all manner of political, cultural and professional concerns, not all of them apparent. . . . Modern institutions of public health, so busy keeping up with ordinary business in an era of budgetary constraint, can scarcely consider long-term goals, much less new concepts of health.[41]

---

38 Hansard, 19 April 1898, vol. 56, col. 454.
39 Porter (n 5), 112.
40 Rob Baggott, Public Health: Policy and Politics (2nd edn., Basingstoke: Palgrave Macmillan 2011) 41.
41 Christopher Hamlin, 'State Medicine in Great Britain' in Dorothy Porter (ed), The History of Public Health and the Modern State (Amsterdam: Rodopi 1994) 154.

Hamlin's downbeat analysis of the state of public health as a field of public policy in Britain during the last century could equally well be applied to the subcategory of public health law. Whereas statutory intervention was a well-used instrument for the pursuit of public health goals in the nineteenth century, the twentieth century was characterised – as will be seen – by legislation that was increasingly out of step with the health and social context. Certain trends emerging from the Victorian era can be seen as impacting on the growing marginalisation of public health legislation over the course of the following century.

In particular, the discovery of the bacteriological causes of disease at the end of the nineteenth century carried important implications for the scope and frequency of legislative activity. Two dimensions may be discerned here. On the one hand, it might be argued that, in light of the evolution of this 'correct' form of understanding of the nature of disease, there was no further need for changes in the mode or objects of regulation adopted by the state in response (as had been the case, for example, when the miasmatic approach, which necessitated the removal of 'filth', superseded the contagionist approach, with its emphasis upon quarantine and isolation). However, such a conclusion somewhat overlooks two factors: first, that (as discussed in the following subsection and also Chapter 1) there have been shifts in the understanding of *public health itself* – that is, its functions, objectives, and scope – that might conceivably have been granted attention in legislation and, second, that the concerns of the public health community gradually shifted over the course of the twentieth century, both from communicable to non-communicable diseases and from absence of disease to 'wellbeing'.

The second repercussion of the emergence of bacteriology upon public health, and by extension, the law relating to it, was that a 'shift in emphasis took place from the environment to the individual as the vector of transmission'.[42] That is, there was 'an emphasis on the manifestation of disease in individuals and subgroups within the population, rather than the health of the population as a whole'.[43] The novelty of this development can be overstated: the sanitary movement had also emphasised the need for interventions in relation to a vulnerable group – the poor – but as Porter notes, this represented a much more 'generalised concept of the population' than that targeted as a consequence of bacteriological understanding, where subgroups might include those affected with tuberculosis, infants at risk from diarrhoea, etc.[44] Moreover, it will be noted that this greater degree of specificity connected to particular conditions as well as to smaller population subgroups. We might therefore discern an increased importance attached to *medical knowledge* in the practice of public health.

This trend was exacerbated by the establishment of the National Health Service (NHS) after the Second World War, as will be discussed further below, but at the dawn of the twentieth century, its consequence was, as Baggott notes,[45] a degree of bifurcation between those who retained some commitment to the ideals of the sanitary approach and those who subscribed more fully to 'germ theory'. The former were increasingly drawn into a broader movement and discourse on social welfare in general terms, while the latter evinced growing interest in the curative possibilities of medical treatment. This last came to dominate the public health community, in part because 'medical intervention . . . could be more easily measured and quantified, over social intervention, which was more difficult to evaluate'.[46] But it also diminished the value of regulatory activity, which was much more readily and usefully directed (whether successfully or not) toward alleviation of negative socio-economic conditions than to the prescription, or proscription, of certain types of scientific knowledge.

---

42 Porter (n 5), 140.
43 Baggott (n 40), 38.
44 Porter (n 5), 140.
45 Baggott (n 40), 38.
46 ibid.

Hence, while (as will be noted below), legislation continued to be enacted to address specific public health problems through particular regulatory mechanisms, arguably a more important way in which legislation impacted upon public health in the early twentieth century was more indirect, through the *establishment of institutional frameworks* through which public health goals might subsequently be realised. Two statutes are worthy of attention in this regard. The Ministry of Health Act 1919 created, for the first time, a central government department with the potential to rationalise and manage those public health functions that had developed as a 'patchwork of ramshackle and uncoordinated services' during the nineteenth century,[47] as well as providing leadership on policy priorities. The Act imposed a wide-ranging duty upon a Minister of Health to:

> take all such steps as may be desirable to secure the preparation, effective carrying out and co-ordination of measures conducive to the health of the people, including measures for the prevention and cure of diseases, the avoidance of fraud in connection with alleged remedies therefor, the treatment of physical and mental defects, the treatment and care of the blind, the initiation and direction of research, the collection, preparation, publication, and dissemination of information and statistics.[48]

In addition to overall coordination, the Ministry acquired specific responsibilities in relation to the public health responsibilities exercised under the Local Government Board Act 1871 (which had united such functions with administration of the Poor Law under the aegis of the Board): environmental health; water supply and sanitation; housing; child and maternal welfare; and the National Health Insurance scheme established by the National Insurance Act 1911 (which provided sickness, disablement, and maternity benefits; free treatment for tuberculosis; and a general practitioner service, albeit only for the insured and not for dependents).

A further 'capacity-building' statute was the Local Government Act 1929, which finally replaced the Poor Law Boards with 'public assistance committees' of the council. The consequence was that the public health functions exercised by Boards of Guardians in the Victorian era, together with control of most public hospitals, were transferred to local government. This represented a further, and more general, extension of the role of local government that had been steadily increasing since the turn of the century – and continued to do so until the Second World War – with obligations to take action and to provide services in areas as diverse as provision of school meals;[49] inspection and treatment of pupils;[50] treatment of tuberculosis;[51] diagnosis, treatment, and education in respect of venereal disease;[52] maternity and child welfare;[53] care of the blind;[54] health education;[55] smoke emissions;[56] care of patients with mental health problems;[57] and diagnosis and treatment of cancer.[58]

---

47   Walter Holland and Susie Stewart, *Public Health: The Vision and the Challenge* (London: Nuffield Trust 1998) 30. The authors note that 'one family, for example, might receive care from as many as nine different doctors working under five different departments': 32.
48   s. 2.
49   Education (Provision of Meals) Act 1906.
50   Education (Administrative Provisions) Act 1907.
51   Public Health (Prevention and Treatment of Disease) Act 1913; Public Health (Tuberculosis) Act 1921.
52   Public Health (Venereal Diseases) Regulations 1916.
53   Maternity and Child Welfare Act 1918.
54   Blind Persons Act 1920.
55   Public Health Act 1925, s. 67.
56   Public Health (Smoke Abatement) Act 1926.
57   Mental Treatment Act 1930.
58   Cancer Act 1939.

This legislative catalogue clearly demonstrates how, 'during the 1920s and 1930s the work of the local public health departments grew significantly in range and importance',[59] a fact that has led some to label this a 'proud era' for public health.[60] However, it will be noted that there appeared to be little by way of coherent planning underlying the allocation of statutory tasks to local bodies; this was a 'ragbag of activities', 'with little philosophical underpinning'.[61] In some respects, this was no different to the Victorian era – then, too, much legislation had been enacted that 'regulated isolated health threats in an uncoordinated way'.[62] Yet, it might be argued that the Victorian period had been characterised by a 'vision' on the part of the state (notably, that of specific reformers such as Chadwick), in which 'the Public Health Acts were permitted to serve as a filter for more general social reform'.[63] Such vision appeared to be lacking in the early twentieth century; it appeared that there was a:

> lack of a firm philosophy to guide it [public health] in approaching health problems. During the early twentieth century, those active in the field worked out what looked very much like an *ex post facto* rationalisation of public health's increased involvement in the work of personal, preventive services.[64]

In light of the focus upon individuals as carriers of disease, there seemed little to distinguish the work undertaken by the Medical Officer of Health as a consequence of his statutory responsibilities from that of the independent general practitioner, such that it was claimed in 1925 that 'public health work is mainly clinical medicine, but clinical medicine of a special kind'.[65] The lack of distinctiveness was exacerbated by the assumption of responsibility for hospital administration following the Local Government Act 1929, since much time was spent on this activity to the detriment of the traditionally broader, preventive role of the Medical Officer of Health.[66]

The statute that has been described as 'the foundation' of contemporary public health law,[67] the Public Health Act 1936, both exemplified and reinforced the uncertain position occupied by the activity of public health. This was a consolidating statute, containing 347 sections and three Schedules, which set out the powers and responsibilities of local authorities in relation to public health. It contained provisions relating to sanitation and buildings (covering sewerage; sanitary conveniences for buildings; powers and byelaws relating to buildings; drains and cesspools; removal of refuse, scavenging, and keeping of animals; filthy or verminous premises or articles and verminous persons and public conveniences); nuisances and offensive trades; water supply; prevention, notification, and treatment of disease; hospitals and nursing homes; notification of births, maternity, and child welfare and child life protection; baths, washhouses, and bathing places; common lodging houses; canal boats; watercourses, ditches and ponds; and tents, vans, and sheds. As Coker and Martin

---

59 Jane Lewis, *What Price Community Medicine? The Philosophy, Practice and Politics of Public Health since 1919* (Brighton: Wheatsheaf 1986) 15.

60 Holland and Stewart (n 47), 58.

61 Lewis (n 59), 11, 26.

62 Robyn Martin, 'Domestic Regulation of Public Health: England and Wales' in Robyn Martin and Linda Johnson (eds), *Law and the Public Dimension of Health* (London: Cavendish 2001) 76–77.

63 Lewis (n 59), 6.

64 ibid, 3.

65 'The Public Health Service' (1925) 34 *Medical Officer* 99.

66 See Lewis (n 59), 26–27. Contrast this with the much broader definitions of public health adopted by Winslow and others, discussed in Chapter 1.

67 Martin (n 62), 77. Coker and Martin also note that, through British colonial influence, this statute constitutes the foundation of public health law in many other parts of the world; see Richard Coker and Robyn Martin, 'Introduction: The Importance of Law for Public Health Policy and Practice' (2006) 120 (Supplement 1) *Public Health* 2, 3–4.

note, this statute was largely (albeit, not exclusively) rooted in a 'nuisance model', in which contagious disease was limited by regulating waste, refuse, and poor systems of drainage, through removal, control, and licencing;[68] thus, the 'concern is with inadequate premises, on an understanding that ill health results from identifiable bodies escaping from a physical source' (see also Chapter 5).[69] In some respects, this was beneficial because it rendered the methods and targets of public health (and its associated legal framework) clearly distinguishable from those of clinical medicine, thus reinforcing the distinctiveness of the field. But the approach taken by the Act was also anachronistic, reflecting the continuing influence of the miasmatic reading of disease causation at a time when the increasing focus of the medical profession was upon the development of therapeutic agents for the treatment of disease.[70] Hence, the legislation, while clearly of utility in rationalising an extraordinary patchwork of statutory powers and responsibilities, also served to underline a growing perception of the irrelevance of public health at this period in history.

Paradoxically, while 'the creation of the NHS in 1948 can be regarded as a major public health achievement in its own right',[71] its establishment, by way of the National Health Service Act 1946, also served to confirm the impression of the marginalisation of wider state responsibilities concertedly to protect and promote population health. This was the case in two senses. First, those working in public health were accorded little say in the operation of the new Service. Although the 1944 White Paper, *A National Health Service*,[72] had envisaged local authority control, the final scheme entailed a nationalised hospital service administered by regional boards appointed by the Minister; this was 'the result of a negotiated compromise between a Labour government determined to create a comprehensive service, funded by taxation and free at the point of delivery, and a medical profession which preferred nationalisation to multipurpose local government control'.[73] Medical appointees to the boards came overwhelmingly from clinical medicine, not public health;[74] while local authorities did retain a role, it was 'substantially reduced',[75] amounting to 'a range of environmental and personal health services, including maternity and child welfare clinics, health visitors, midwives, health education, and vaccination and immunisation. They were also in charge of the ambulance service'.[76] Lewis reports that the Medical Officer of Health for Bournemouth bemoaned that, having been 'for 21 years . . . medical superintendent of all the institutions controlled by the Public Health Committee . . . he has not opportunity of expressing his views to a Hospital or Sanatorium Management Committee or even of hearing the opinions expressed by others'.[77]

Second, there was a widespread belief 'that the NHS was constituted as a sickness rather than a health service',[78] a view that largely prevails to the present day.[79] Another Medical Officer of Health, for Salford, opined that 'a tragedy of our times is that so much is being spent on negative health; so comparatively little on positive health'.[80] This was reflected

68 ibid, 3.
69 Martin (n 62), 79.
70 See Holland and Stewart (n 47), 59.
71 Baggott (n 40), 48.
72 Cmd 6502.
73 Porter (n 6), 215–216.
74 Holland and Stewart (n 47), 100.
75 Lewis (n 59), 46.
76 Holland and Stewart (n 47), 96.
77 Quoted in Lewis (n 59), 47.
78 Baggott (n 40), 49.
79 See e.g. HM Government, *Healthy Lives, Healthy People: Our Strategy for Public Health in England* (CM 7985 2010): 'one of the great challenges of our generation [is] how we can create a public health service, not just a national sickness service': [1.5].
80 Quoted in Lewis (n 59), 48.

in the legislation; as Holland and Stewart note, 'the Act placed the emphasis squarely on curative medicine'.[81] Although the general duties to promote a comprehensive health service imposed upon the Secretary of State for Health by section 1 of the Act included 'improvement in the physical and mental health of the people of England and Wales' and the 'prevention' as well as the 'diagnosis and treatment of illness', the priority accorded to the latter was indicated by the pre-eminence placed upon hospital and general practitioner services, in Parts II and IV of the legislation respectively. Only section 28, which empowered local authorities to 'make arrangements for the purpose of the prevention of illness' seemed, albeit in rather opaque manner, to speak to the traditional role for public health; and even these arrangements necessitated approval by the Minister. One Medical Officer of Health wrote, perhaps somewhat optimistically, that 'there is all the world of preventive medicine in these permissive clauses. . . . [I]t appears to me that anything can be provided as long as it is reasonably provided with the object of preventing disease, or for the welfare of the patient'.[82]

The period following the establishment of the NHS might be viewed as one in which the overwhelming focus was upon the potential of curative services to address the health problems of the British population. Such limited public health legislation as was enacted remained embedded in the dated concepts of disease and the attendant regulatory mechanisms exemplified by the 1936 Act. For example, the Prevention of Damage by Pests Act 1949 placed a duty upon local authorities to keep their districts free from rats and mice, and upon those manufacturing, storing, transporting or selling food to give notice of infestation, while the Public Health (Recurring Nuisances) Act 1969 addressed problems of smell and noise that frequently recurred. The Public Health Act 1961 extended the ambit of the 1936 Act but remained firmly grounded in the model of regulation of individual nuisances.[83]

It was not simply the understanding of the causes of disease embodied by such legislation that appeared outdated. The major threats to public health were quite distinct from those that had been prevalent in the Victorian era. It has been calculated that approximately 75% of the decline in mortality between 1901 and 1971 can be attributed to a reduction in deaths from infectious water-borne, air-borne, food-borne, and other diseases.[84] Proportionately, therefore, non-communicable conditions, such as heart disease and cancer, were a much greater threat to population health by the 1960s than had been the case in the nineteenth century: deaths from the former condition overtook those from infectious diseases around 1916 in the UK, while cancer did so around 1931.[85] There was, therefore, a significant 'epidemiological transition', to which, of course, the public health interventions of the nineteenth and early twentieth centuries had made an important contribution.

However, the legislative response to this shift during the twentieth century was minimal at best. There was certainly no attempt made to enact legislation, along the lines of the Public Health Act 1936, which conferred powers and duties to act in a broad variety of circumstances germane to differing forms of non-communicable disease. Rather, there was limited legislative response to particular public health threats. For example, in respect of the health harms caused by tobacco, sales to children were banned, initially by the Children's Act 1908 and subsequently and progressively by the Children and Young Person's Act 1933,

---

81 Holland and Stewart (n 47), 100.
82 Kenneth Macdonald, 'The Challenge of Section 28' (1947–48) 61 *Public Health* 27, 27–28.
83 See Martin (n 62), 80.
84 Thomas McKeown, R.G. Record, and R.D. Turner, 'An Interpretation of the Decline in Mortality in England and Wales during the Twentieth Century' (1975) 29 *Population Studies* 391.
85 Scott Mann, *Bioethics in Perspective: Corporate Power, Public Health and Political Economy* (New York: Cambridge University Press 2010) 108.

the Protection of Children (Tobacco) Act 1986, and the Children and Young Persons (Protection from Tobacco Act) 1991; cigarette advertising on television was banned under the Television Act 1964, and advertising for all forms of tobacco was banned by the European Union 'Television without Frontiers' Directive from 1991;[86] there were also regular increases in duty (i.e. taxation) under the annual Finance Acts during the century. Another illustration is intervention in relation to asbestos: the Asbestos Industry Regulations 1931 (made under section 79 of the Factory and Workshop Act 1901, which regulated 'dangerous and unhealthy industries') imposed duties upon factory owners and employers, including provision of ventilation and other equipment,[87] but only applied in the asbestos industry. The Asbestos Regulations 1969 extended the statutory duty to employers in other workplaces;[88] this duty was further extended to visitors and other persons by the Control of Asbestos at Work Regulations 1987;[89] and a duty to manage asbestos in all non-domestic premises was imposed by the Control of Asbestos at Work Regulations 2002.[90] In addition to legislative intervention, civil litigation has also played an important role in shaping public health law in this field.[91] Mention might also be made of the increasingly voluminous body of environmental law and legislation, a field of activity that clearly interweaves with public health law, but that, in an 'unstable wedding', combines the role of protection of population health with that of protection of natural resources.[92] For example, as Martin notes, much of the Public Health Act 1936 has been subsumed into the Environmental Protection Act 1990.[93] However, since the definition of 'harm' in this statute is expressed primarily in ecological terms, while, in respect of harm to 'man', no specific mention is made of health,[94] it appears difficult to construe this legislation as 'public health law' at all (see also Chapter 5).

As we reached the end of the twentieth century – and in stark contrast to its central role in the preceding period – it was therefore hard to resist the conclusion that public health legislation had become of merely peripheral importance in addressing the health problems of the population of the UK. This impression is confirmed by a consideration of the final major statute of the period, the Public Health (Control of Disease) Act 1984, of which Martin remarks that it 'is not a 1984 Act as such but a consolidation of 19th century legislation'.[95] Consonant with the approach taken in earlier legislation, the statute encompasses a wide range of very specific powers, duties, and prohibitions, the epidemiological basis for many of which appears crude and outdated. For example, sections 24 and 25, respectively, provide that:

> A person shall not send or take to any laundry or public washhouse for the purpose of being washed, or to any place for the purpose of being cleaned, any article which he

---

86 Directive 89/552/EEC of 3 October 1989 on the coordination of certain provisions laid down by Law, Regulation or Administrative Action in Member States concerning the pursuit of television broadcasting activities, [1989] OJ L 298/23, Article 13. The Directive was given effect in the UK by the Broadcasting Act 1990.

87 SI 1931/1140. For a critique, see Nick Wikeley, 'The Asbestos Regulations 1931: A Licence to Kill?' (1992) 19 *Journal of Law and Society* 365.

88 SI 1969/690.

89 SI 1987/2115.

90 SI 2002/2675. Much of the law relating to asbestos exposure was consolidated by the Control of Asbestos Regulations 2006, SI 2006/2739.

91 See e.g. *Smith v Central Asbestos Co. Ltd.* [1972] 1 QB 244.

92 See A. Dan Tarlock, 'The Future of Environmental "Rule of Law" Litigation' (2000) 17 *Pace Environmental Law Review* 237, 238.

93 Martin (n 62), 80.

94 s. 1(4).

95 Robyn Martin, 'The Limits of Law in the Protection of Public Health and the Role of Public Health Ethics' (2006) 120 (Supplement 1) *Public Health* 71, 74.

knows to have been exposed to infection from a notifiable disease, unless that article
has been disinfected by or to the satisfaction of the proper officer of the local authority
for the district or a registered medical practitioner.

A person who knows that he is suffering from a notifiable disease shall not take any
book, or cause any book to be taken for his use, or use any book taken, from any public
or circulating library. A person shall not permit any book which has been taken from a
public or circulating library, and is under his control, to be used by any person whom
he knows to be suffering from a notifiable disease. . . . A person shall not return to any
public or circulating library a book which he knows to have been exposed to infection
from a notifiable disease, or permit any such book which is under his control to be so
returned.

Similarly anachronistic provisions are to be found in sections 45 ('it shall not be lawful to
hold a wake over the body of a person who has died while suffering from a notifiable disease') and 55 ('no person who collects or deals in rags, old clothes or similar articles, and
no person assisting or acting on behalf of any such person, shall . . . sell or deliver . . . any
article of food or drink to any person, or any article whatsoever to a person under the age of
14 years'), amongst others.[96]

The powers set out in Part II of the Act apply in relation to 'notifiable diseases', defined
in section 10 as cholera, plague, relapsing fever, smallpox, and typhus; food poisoning
is made separately notifiable under section 11. This catalogue is both dated – the World
Health Organization had declared smallpox to have been eradicated in 1980[97] – and narrow, although a number of other conditions were added by way of secondary legislation.[98]
Notably, it does not include HIV/AIDS.[99] Surveillance of this condition is addressed by way
of the AIDS (Control) Act 1987, which requires health authorities to make reports to the
Secretary of State on various matters, including numbers of diagnoses and deaths, while
the Public Health (Infectious Diseases) Regulations 1988 enabled detention in hospital to
prevent spread of the disease.[100]

While the emergence of HIV/AIDS (and later, avian influenza and SARS, coupled with a
resurgence of the incidence of tuberculosis), indicated that a legislative focus upon communicable disease was not entirely inappropriate even at the end of the twentieth century, the
1984 Act may nonetheless be criticised for its inflexibility. The specificity of the powers and
duties that it confers militate against use for new and unforeseen threats to public health;[101]
and they are clearly inapplicable to those non-communicable diseases that represent the
greatest contemporary threat to population health and that form central concerns of the
emerging 'new public health' paradigm (to be considered in the next subsection). Hence, at
the dawn of the new millennium, public health legislation in the UK appeared to be wholly
unfit for purpose.

---

96 For a comprehensive critique of the Act, see Stephen Monaghan, *The State of Communicable Disease Law* (London: Nuffield
    Trust 2002).
97 Resolution of the World Health Assembly, WHA 33.3, 8 May 1980.
98 Primarily, the Public Health (Infectious Diseases) Regulations 1988, SI 1988/1546. The current list of notifiable
    diseases in England is contained in Schedule 1 of the Health Protection (Notification) Regulations 2010, SI
    2010/659.
99 For a scholarly analysis of the law in this context, see James Chalmers, *Legal Responses to HIV and AIDS* (Oxford: Hart
    Publishing 2008).
100 SI 1988/1546, reg. 5, modifying s. 38 of the 1984 Act.
101 See Martin (n 95), 74, and see further the discussion in Chapter 7 below.

3.1.4 The twenty-first century: public health legislation revitalised?

While the continued threat posed by communicable diseases should not be understated – in addition to those outlined in the preceding paragraph, the outbreaks of 'swine flu' in 2009, Ebola in 2014, and Zika in 2016 have underlined the continuing need for nation states and international organisations to remain vigilant (although the direct effects upon the UK have been minimal) – the primary public health concern of government in the early twenty-first century is now non-communicable disease. By 2014, UK deaths from such diseases were estimated to amount to 89% of the total, with the probability of early death (after age 30, but before age 70) from the four main non-communicable diseases (cancer, diabetes, cardiovascular disease, and chronic respiratory disease) standing at 12%.[102] However, it is not simply mortality that poses a policy problem. While communicable diseases tend to be acute, resulting in relatively swift death, non-communicable diseases are chronic in character and thus place greater pressure on health system resources, exacerbating the inevitable mismatch between the demand for, and supply of, services and treatments. Measures to reduce their incidence are therefore imperative not only from a social perspective but also – in similar fashion to the Victorian era[103] – for economic reasons.

The focus (albeit not an exclusive one) upon non-communicable diseases forms one part of the so-called new public health (NPH) paradigm that began to emerge from the 1970s onwards,[104] finding its most influential expression in the 'Ottawa Charter' of 1986.[105] Stated briefly, this conception of the role of public health 'is an integrative approach to protecting and promoting the health status of both the individual and the society . . . recognizing the interdependency and interrelationship of the health of people, communities, and nations',[106] which is 'based not only on responsibility and accountability of national, regional, and local governments for the health and well-being of society'[107] but which also 'involves the voluntary organizational and private sectors, such as food, medical equipment, pharmaceutical and vaccine manufacturers' (see also Chapter 1).[108]

The extent to which NPH is genuinely 'new' – a paradigm shift – is debateable. Awofeso convincingly argues that it draws heavily upon forms of knowledge and interventions from previous eras;[109] to give just one example, NPH's emphasis upon the manner in which 'upstream' factors such as poverty or the built environment are determinative of health inequalities is reminiscent of the approach taken by Victorian reformers such as Chadwick. Nor is NPH driven primarily by evolving understandings of the nature of disease, as was the case in the latter half of the nineteenth century. If anything, the novelty of NPH appears to reside in its explicitly integrative agenda. This is so both in respect of its epistemology – an 'increasing acknowledgement that public health epidemiology . . . must interact with

---

102 World Health Organization, *Non-Communicable Diseases Country Profiles 2014* (Geneva: WHO 2014).

103 The financial imperative is expressed, not merely in respect of the impact of non-communicable diseases upon health system resources, but also, in a manner akin to the Victorian rationale, as directly affecting economic activity and, therefore, national wealth; see e.g. HM Government (n 79), 5 reporting that £100 billion a year could be saved by reducing working-age ill health.

104 See e.g. Theodore Tuchinsky and Elena Varikova, *The New Public Health: An Introduction for the 21st Century* (3rd edn., London: Academic Press 2014), especially chapter 5; Helen Halpin, Maria Morales-Suárez-Varela, and José Martin-Moreno, 'Chronic Disease Prevention and the New Public Health' (2010) 32 *Public Health Reviews* 120.

105 See World Health Organization, Regional Office for Europe, <www.euro.who.int/__data/assets/pdf_file/0004/129532/Ottawa_Charter.pdf> accessed 5 April 2016.

106 Theodore Tuchinsky and Elena Varikova, 'What is the "New Public Health"?' (2010) 32 *Public Health Reviews* 25, 26.

107 ibid.

108 ibid.

109 Niyi Awofeso, 'What's New about the "New Public Health"?' (2004) 94 *American Journal of Public Health* 705.

qualitative methodology, and public health must integrate a variety of disciplines, including sociology, social psychology, health economics, environmental health, systems analysis and political science'[110] – and, perhaps more crucially for the purposes of this chapter, in respect of the institutional framework for the realisation of public health goals. The latter entails a multisectoral, "whole of society" approach involving ministries and stakeholders beyond health, perhaps best captured by the 'Health in All Policies' strategy.[111]

What is the role for public health law (or, perhaps, law in general, since under 'Health in All Policies', laws in every sector have the potential to impact upon population health) in this 'new' model? As with NPH itself, there are legacies of previous approaches embedded within the twenty-first-century framework. For example, Part 1 of the Health Act 2006 confers powers to make regulations prohibiting smoking in public and workplaces that are enclosed or substantially enclosed;[112] the Children and Families Act 2014 extends these powers to permit prohibition of smoking in private vehicles where a person under 18 is present in the vehicle.[113] Smoke-free legislation, which is considered to have been highly successful,[114] may in some regards be seen as the culmination of the targeted responses to this particular risk factor for non-communicable disease that had commenced in the twentieth century. It is progressive not because of the subject-matter nor the employment of a 'command and control' mode of regulation to achieve public health goals, but rather in its overt subordination of individual autonomy to the interest of protecting others from harms to their health, a step that had proved too daunting for previous governments and legislatures to take. Yet, even here, one might detect echoes of the debates surrounding the vaccination legislation of the Victorian era, which were outlined above.

General powers to address public health threats, broadly comparable to those contained in the 1936 and 1984 Acts, are now set out in Part 3 of the Health and Social Care Act 2008, which acts as an amendment to the 1984 Act. This seeks to address the anachronism of the preceding legislation by adopting an 'all hazards' approach to public health threats, bringing English law in line with the revised International Health Regulations of 2005 (see further: Chapter 8). In consequence, the powers are no longer addressed solely to certain specified forms of communicable disease but are exercisable in respect of other forms of risk, such as contamination by chemicals or radiation.[115] Additionally, as will be noted in Chapter 7, the legislation confers powers of a more general nature than those contained within the very specific provisions of the 1984 Act. However, in other respects, the statute does not fit the NPH paradigm. It confers no authority upon the state to take steps to respond to the public health threats presented by non-communicable diseases, nor those that arise somewhat more indirectly from significant contemporary risk factors such as climate change.[116] Nor does it address 'upstream' determinants such as poverty or speak to inequalities in health status.

---

110 Tuchinsky and Varikova (n 104), 106.

111 See e.g. Timo Ståhl, Matthias Wismar, Eeva Ollila, Eero Lahtinen, and Kimmo Leppo, *Health in All Policies: Prospects and Potentials* (Helsinki: Ministry of Health 2006).

112 The primary Regulations enforcing the smoking ban in England were the Smoke-Free (Premises and Enforcement) Regulations 2006, SI 2006/3368.

113 s. 95. The Smoke-Free (Private Vehicles) Regulations 2015, SI 2015/286 give effect to the prohibition.

114 See Linda Bauld, *The Impact of Smokefree Legislation in England: Evidence Review* (Bath: University of Bath 2011) 16. However, while the prevalence of smoking has been falling gradually, the number of deaths of all adults over 35 estimated to have been caused by smoking has remained unchanged: see Health and Social Care Information Centre, *Statistics on Smoking: England 2014* (Leeds: Health and Social Care Information Centre 2014).

115 See especially Public Health (Control of Disease) Act 1984, s. 45A, inserted by Health and Social Care Act 2008, s. 129.

116 In the case of climate change, the Civil Contingencies Act 2004, which confers very broad powers upon government to respond to emergencies, may be of some relevance; although this is not specifically oriented towards public health. See further: Chapter 7 below.

These issues may be addressed through legal and regulatory interventions elsewhere, as discussed further in Part II of this book.

Other legislative developments appear, however, to move public health law more closely into step with the NPH approach. In particular, significant 'capacity-building' changes have recently taken place as the institutional framework for public health in England has been overhauled by means of the Health and Social Care Act 2012. These entail the establishment of Public Health England, described as 'a new, dedicated and professional public health service',[117] and the imposition of a statutory duty (for the first time) upon the Secretary of State for Health to take such steps as are considered appropriate for the protection and improvement of public health.[118] However, the most significant development was the return of public health responsibilities to local authority control, effected by section 12 of the Act,[119] a step justified by government on the basis that:

> There has not been enough focus on the root causes of ill health. Mental and physical health and wellbeing interact, and are affected by a wide range of influences throughout life. Central government can play a part in shaping some of these influences and must have a firm grip both on protecting people against serious health threats and on preparing for emergencies. However, top-down initiatives and lectures from central government about the 'risks' are not the answer. And while the NHS will continue to have a critical role to play, it cannot tackle all the wider factors on its own. . . . Local government is best placed to influence many of the wider factors that affect health and wellbeing. We need to tap into this potential by significantly empowering local government to do more through real freedoms, dedicated resources and clear responsibilities, building on its existing important role in public health.[120]

Thus, while superficially in large part a restoration of a framework familiar from the Victorian era, the institutional structure established by the 2012 Act appears to have an NPH rationale insofar as it is designed to facilitate action on the 'upstream' determinants of health.

Further provisions of the 2012 Act also serve to align the public health institutional framework in England more closely with the NPH agenda. Thus, the duty to protect public health contained in section 11 applies in relation to 'disease or other dangers to health'. It will be noted that this is not restricted to communicable diseases and that an 'all hazards' approach is taken – the explanatory notes to the Act identify the health risks of climate change as one of the 'other dangers' covered by the section and observe that 'the provision will continue to be effective as new threats to health emerge'. Furthermore, section 4 of the 2012 Act imposes a duty upon the Secretary of State, when exercising public health functions, to 'have regard to the need to reduce inequalities between the people of England with respect to the benefits that they can obtain from the health service'.[121] Moreover, each upper-tier local authority in England must establish a Health and Wellbeing Board that is placed under a duty to encourage integrated working 'for the purpose of advancing the health and

---

117 HM Government (n 79), [4.3]. Public Health England is an executive agency of the Department of Health.
118 ss. 11 and 12, inserting ss. 2A and B into the National Health Service Act 2006. Examples of such steps are provided in ss. 2A(2) and 2(B)(3). In practice, the Secretary of State will delegate the exercise of such duties at a national level to Public Health England and, at a local level, to local authorities, while ultimately retaining responsibility for the discharge of such duties to Parliament.
119 Inserting s. 2B into National Health Service Act 2006.
120 HM Government (n 79), [2.1]–[2.2], [2.5].
121 Inserting s. 1C in National Health Service Act 2006.

wellbeing of the people in its area'; this extends not just to those working within the health sector but also to those providing 'health-related services [which] may have an effect on the health of individuals but are not health services or social care services' – which might therefore include those with responsibility for housing, transport, planning, parks and green spaces, etc.[122]

Thus far, the discussion has centred upon England; however, one of the most significant developments since the end of the twentieth century has been the devolution of public health responsibilities to Scotland, Northern Ireland, and Wales. This issue will be revisited in Chapter 7, but a brief outline will prove of value here. The Public Health etc (Scotland) Act 2008 is, in essence, an update of late nineteenth-century legislation to bring the law in line with the requirements of the International Health Regulations. It adopts a relatively narrow view of public health as concerned with infectious diseases, contamination, or 'other such hazards which constitute a danger to human health'[123] and thus makes little concession to an NPH agenda, although it does impose a duty upon health boards and local authorities to cooperate 'with any relevant person that appears . . . to have an interest in or function relating to the protection of public health'.[124] Modernisation for a similar purpose has been undertaken in Northern Ireland, although here the governing legislation remains of twentieth-century origin,[125] albeit amended.[126] To date there has been little by way of legislative alignment with NPH, although there is evidence of commitment in this regard from political actors.[127]

Matters are, however, radically different in Wales. Here, three distinct strands may be detected. First, as in the other nations, there has been an updating of legislation to bring it in line with the revised International Health Regulations.[128] Second, the Welsh Government has put forward proposals for a broad-ranging public health statute targeted at a diverse range of risk factors for non-communicable disease or harms, although it has yet to secure political support for such a measure.[129] And third – and most radically – the Well-being of Future Generations (Wales) Act 2015 imposes a duty upon public bodies to pursue wellbeing goals, which include working towards 'a society in which people's physical and mental well-being is maximised and in which choices and behaviours that benefit future health are understood',[130] 'in a manner which seeks to ensure that the needs of the present are met without compromising the ability of future generations to meet their own needs'.[131] In applying this 'sustainable development principle', public bodies are required to work for the long term, to prevent problems from occurring or getting worse, while considering how pursuit of one objectives may impact upon other objectives, collaborating with other persons or bodies who might help the body reach its objectives, and involving all of those

---

122 s. 195.
123 s. 1(2).
124 s. 6(1).
125 Public Health Act (Northern Ireland) 1967.
126 Public Health (Amendment) Act (Northern Ireland) 2008.
127 See especially Department of Health, Social Services and Public Safety, *Making Life Better: A Whole System Framework for Public Health* (Belfast: DHSSPS 2014).
128 In this respect, Part 3 of the Health and Social Care Act 2008 applies to Wales.
129 See Public Health (Wales) Bill 2015, which addresses tobacco and nicotine products; acupuncture, body piercing electrolysis and tattooing; intimate piercing of children and young people; planning and delivery of pharmaceutical services; and provision of toilets. The Bill was rejected by the Welsh Assembly on 16 March 2016, largely because of party political factors, although there was strong opposition to the proposal for a partial ban on the use of e-cigarettes in public places.
130 s. 4.
131 s. 5(1).

with an interest in achieving the goals.[132] While this is not a straightforward application of the 'Health in All Policies' approach – not least because health is only one of seven 'well-being goals', which are accorded equal weight – it goes much further in this direction than anywhere else in the UK has done.

3.1.5 Beyond legislation, beyond law?

The focus here has been upon legislation, the most direct (and, perhaps, blunt) means by which the state can seek to address public health threats or achieve goals. But, as will be explored in more depth in the next section of this chapter, legislation – indeed, law in general – is merely one mode of regulation. As Magnusson notes, 'an emerging and important feature of public health regulation concerns the role of the private and non-government actors . . . to improve the health of the workforce and the wider community'.[133] Although this approach will be analysed in greater detail in Chapters 5 and 9, a brief codicil to the above historical account will serve as illustration of its place within the contemporary public health regulatory framework.

In its White Paper on public health strategy, published in 2010, the Conservative–Liberal Democrat Coalition Government underlined its desire to 'balance the freedoms of individuals and organisations with the need to avoid harm to others, use a "ladder" of interventions to determine the least intrusive approach necessary to achieve the desired effect and aim to make voluntary approaches work before resorting to regulation'.[134] This took concrete form in a 'Public Health Responsibility Deal' agreed between government, industry, and the voluntary sector, by which the latter signed up to 'pledges' to take voluntary action in one or more of the areas of alcohol, food, health at work, and physical activity.[135] The Deal also reflected the Coalition Government's interest in theories and practices of behavioural science; it promised,

> we will in particular seek to use approaches that focus on enabling and guiding people's choices wherever possible. This includes changing social norms and default options so that healthier choices are easier for people to make. There is significant scope to use approaches that harness the latest techniques of behavioural science to do this – nudging people in the right direction rather than banning or significantly restricting their choices.[136]

The Responsibility Deal, and the 'nudge' approach that underpins it, was sharply criticised by many public health organisations,[137] and a parliamentary select committee report on the new English public health framework observed that 'those with a financial interest must not be allowed to set the agenda for health improvement'.[138] Evidence on its effectiveness

---

132 s. 5(2).
133 Roger Magnusson, 'Mapping the Scope and Opportunities for Public Health Law in Liberal Democracies' (2007) 35 Journal of Law, Medicine and Ethics 571, 578.
134 HM Government (n. 79), [9(e)].
135 See Department of Health, The Public Health Responsibility Deal (London: Department of Health 2011).
136 HM Government (n 79), [2.33]–[2.34].
137 See e.g. Royal College of Physicians, <www.rcplondon.ac.uk/press-releases/key-health-organisations-do-not-sign-responsibility-deal> accessed 5 April 2016; and British Medical Association Ethics Department, Behaviour Change, Public Health and the Role of the State – BMA Position Statement (London: BMA 2012).
138 House of Commons Select Committee on Health, Public Health, (HC 2010–12, 1048-I), [287].

appears to be limited,[139] and its status following the Conservative Party's victory in the 2015 general election remains unclear at the time of writing. Nonetheless, as an exemplar of a form of public health regulation of a very different, and much less intrusive, character to that embodied by the legislation analysed above, it remains of considerable interest. There is further discussion in Chapter 9.

3.2 Public health actors

The history outlined in the preceding section shows that the *dramatis personae* of public health in the United Kingdom has fluctuated considerably over time; moreover, given that it was as recently as 2012 that a fundamental reallocation of responsibilities between National Health Service and local government took place in England, we should certainly not presume that the story has ended. Identifying precisely which institutions or individuals have a role to play in the framework of public health law is, therefore, challenging, but nonetheless, a brief account can be provided here, which should serve to illuminate the analysis contained in Part II of this book.

At the most fundamental level, in order to develop an understanding of the relevant players, we might first wish to disentangle the meaning of the word 'public' in 'public health law'. Gostin and Wiley have observed that, in this context, the word 'has two overlapping meanings: one that explains the entity that takes primary responsibility for the public's health, and another that explains who has a legitimate expectation of receiving the benefits'.[140] The latter refers to the population focus of the legal and other forms of regulatory intervention in this area: this aspect is discussed further in Chapter 1 and will not be developed further here, although parenthetically it may be noted that it is simplistic to assume that the population is always merely the passive 'target' of public health interventions – the success or otherwise of a regulatory intervention turns, ultimately, upon the public's response to it; thus, even forms of 'command and control' regulation that appear to leave little space for autonomous action can be undermined by popular resistance, as the history of vaccination legislation in the Victorian era emphasises.

The first meaning attributed to the word 'public' is explained by Gostin and Wiley in these straightforward terms:

> The government has primary responsibility for the public's health. The government is the public entity that acts on behalf of the people and gains its legitimacy through a political process. A characteristic form of "public" or state action occurs when a democratically elected government exercises powers or duties to protect or promote the population's health.[141]

139 See e.g. Mark Petticrew, Elizabeth Eastmure, Nicholas Mays, Cécile Knai, Mary Alison Durand, and Ellen Nolte, 'The Public Health Responsibility Deal: How Should Such a Complex Public Health Policy be Evaluated?' (2013) 35 *Journal of Public Health* 495; Cécile Knai, Mark Petticrew, Mary Alison Durand, Courtney Scott, Lesley James, Anushka Mehrotra, Elizabeth Eastmure, and Nicholas Mays, 'The Public Health Responsibility Deal: Has a Public-Private Partnership Brought about Action on Alcohol Reduction?' (2015) 110 *Addiction* 1217.
140 Lawrence Gostin and Lindsay Wiley, *Public Health Law: Power, Duty, Restraint* (3rd edn., Berkeley: University of California Press 2016) 5–6.
141 ibid 6.

However, the simplicity of this account masks a number of more complex issues, many of which have been analysed in detail elsewhere by one of the present authors.[142] First, we may wish to note that 'government' need not only signify the executive branch. Although this branch is by far the dominant player in the British political system, no legislation can be enacted without the signification of consent by the legislative branch (i.e. Parliament): while electoral majorities and party discipline usually have the consequence that Parliament ultimately assents to the government's wishes, the process of debate and amendment may yield important alterations to the content of public health laws. Perhaps more significantly, the third governmental branch, the judiciary, is an important actor on the public health law stage. As will be noted in Part II of this book, in certain areas, the evolution of common law – such as that relating to the tort of nuisance – has had a significant impact upon the legal framework of public health in the UK. The judiciary also carries the potential to affect the public health landscape through the exercise of its functions of statutory interpretation.

Second, where the focus of attention lies with the executive branch, it is possible to identify more precisely the governmental institutions that play a particularly significant role in public health. To this end, it should be noted that some commentators take a relatively narrow 'jurisdictional' approach,[143] which might limit governmental public health actors to those with specific competence in, and a mandate to act upon, health questions, such as Ministries of Health or public health officials. In the UK, this approach would allocate primary responsibility for public health at national level to the Department of Health in Whitehall and its equivalents in Scotland, Wales, and Northern Ireland and to dedicated agencies such as Public Health England, NHS Health Scotland, Public Health Wales, and the Public Health Agency in Northern Ireland, all of which work to improve population health and reduce health inequalities. At local level, one might anticipate the main actors to be organisations responsible for planning and commissioning health services for defined geographical populations, currently Clinical Commissioning Groups in England, NHS Boards in Scotland, Local Health Boards in Wales, and Local Commissioning Groups in Northern Ireland.

This 'map' is misleading both descriptively and, it may be claimed, normatively. From the latter perspective, it would not appear consonant with the NPH paradigm, which places emphasis upon the interrelationships between population health and other social and environmental factors, and consequently upon an 'all of government' approach to addressing public health problems. As one of us writes:

> As 'health' or 'public health' arise increasingly in discussions of departments other than those whose stated competence relates to health, where public health as a governmental matter is being considered, it is best not to limit the scope by government department.[144]

It is descriptively inaccurate because, while the central governmental institutions previously listed do play a highly significant part in establishing and administering the framework of public health law in the UK, the primary actor at local level for most of the past two centuries, save for a period from just after the Second World War until 2012, has been local

---

142 See John Coggon, *What Makes Health Public? A Critical Evaluation of Moral, Legal and Political Claims in Public Health* (Cambridge: Cambridge University Press 2012), especially chapter 3.
143 ibid, 54.
144 ibid, 58.

government, rather than the NHS.[145] Historically, the Medical Officer of Health appointed by many local authorities from the Public Health Act 1848 onward was a key figure;[146] the lead local role in the contemporary local public health structure is played by the Director of Public Health. However, as noted above and consistently with the apparent NPH underpinnings of the institutional structure established by the Health and Social Care Act 2012,[147] integrated working is envisaged between local public health officials and others whose work concerns health either directly (such as representatives of Clinical Commissioning Groups) and those who provide services that may have an impact upon health (such as housing or transport). It seems probable that comparable arrangements will become more common in the future if greater devolved powers are allocated to urban areas or regions. For example, an important aspect of the so-called 'Devo Manc' agreement was a Memorandum of Understanding between NHS England, all local authority members of the Association of Greater Manchester Authorities, and all Clinical Commissioning Groups in the Greater Manchester region, which has as its overriding purpose,

> to ensure the greatest and fastest possible improvement to the health and wellbeing of the 2.8 million citizens of Greater Manchester, [which] requires a more integrated approach to the use of the existing health and care resources . . . as well as transformational changes in the way in which services are delivered.[148]

Yet, while the 'publicness' of public health inevitably focuses attention upon government – in whatever manifestation – as a key player, the discussion of the Coalition Government's 'Responsibility Deal' in the preceding section should alert us to the growing involvement of other stakeholders from civil society and the private sector (and, correspondingly, to a broad understanding of the nature of contemporary public health law, as adopted in this book). There is a connection here to the epidemiological transition of the second half of the twentieth century, and the subsequent emphasis within the NPH paradigm upon non-communicable disease. That is, since many of the conditions with which public health practitioners and policy-makers are currently concerned are so-called 'lifestyle diseases' associated with consumption of products including sugar, salt, tobacco, processed meat, saturated fats, and alcohol, engagement with industry and/or third-sector organisations (such as those promoting physical activity or alcohol awareness) would appear to offer the best prospect of success. For example, the Coalition Government's strategy for tackling obesity contains the following passage:

> We believe that we can achieve the most, and do so most quickly, by bringing together key partners from business and the charitable and public sectors. All sectors of the food industry – retailers, manufacturers, trade associations, caterers and suppliers to the

---

145 There are distinctions between the nations of the UK in this respect. Broadly, the NHS in Scotland and Wales retains a greater role in delivery of public health than is the case in England: for example, Directors of Public Health continue to work within the NHS in both nations. The pattern in Northern Ireland is more centralised, with the Public Health Agency being the key actor. However, there are a number of initiatives and mechanisms for integrated working with local authorities and other relevant bodies and stakeholders in each case.

146 For discussion, see e.g. John Welshman, 'The Medical Officer of Health in England and Wales, 1900–1974: Watchdog or Lapdog?' (1997) 19 *Journal of Public Health Medicine* 443.

147 See (n 122) and accompanying text.

148 Association of Greater Manchester Authorities/NHS England/Greater Manchester Association of Clinical Commissioning Groups, *Greater Manchester Health and Social Care Devolution: Memorandum of Understanding* (2015) 2. The transfer of control over health and social care funding came into effect on 1 April 2016.

catering industry – can help and support people to make healthier choices. The food industry has unparalleled ability to influence our diet through the food it offers and the way it promotes and markets it. Yet up to now we have not made enough use of its reach as a force for good in nutrition. . . . The food and drink industry has a particularly crucial part to play in view of its reach and influence on our diet. . . . The contribution of the food industry might, for example, include reformulation of products to make them less energy dense, portion control, and actions to encourage consumers to choose these products through a responsible balance of promotional activity. This initiative calls for a real step-change in the public health contribution of the food and drink industry and we are expecting to see significant commitments and will keep progress under review. We will support these efforts through relevant consumer-focused . . . campaigns and look to other partners – for example, third sector organisations – also to play a crucial part.[149]

There has, therefore, been a shift from government to *governance* in public health – the latter term capturing 'the totality of interactions, in which government, other public bodies, private sector, and civil society participate, aiming at solving societal problems or creating societal opportunities' (see further: Chapter 9).[150] As the discussion in the preceding section of this chapter suggests, this is far from unproblematic, especially in the case of industry, for which the acceptance of a broad commitment to the community that sustains its existence is almost always a much weaker imperative than making profit, notwithstanding the rise of 'corporate social responsibility'. Moreover, at a more fundamental level, harnessing the private sector in the service of public health diverges significantly from the traditional understanding of the subject-matter, in which public good (population health) is pitted against private interest (individual autonomy). Nonetheless, we might conclude, with Kaul, that in this context:

'Public' today no longer refers only to the state. Rather, it means bringing the public, with all its different elements, together for a joint exploration of concerns, a determination of common preferences, and a fair bargain for all – a task that apparently cannot be simply delegated to elected representatives or national and international bureaucracies.[151]

3.3 Regulatory approaches and public health

The discussion in the first section of this chapter was centred upon legislation, largely because, as the most deliberate and considered mode of state intervention, this provides the clearest insight into the changing targets, objectives, and strategies of government in the public health arena over a historical period. Of course, this is not the only form of legal intervention. Part II of this book will additionally examine other types, such as common law, international law, and 'soft law'.

---

149 Department of Health, *Healthy Lives, Healthy People: A Call for Action on Obesity in England* (London: Department of Health 2011) [6.7], [6.11].
150 Louis Meuleman, *Public Management and the Metagovernance of Hierarchies, Networks and Markets* (Heidelberg: Physica-Verlag 2008) 11.
151 Inge Kaul, 'Global Public Goods: What Role for Civil Society?' (2001) 30 *Nonprofit and Voluntary Sector Quarterly* 588, 594–595. See also Magnusson (n 133), 578.

Gostin and Wiley have provided a highly influential categorisation of legal intervention as a mode of regulation in the public health context, albeit one which is oriented particularly toward the US.[152] It centres upon powers that are exercised by means of legislation or executive action, although it does extend further. In brief, it consists of (a) the power to tax and spend (the latter being read more broadly by Magnusson to include 'capacity-building' activities such as establishment of public health agencies and the conferral of mandates);[153] (b) the power to alter the informational environment (including facilitation of what Magnusson describes as 'public health "information assets"', such as reporting systems for surveillance, health registers, and health impact assessments);[154] (c) the power to alter the built environment; (d) the power to alter the socio-economic environment; (e) direct regulation of persons, professions, and businesses (within this category, Gostin and Wiley enumerate laws requiring use of seatbelts and motorcycle helmets, licencing, and inspection; Magnusson additionally observes that laws [such as those on consumer protection], which are not ostensibly concerned with public health may, nonetheless, impact upon it);[155] (f) indirect regulation through the tort system; and (g) deregulation, i.e. repeal or amendment of laws that are harmful to population health.

Another taxonomy of regulatory approaches, adopted by Reynolds in analysis of public health law in Australia,[156] lists 'command and control' strategies, which entail some form of compulsion, self-regulation, informational strategies, regulation through administrative powers (such as licencing and administrative penalties), economic instruments (such as taxation or incentives), and civil liability. Later work by the same author focuses more upon the objectives of regulation than the instruments or mechanisms used.[157] Thus, he distinguishes the imposition of particular requirements (a prescriptive approach) from an outcomes-based approach that specifies a broad goal but that allows for some discretion in the manner in which it is achieved, from that which 'focuses its regulatory efforts in a way that ensures that problems receive attention in proportion to the risks of harm that they present' (harm- or risk-based regulation).[158]

Both Gostin and Reynolds are concerned primarily to classify forms of legal intervention, but a broader approach – noted in the previous chapter of this book – is taken by the Nuffield Council on Bioethics. The Council's 'ladder of intervention' offers a means of choosing between policy options in public health, only certain of which need entail the use of legal measures.[159] The ladder presents a series of interventions, progressively ordered in the degree of their intrusiveness upon individual freedom and accordingly requiring increasingly strong justification in order to be publicly acceptable. It ranges from doing nothing or merely monitoring the situation, through provision of information, enabling choice, guiding choices through changing the default policy, guiding choices through incentives, and through disincentives, to restriction of choice and, finally, elimination of choice. It should be noted that regulation through law need not necessarily occur solely at the highest rungs of the ladder: for example, legal measures obliging provision of information, while coercive

152 Gostin and Wiley (n 139), 27–33.
153 Magnusson (n 133), 576.
154 ibid, 577.
155 ibid.
156 Christopher Reynolds, *Public Health Law and Regulation* (Sydney: The Federation Press 2004) 100–130.
157 Christopher Reynolds, *Public and Environmental Health Law* (Sydney: The Federation Press 2011) 147–152.
158 ibid, 148.
159 Nuffield Council on Bioethics, *Public Health: Ethical Issues* (London: Nuffield Council on Bioethics 2007) [3.37]–[3.38].

to some (such as businesses required to provide information on food packaging) would not eliminate choice for others (here, consumers).

The Nuffield model found favour with the Conservative–Liberal Democrat Coalition Government, being utilised in White Papers on sustainable transport[160] and setting out its overall strategy on public health.[161] In these contexts, it appeared to be deployed to underpin an ideological commitment to enhancing autonomy (of individuals and businesses) and limiting regulatory intervention as far as possible. In this respect, there was a connection to 'nudge' and the Responsibility Deal, discussed above. This is further apparent in a Lords Select Committee Report on 'behaviour change', which presents a taxonomy that builds upon the Nuffield ladder, dividing interventions into those that regulate the individual (through elimination or restriction of choice); those that have a fiscal impact upon the individual (disincentives and incentives); and non-regulatory and non-fiscal measures in relation to the individual (such as persuasion, provision of information, changes to the default policy, and use of social norms), some of which would entail regulation of other actors, such as businesses, to guide individual choices.[162] Notably, however, the Select Committee does not accord precedence to non-regulatory interventions, urging 'ministers to ensure that policy-makers are made aware of the evidence that non-regulatory measures are often not likely to be effective if used in isolation and that evidence regarding the whole range of policy interventions should be considered before they commit to using non-regulatory measures alone'.[163]

We return to discuss the Nuffield ladder briefly in the next chapter, but in greater detail in Chapter 9, when we will analyse forms of regulation beyond 'hard' law. In the next chapter, we seek to set out a definition of what we understand 'public health law' to be and explain how we approach our discussion of the field in the remainder of the book.

Chapter 3: Summary

- The origins of modern public health law in the UK lie in the Victorian era, with a wide variety of statutes according primary responsibility to local government to act in respect of the health of the population. This period also witnessed the first manifestations of a tension between state intervention and individual autonomy in the field of public health that continues to the present day.
- For much of the twentieth century, public health played a subsidiary role to clinical medicine delivered through the NHS, which functioned, in effect, as a 'sickness service'. By the end of the century, public health law in the UK was significantly out of step with the major threats to the health of the population.
- More recently, greater interest has been shown by government in utilising legal measures to address risk factors for non-communicable disease and to build institutional capacity to address a range of issues – not all of which fall within the traditional domain of health – that impact upon the public's health. Devolution of responsibility for public health to constituent parts of the UK is providing space for some further rethinking of the state's role.

---

160 Department for Transport, *Creating Growth, Cutting Carbon: Making Sustainable Local Transport Happen*, Cm 7996 (2011) [1.10].
161 HM Government (n 79), [2.25]–[2.35].
162 Science and Technology Select Committee, *Behaviour Change* (2010–12, HL 179) [2.3].
163 ibid, [8.16].

- While the key actor in public health is government – and, in England (though not to the same extent elsewhere in the UK), continues to be *local government* – *there* is an important role for the private sector, well illustrated by the 'Responsibility Deal' established between the UK government, industry, and voluntary organisations in 2010.
- Legislation, which may pursue public health goals through a number of approaches including informational, fiscal and 'command and control' means, is merely one form of regulatory activity undertaken by the state. Legal intervention may take other forms, such as judge-made law; while there are other types of intervention that do not resemble 'law', as traditionally understood, at all. These issues are analysed subsequently in this book.

3.4 Further readings

Niyi Awofeso, 'What's New about the "New Public Health"?' (2004) 94 *American Journal of Public Health* 705.

Walter Holland and Susie Stewart, *Public Health: The Vision and the Challenge* (London: Nuffield Trust 1998).

Roger Magnusson, 'Mapping the Scope and Opportunities for Public Health Law in Liberal Democracies' (2007) 35 *Journal of Law, Medicine and Ethics* 571.

Nuffield Council on Bioethics, *Public Health: Ethical Issues* (London: Nuffield Council on Bioethics 2007), especially chapter 3, available at www.nuffieldbioethics.org/project/public-health/.

Diana Porter, *Health, Civilization and the State* (London: Routledge 1999), especially chapters 2, 3, 5, 7, and 8.

Michael Warren, *A Chronology of State Medicine, Public Health, Welfare and Related Services in Britain 1066–1999* (London: Faculty of Public Health Medicine 2000), available at www.fph.org.uk/uploads/r_chronology_of_state_medicine.pdf.

Part II
The field of public health law

Chapter 4

Defining the scope of public health law

4.1 Towards a definition of, approach to, and application of public health law

This chapter outlines and explains our substantive understanding of public health law and explains how Part II of this book will work. Overall, the chapter serves two main ends. First, reflecting back on Part I, we present with more detail our definition of public health law, including a fuller rationale for conceiving it as we do. Following this, we describe how Chapters 5 to 9 are devised, explaining in particular our approach to examining the ways in which law can support or constrain public health agendas. Bearing in mind the practical knowledge and foundational skills that this book aims to help develop and its key purpose as a general reference on public health law and legal approaches to public health, Part II explains different manners of and approaches to law and regulation. The next five chapters introduce private law, criminal law, public law, EU and international law, and 'softer' modes of regulation, respectively. As well as explaining the nature, effect, and functions of different legal subdisciplines, we give practical examples of how they might be used in the service of, or to place limits on, actual and potential public health agendas and practices.

Our approach to presenting public health law may be contrasted with a purely *problem-based* study of public health law, which would introduce the subject by looking at how laws apply to specific public health problems with chapters on, for example, tobacco control, regulation of foods, and environmental regulations. To be clear, we recognise the value of a purely problem-based approach. However, to give this work its deepest and widest application, we perceive greater utility in the approach-led rather than issue-led overview and analysis of public health law. As we have shown in Part I, the 'mission' of contemporary public health is a very broad-reaching one. Practitioners and scholars may find it relatively easy to find authoritative texts on, say, the ethics, politics, or regulation of tobacco.[1] However, this book aims to provide a *general* overview of public health law and to explain the field in a way that develops transferable knowledge and understanding. We hope that the way we have framed things will be as useful to someone, for example, who is interested in tobacco control as someone concerned with the containment of a pandemic, or someone aiming to see that people exercise more, or someone advocating that we conceive of a component of

---

1 See e.g. Robert Goodin, *No Smoking: The Ethical Issues* (2nd edn., Chicago: University of Chicago Press 1990); Andrew Mitchell and Tania Vonn (eds), *The Global Tobacco Epidemic and the Law* (Cheltenham: Edward Elgar 2014).

mental health as a public health matter, or someone who is interested in the regulation of food or in the built environment. Therefore, having presented our chosen approach for Part II, the final part of this chapter explains briefly how the content and structure of the work as a whole might be used in projects targeting different specific problems. We emphasise how the separation of legal approaches here serves an educational goal, but in application, study, and practice, public health law requires consideration of 'joined-up methods' that potentially draw from any or all of the different legal approaches that we identify.

4.2 Public health law: our definition and understanding of the field

In Chapter 1, we explained why contemporary theory and practice present a very broad definition of public health and therefore give rise to an imperative – at least when considering twenty-first-century public health agendas and practices – to work with an understanding of the field that is very wide in its reach. This imperative is reinforced given the scope of public health ethics presented in Chapter 2, and the search for an ethical (and political) mandate that is claimed by key actors such as the World Health Organization (WHO), Public Health England (PHE), and the Faculty of Public Health (FPH). Furthermore, in Chapter 3, we demonstrated the evolution of public health legislation and explained the synergies and flaws in the way that such laws have developed against the backdrop of parallel developments of the idea and practice of public health itself. This broad groundwork in Part I leads to our rationale for and understanding of the directions in which the study of public health law and regulation should now be moving.

The nature of the challenges that confront public health practitioners and policy-makers is very diverse. Necessarily, potential responses to these challenges are also varied. Contemporary public health practice is not limited to containment of contagious disease: indeed, it is not limited to containment of disease at all. Rather, it focuses too on questions of prevention, including prevention of risk factors, contextualised within understandings of the social determinants of health and population-level research and regulatory approaches. Finally, we have noted how public health agendas have evolved not simply to counter ill health – states of disease – but also aim to advance positive states of health: FPH, for example, claims a mandate to protect and promote wellbeing, a much broader (if unexplained) concept than just health. The breadth of these mandates is caught under the umbrella of three areas of governmental responsibility: health care, public health infrastructure, and the social determinants of health.

Within the evolving public health agenda, we find an expanding claim to 'jurisdiction' intrinsic to the idea of public health itself. While medical law is widely viewed as imposing external norms (i.e. legal rules and regulation) on a contained practice (i.e. medicine), definitions of public health include law and regulation within them, with their attention on modes of social coordination (see also the discussion of the controlling and facilitative functions of public law in Chapter 7). Think, for example, about how law and regulation are captured by Winslow's representation of public health, presented in Chapter 1.[2] In that purposive definition of the field, and others that have evolved from it, a subtle array of regulatory measures is implicated. These range from the 'hardest' of coercive laws ('police powers'), through other legal and policy measures (e.g. in maintaining a clean environment, ensuring

---

2 Charles-Edward Winslow, 'The Untilled Fields of Public Health' (1920) 51 (1306) *Science* 23.

good health care systems are in place, or supporting sound education in personal health), and even incorporating 'softer' means of social control ('development of social machinery'). It is our argument that the field of public health law, to be adequate to its task, must be able to encompass this very disparate range of practical approaches.[3] And, whilst we would argue that public health practice naturally includes law, it is also necessarily contained and constrained by law.

4.2.1 Defining the field: drawing from Martin, Bennett, Magnusson, Gostin, and Wiley

Given the scope of public health and public health agendas, how might we address the task of characterising public health law? It is helpful to advance our discussion with reference to three associated, influential framings of public health law, generated in the works of leading public health lawyers in the UK, the US, and Australia. We consider each of these, critically reflecting on the framings that we find and noting where we follow, and how we differ, in our approach to defining the field. First, we refer to the scholarship of Robyn Martin, the leading pioneer of public health law since its re-emergence as an area of study and practice in its own right in the UK. Writing with Richard Coker in 2006, she observes that:

> As a consequence of the paucity of scholarship on public health law, the focus and boundaries of public health law have been far from clear. British law schools which offer 'Health Law' programmes at undergraduate and postgraduate level have addressed almost exclusively issues pertaining to the treatment of the individual patient, issues that are easily identifiable and easily defined.[4]

The authors go on to say: 'Few health law programmes have ventured into the obscure and unbounded terrain of public health law because of difficulties of knowing where to start'.[5] A common theme to Martin's legal analysis in public health concerns the different roles that we might expect of legal and regulatory powers and influence. Indeed, our textbook follows her approach to conceiving of law as one part of a wider array of governance 'tools' in public health and looking to the whole range of available legal and regulatory measures given the context of public health concerns. Like Martin, we strongly resist limiting public health law to any given single type of legal subdiscipline, such as administrative law.[6]

Within Martin's evaluation and presentation of the field, we might contrast two separate collections of ideas, both of which we follow. First, we find reference to what may be considered more purposively or positivistically *as* public health laws: these are laws that impose public health duties on public officials, for example, to report notifiable diseases; laws that empower public authorities to limit individual freedoms in order to contain an outbreak of disease; and laws that create public health offences, for example, regarding the conduct of individuals who suffer from a notifiable disease[7] (see also Chapter 3). Second, we find reference to the wider legal, ethical, and political context and to the potential constraints on

---

3 cf Robyn Martin, 'The Limits of Law in the Protection of Public Health and the Role of Public Health Ethics' (2006) 120 *Public Health* 71.

4 Robyn Martin and Richard Coker, 'Conclusion: Where Next?' (2006) 120 *Public Health* 81, 81.

5 ibid.

6 Consider also John Harrington, 'Commentary on "Legal Foundations of Public Health Law and Its Role in Meeting Future Challenges' (2006) 120 *Public Health* 14.

7 Robyn Martin, 'Law as a Tool in Promoting and Protecting Public Health: Always in Our Best Interests?' (2007) 121 *Public Health* 846, 847–848.

public health activity given concern, for example, for individual rights,[8] and the relevance and applicability of wider bodies of law to the study of, and practice in, public health law.[9] In other words, we are concerned both with explicitly designated public health laws and with laws and regulations that (whether by design or not) are relevant to public health practice. Overall, Martin presents a compelling case for the subject and practice of public health law to require the broadest of understandings and approaches. Again, drawing from her work with Coker:

> It is the diversity of available tools that will intimidate legal scholars who have tradi-
> tionally focused their research on narrowly defined areas of law. Knowledge of public
> health law requires understandings of taxation law (the power of the state to tax and
> spend), law regulating use of information (the power to alter the informational environ-
> ment), occupational health, traffic and environmental law (the power to alter the built
> environment), the economic, political and social context of law (the power to alter the
> socio-economic environment), public and administrative law regulatory tools (direct
> regulation of persons, professions and businesses) and tort law (indirect regulation
> through the tort system).[10]

We fully endorse this viewpoint and work towards our definition of the field, and our approach to the remainder of this book, accordingly. However, it is useful, before provid-ing that definition, to look to the definitions found in a definition of *public health governance* advanced by Martin with Belinda Bennett, Lawrence Gostin, and Roger Magnusson and then to consider the famous definition of public health law in Gostin and Wiley's leading textbook on the subject.

Bennett, Gostin, Magnusson, and Martin say:

> Public health governance is the means by which society collectively seeks to assure
> the conditions under which the population can live with the highest possible level of
> health and wellbeing. The conditions for the public's health are broad, spanning mul-
> tiple spheres – informational (health communication, advertisements, labelling), envi-
> ronmental (air, water), built (rural, urban, and suburban), and socioeconomic (taxes,
> spending, housing, poverty). Public health governance entails direct regulation of busi-
> nesses (inspections, nuisance abatements, and occupational health and safety) and of
> individuals (seatbelts, motorcycle helmets, quarantine). And it encompasses indirect
> regulation through the tort system (tobacco, firearms, toxic substances). Finally, given
> the complexity of many public health threats and challenges – from global warming,
> to obesity, to pandemic influenza – governance also has an 'inward dimension' that
> relates to the organisational structures, agencies and legal mandates through which
> governments exercise their own public health regulatory functions.[11]

We again endorse and draw from the approach presented. In particular, take note of the way different modes of social coordination – governance – are explained, and the justification

8 ibid.
9 See Martin and Coker (n 4); Richard Coker and Robyn Martin, 'Introduction: The Importance of Law for Public Health Policy and Practice' (2006) 120 *Public Health* 2.
10 Martin and Coker (n 4), 81.
11 Belinda Bennett, Lawrence Gostin, Roger Magnusson and Robyn Martin, 'Health Governance: Law, Regulation and Policy' (2009) 123 *Public Health* 207, 207 (reference omitted).

for including them. First, we share Bennett and colleagues' view that governance is 'primarily, but not exclusively, within the domain of government'.[12] Government may be the key actor, but other stakeholders have roles too. The stakeholders listed in the article are business, employers, academia, charitable foundations, the media, and civil society.[13] Second, an interest in public health governance is driven not by a focus solely on one means of control: rather, as echoed in our approach, it requires a consideration of the whole range of measures that are relevant to providing the conditions in which people can be healthy.[14] Thus, for Bennett et al, governance for public health includes 'direct regulation', which covers both hard laws and the exercise of legal powers whose purpose is to govern public health; 'indirect regulation', which entails the employment of legal measures that are not archetypally 'public health laws', for example, laws of tort, which govern the standards owed by private actors and in practice can serve public health; and the regulation by different agencies. A concern for ethics also enters their characterisation of the field.

In what follows, we also work on the basis that these diverse matters need to be covered. Like Bennett and colleagues, we remain attentive to the question of specifically designated public health powers, roles, and responsibilities and to the institution of measures that serve public health ends even if that is not their clear purpose. In our presentation of these ideas, we look to the ways different areas of law serve or constrain public health ends (Chapters 5 to 8) and then consider softer modes of regulation (Chapter 9). Although this includes our highlighting specific public health laws and policy, we are not concerned to distinguish in every case what is 'truly' a public health law. Rather, we are concerned to explain different possible legal and governance approaches and to 'map' them onto discussions of public health.

Although in a strict sense the label 'public health governance' might more appropriately capture the area of study that we are presenting in this book, we will continue with the designation public health law. For some legal purists, this may be problematic (see also Chapter 9), but it is in keeping with our approach as emanating from law-based concerns and is consistent with perhaps the most famous framing of the field: that provided by Lawrence Gostin in his seminal, US-focussed, textbook, Public Health Law: Power, Duty, Restraint, which is now co-authored with Lindsay Wiley:

> Public health law is the study of the legal powers and duties of the state, in collaboration with its partners (e.g. health care, business, the community, the media, and academe), to ensure the conditions for people to be healthy (to identify, prevent, and ameliorate risks to health in the population), and of the limitations on the power of the state to constrain for the common good the autonomy, privacy, liberty, proprietary, and other legally protected interests of individuals. The prime objective of public health law is to pursue the highest possible level of physical and mental health in the population, consistent with the values of social justice.[15]

There is clear overlap between the concerns expressed in the previous definition of public health governance and those found in Gostin and Wiley's definition of public health law.

---

12 ibid.
13 ibid.
14 See Chapter 1, section 1.3, and the World Health Organization's statement at <www.who.int/trade/glossary/story076/en/> accessed 5 April 2016.
15 Lawrence Gostin and Lindsay Wiley, Public Health Law: Power, Duty, Restraint (3rd edn., Berkeley: University of California Press 2016) 4.

Given the importance and influence of their textbook, but also given public health law's status as an 'outlier subject' within legal studies, we reflect here, finally, on different components of Gostin's definition[16] and explain how we then come to our own characterisation of the field.

First, as with the other definitions above, we note that Gostin and Wiley's focus is on each and every area of law that might impact health. In legal education, 'core' areas of law are separated, in essence, by reference to different sorts of systems of legal governance. For example, public law modules explore constitutional and public administrative rules and principles that constrain and empower the authority of the state and governmental actors, modules in the laws of tort examine the standards that we may reasonably expect of one another as private actors, and modules in criminal law explain what it means to commit a public wrong and how the coercive and morally-loaded mechanisms of the criminal justice system define social standards and allow for punitive responses when these are breached. Gostin and Wiley's idea of public health law does not confine itself to any one such area of law. Their analysis shows how the law, taken in its entirety, empowers public health actors and shows how it constrains their capacity to act. As such, they are interested, for example, in how tort law approaches might advance public health agendas in relation to smoking tobacco through class actions against tobacco manufacturers.[17]

As will be evident from the manner in which we have outlined this book, we agree with Gostin and Wiley that public health law needs to look across the legal landscape. Given the breadth of public health, it would be artificial to limit or exclude any given area of law if it has a bearing on population health. Simply put, we believe that readers of this book will be interested to learn of the full legal 'armoury' that might serve or limit public health agendas or apparently conflicting alternative agendas. It would be too limiting to work with an approach that considers just a narrow tranche of legal powers and competences (e.g. powers to interfere with individual liberties in instances of pandemic emergency). From a twenty-first-century public health perspective, there is practical relevance in, for example, how we define and protect consumer rights in relations to foods and other products, or the health and safety standards we might expect from employers, or the freedoms (or otherwise) to participate in risky or dangerous activities, and so on.

A second feature of Gostin and Wiley's definition, which we draw upon when coming to our own representation of public health law, is that it focuses on legal and other forms of regulation. This is hinted at by Gostin and Wiley when they refer, not just to the 'powers and duties of the state', but also the role of its 'partners' in providing conditions in which people may be healthy. As per the discussion of Bennett et al's definition, in our own development of this perspective, we see two key heads of activity, each of which is explored in detail in Chapter 9.

The first such area of governance is found in formal, but strictly speaking 'soft', modes of regulation. 'Hard law' in this jurisdiction is found in *primary legislation* (i.e. Acts of Parliament, such as the Health Act 2006) or authoritative judicial pronouncements found in the body of case law that constitutes our *common law* (e.g. the binding decision of the Court of Appeal in the Rampton smokers' case, which determined the legality of an aspect of the

---

16 See also ibid, chapter 1, where Gostin and Wiley expand in depth on their definition, and further, John Coggon and
    Lawrence Gostin, 'Beyond Medicine, Patients and the Law: Policy and Governance in 21st Century Health Law' in
    Catherine Stanton, Sarah Devaney, Anne-Maree Farrell, and Alexandra Mullock (eds), *Pioneering Healthcare Law: Essays in
    Honour of Margaret Brazier* (Abingdon: Routledge 2015).
17 See Gostin and Wiley (n 15), 255–263.

smoking ban in England and Wales).[18] Chapters 5 to 8 explore and explain how hard law approaches apply in the field of public health law. But it is also important to recognise other forms of regulatory measures that emanate from public authority. Here, we might consider *secondary legislation*, for example, Regulations promulgated by a Secretary of State on the basis of powers delegated through primary legislation (e.g. the Smoke-free (Exemptions and Vehicles) Regulations 2007,[19] which were issued by the Secretary of State for Health in accordance with sections 3, 5, and 79(3) of the Health Act 2006 and which provide detail on where the smoking of tobacco may be permissible within enclosed public spaces). We might also here consider policies and guidance documents issued by government departments and other executive agencies (e.g. Department of Health guidelines on alcohol consumption).[20]

The second area of governance, which we address in Chapter 9, is 'softer' still, yet also of enormous importance in terms of its impact on population health. Beyond social controls administered through legal and political actors and agencies, there is also a great deal of social regulation ('social machinery') that functions through the norms and activities of private organisations and actors. The policies and approaches, for example, of supermarkets have the clear potential to impact on people's decisions to consume (or not) particular products. Equally, 'voluntary' subscription to publicly endorsed regimes, such as the 'Responsibility Deal' established by the Conservative–Liberal Democrat Coalition Government (see also Chapter 3), suggest public health governance roles that are assumed by private, rather than public, actors. Equally, we might consider how individuals themselves possess personal responsibility for health. To complete the picture of public health law, it is crucial to develop an understanding of how institutions and actors that are not 'public' bodies, but which have an enormous public reach or public health impact, are governed and self-govern, how their exercise of power might impact population health, and how constraints may be put on their decision-making.

Whilst our approach therefore owes much to Gostin and Wiley's work, a point of tension between our approach and theirs bears emphasis.[21] Gostin and Wiley conclude their definition by saying: 'The prime objective of public health law is to pursue the highest possible level of physical and mental health in the population, consistent with the values of social justice'. As indicated by our discussion of public health ethics in Chapter 2, we see a real need for different theories of justice if we are to establish a full understanding of the legitimacy of public health activity. Questions of political morality and ethical practice are fundamental in the study of public health law. However, there is not one single unifying theory of justice that can be said to underpin public health activity. Everyone can agree that public health law ought to accord with sound moral principles, but there is radical disagreement about what those are. We have shown how there are participants to debates on the proper scope of public health, and public health law, such as Richard Epstein, who would disavow a commitment to governmental pursuit of better population health and wellbeing; some protagonists even deny the coherence of the very idea of population health.[22]

In his work, Gostin links his understanding of public health law to a particular normative argument regarding the fundamental importance of health and, from there, links his

---

18 See R (on the application of G) v Nottinghamshire Healthcare NHS Trust [2009] EWCA Civ 795.
19 SI 2007/765.
20 See Department of Health, *Alcohol Guidelines Review – Report from the Guidelines Development Group to the UK Chief Medical Officers* (London: Department of Health 2016).
21 See also Angus Dawson, 'Commentary on "The Limits of Law in the Protection of Public Health and the Role of Public Health Ethics"' (2006) 120 *Public Health* 77.
22 cf Richard Mohr, 'AIDS, Gays, and State Coercion' (1987) 1 *Bioethics* 35, 47.

prescriptions of what public health law should do to a firm theory of justice. For our purposes, we prefer not to suggest a 'prime objective' for public health law. For the purposes of this work, we do not advocate for a particular agenda; instead, we aim to present a groundwork from which readers, potentially of quite conflicting political viewpoints, might draw. And, so, we now present our definition of the field, with a summary of its implications for the field of study.

4.2.2 A definition of public health law

Given the different considerations covered in Part I, and the ideas explored above in this chapter, we advance and work with the following definition of public health law:

> *Public health law is a field of study and practice that concerns those aspects of law, policy, and regulation that advance or place constraints upon the protection and promotion of health (howsoever understood) within, between, and across populations.*[23]

As we have explained, such a definition provides the different necessary conditions for the study and practice of public health law. Our definition:

- Covers the very broad, but necessary, embrace that is claimed by contemporary public health activity, which includes the provision of a health care system, public health infrastructure, and measures that respond to social determinants of ill health.
- Provides a breadth in its concept of law: we are not simply focussed on 'hard law' measures but look also to social policy broadly conceived to include the governance roles of public and private actors and institutions.
- Embraces different legal and regulatory measures and approaches and reaches across sectors.
- Emphasises the role of law and governance both as means to promote public health agendas and as means to limit what may be done in the name of public health.
- Permits an open interpretation of 'health' allowing analysis of measures that bear not simply on, for example, disease, but also on broader, positive states such as wellbeing.
- Is open to engagement from disciplines outside of legal studies: for example, as emphasised above, we argue that the field should be informed by public health ethics. Our definition of public health law is also compatible, for example, with study informed by disciplines such as anthropology, sociology, psychology, history, and economics.

Although any definition of the field could be contested or modified, our view is that the concise characterisation of public health law here avoids being overly prescriptive about content, whilst also exhibiting the characteristics that we list. Each of these is, we suggest, an essential component of public health law, both as an area of study and as an area of practice. Having explained our position, and the reasons for coming to it, we now move to contrast problem-based engagement in legal studies in public health with approach-based engagement and explain how our approach-based work is designed to serve the ends of users of this book.

---

23 Contrast John Coggon, *What Makes Health Public? A Critical Evaluation of Moral, Legal, and Political Claims in Public Health* (Cambridge: Cambridge University Press 2012), chapter 5, especially 86–91.

4.3 Studying public health law: approach-led *versus* issue-focussed analysis

Part I of this book provides the context to studies in public health law, introducing the field of public health and its key actors, explaining how ethics relates to public health, and presenting a history of public health law in the UK. The legal scholars discussed in this chapter, such as Robyn Martin and Lawrence Gostin, and the philosophers to whom we have referred above, such as Angus Dawson and Marcel Verweij, have helped advance public health ethics and law as fields of study that now enjoy a more significant presence in the academic literatures. Over the last fifteen years, there has been an enormous growth in public health ethics and law research, affording the opportunity to examine in different ways the relationships between ethical theories and public health law and practice[24] and widening analyses of health and law (perhaps especially notably in relation to European Union law and health regulation).[25] In other jurisdictions, there have also been focussed studies on defining public health law itself, with aims that are not altogether different from ours in the production of the current work.[26] Because of the relative novelty of public health law, questions arise about how best to systematise the study.

Given the differences, but also overlaps, between this and cognate works, we consider it important to explain our structuring of the book – in essence, to explain our methods. Public health law cuts across governance approaches, governmental sectors, academic disciplines, and public and private actors. Rather than find coherence to this field of study by reference to a unifying 'philosophy' or legal approach, its boundaries are marked by reference to its subject-matter: public health.[27] Yet, by this sort of reasoning, we could find that, in fact, there is more coherence if we break different areas of public health concern into smaller fields that require their own, individual study. For example, we could identify specific areas and produce a chapter on each, perhaps covering tobacco control, alcohol regulation, obesity and law, pandemic planning, vaccination policy, and so on. Doing this would serve well to explain how public health law works in different areas, 'dissecting' them legally and demonstrating the roles of alternative regulatory approaches.

Although we see considerable merit in this way of framing matters, we have opted instead to systematise the following chapters around five broad headings. These do not exhaust the 'core' areas of legal study but have been selected because we have found them to represent the foundation of relevant legal approaches in the context of public health. The remaining chapters in Part II cover the law as follows. First, under the heading 'private law' we consider laws governing private obligations between citizens (contract and tort) and laws relevant to our home, family, and personal lives (family law and laws governing privacy). We then look to the nature and scope of criminal law and its relationship with public health measures. In Chapter 7, we present the idea of 'public law', which refers to administrative law (laws governing the decision-making and activities of public bodies), constitutional law, and human rights law. Chapter 8 moves to explain the effects of EU and international law on English public health law. And, finally, in Chapter 9, we introduce ideas regarding softer

---

24 See e.g. Sridhar Venkatapuram, *Health Justice: An Argument from the Capabilities Approach* (Cambridge: Polity Press 2011); Coggon, ibid.
25 See e.g. Tamara Hervey and Jean McHale, *European Union Health Law: Themes and Implications* (Cambridge: Cambridge University Press 2015); Mark Flear, *Governing Public Health: EU Law, Regulation and Biopolitics* (Oxford: Hart Publishing 2015).
26 See e.g. Gostin and Wiley (n 15); Wendy Parmet, *Populations, Public Health, and the Law* (Washington: Georgetown University Press 2009).
27 cf Theodore Ruger, 'Health Law's Coherence Anxiety' (2008) 96 *Georgetown Law Journal* 625.

modes of public policy-making, the governance functions of private actors, and the health responsibilities of individual citizens.

Our rationale for taking this approach is that it allows us systematically to achieve three key goals with each chapter. The chapters present examples of substantive rules, principles, and norms in relation to different public health problems; outline how different legal approaches manifest themselves; and discuss them in relation to public health practices and agendas. Doing things this way is designed to allow readers – especially readers who have no or limited background in legal studies – to develop a more straightforwardly generalisable understanding of the basis, reach, and limitations of different legal approaches.

The strength of this approach is the development of a clearer understanding of law and regulation. In addition, it allows us to relate the legal framing to questions in public health ethics when explaining how public health ends might either be served or constrained, and the legitimacy of their being served or constrained. The key potential weakness is that, by building the structure around different approaches, readers may miss the important point that *public health problems will generally be best addressed by multilayered governance approaches*. This is particularly so for large-scale public health problems. For example, take the question of smoking tobacco. From a practical public health perspective, it is necessary to consider how a range of legal approaches might combine here: the potential application or deterrent effect of private law protections against exposure to tobacco smoke (e.g. through the potential to sue for harms caused by such exposure); the role for coercive measures (e.g. making smoking in enclosed public spaces a criminal offence); we will be interested in the regulatory powers of public authorities (e.g. the capacity for the NHS to promulgate non-smoking policies); we will be interested in the EU and international context (e.g. in compliance with any relevant international legal obligations in relation to tobacco control and commercial freedoms); and we will be interested in the scope and application of softer measures of governance (e.g. information campaigns to heighten public awareness and 'nudge' people away from smoking).

This book presents the foundations of public health law, but when a given problem is presented, it must not be thought, without exploration, that a single approach alone is appropriate. Readers should consider the potential to *combine* tools from the different areas of law and also to consider how one area of law might limit a potential measure brought in another area: for example, whether a potential regulation that would advance a public health end would conflict with a trade right under EU or international law. The examples provided in the following chapters are selected with a view to drawing out key points. Of necessity, we cannot present a comprehensive picture of a field as broad as public health law. So instead, we aim to encourage the capacity to think about the merits and effects of different approaches and then to allow the reader to seek means of applying the ideas from across the different areas.

Chapter 4: Summary

- Because of the breadth of public health activity, the study and practice of public health law cannot be limited to single areas of law or legal analysis.
- In examining law and public health, it is potentially necessary to consider any area of law and also to consider non-legal modes of regulation.
- Public health law relates to measures that underpin and facilitate public health activity and measures that may limit public health agendas.

Public health law is therefore defined as a field of study and practice that concerns those aspects of law, policy, and regulation that advance or place constraints upon the protection and promotion of health (howsoever understood) within, between, and across populations.

4.4 Further readings

Lawrence Gostin and Lindsay Wiley, *Public Health Law: Power, Duty, Restraint* (3rd edn., Berkeley: University of California Press 2016).

Linda Johnson and Robyn Martin (eds), *Law and the Public Dimension of Health* (London: Cavendish 2001).

Wendy Parmet, *Populations, Public Health, and the Law* (Washington: Georgetown University Press 2009).

Keith Syrett and Oliver Quick, 'Pedagogical Promise and Problems: Teaching Public Health Law' (2009) 123 *Public Health* 222.

The special issue of *Public Health* (2006) Volume 120, Supplement 1, edited by Richard Coker and Robyn Martin.

Chapter 5

Private law and public health

5.1 Law in the private sphere

In this chapter, we explore private law and public health. We use 'private law' here as a term that refers to various quite distinctive legal relationships, mechanisms, and purposes. It might be thought that archetypically *public* health ends cannot be served by areas of law described as *private* – that, at most, we would be looking at the *constraints* that private rights put on public health activity.[1] However, we aim with this chapter to show both how private law aims and practices may form part of population-health approaches, as well as to consider how the good of collective public health activity can be limited, given individuals' private rights.[2] To demonstrate the breadth of scope here, it is useful to recall the areas of public health responsibility that Lawrence Gostin identifies, and which we presented in Chapter 1 – that there are obligations to assure access to a health care system, to provide a functioning public health infrastructure, and to respond to the social determinants of health.[3] In relation to each of these, laws governing private rights in fact lend a great deal. Furthermore, this is so both through the ways in which the laws themselves interact with public health agendas and how private law actions and evolving common law rules may serve in processes of advancing or limiting public health ends.[4] As such, we emphasise in this chapter the impacts of law, but also the impacts of (threatened) litigation.[5]

The chapter has four substantive sections, which combine to explain various conceptual and practical questions in our framing of private law and public health and outline the relevance of these areas of law to the study and practice of public health law. Of necessity, our presentation cannot be comprehensive. But, as *per* our overall aims and approach outlined in Chapter 4, the legal overview and practical case studies give an indication of the range of

---

1 cf Roger Brownsword, 'Public Health, Private Right, and the Common Law' (2006) 120 *Public Health* 42.
2 See also Keith Syrett and Oliver Quick, 'Pedagogical Promise and Problems: Teaching Public Health Law' (2009) 123 *Public Health* 222.
3 See Gostin's *Foreword*, xi–xii, in John Coggon, *What Makes Health Public? A Critical Evaluation of Moral, Legal, and Political Claims in Public Health* (Cambridge: Cambridge University Press 2012).
4 See also Robyn Martin, 'Public Health and the Scope of the Potential Liability in Tort' (2005) 21 *Professional Negligence* 39: Here, Martin focuses on the potential to find legal liability in relation to four matters: harms that result from following poor health or lifestyle advice, harms resulting from negligently administered public health interventions, harms resulting from a failure to make a public health intervention, and rights-breaches against individuals in the institution of public health interventions.
5 See also Lawrence Gostin and Lindsay Wiley, *Public Health Law: Power, Duty, Restraint* (3rd edn., Berkeley: University of California Press 2016), which contains an overview of the ways in which private law and public health interact in the US context.

ways that law touches our private lives, and the potential implications of this in relation to public health. Our focus in sections 5.2 and 5.3 is on legally protected private obligations that we, as private citizens, owe to one another. We examine both obligations that people assume by private arrangement and obligations that we owe one to another given standards that are set by the law itself. We then move in sections 5.4 and 5.5 to consider how laws serve and constrain public health activity in the context of our personal, family, and home lives.

5.2 Private law as civil obligations

Typically, when legal practitioners and scholars refer to private law, they mean those legal rules that govern what might be termed our 'civil obligations': the rights and duties that we owe to each other as private citizens. In English law, we primarily think of these as being protected by the laws of *contract* and *tort*. Let us consider first the law of contract.[6] Although it offers fewer obvious connections with public health, it is important to have an understanding of its operation. Contract law regulates voluntarily made private agreements, where parties consent to particular terms that are accepted on the basis that each party to the contract offers something of value: a form of *quid pro quo*. If parties form a legally valid contract, the rights and obligations that they thereby assume are governed through law. This means that failures to honour the contract can lead to a legal determination that compensation be provided to the party who is suffering the breach of the contract, that the contract be fulfilled, or even in some cases that additional payments be made to the wronged party based on consequent benefits that have accrued to the wrong-doing party. A clear public interest underpins the role of law here. Rather than leave parties uncertain of their position, or susceptible to being cheated following the formation of agreements, the potential to enforce obligations assumed voluntarily allows members of society to set and work according to clear expectations. This all serves as part of law's role in *setting standards* and *ensuring justice* by aiming to guarantee that we honour the obligations that we owe each other.

   This book does not provide detail on the complexities of creating lawful contracts or formulating valid contract terms. It should, though, be noted that there are important statutory and common law rules designed to assure *fairness* in contract law, for example, by limiting the sorts of clauses that might be included in legally protected contracts. Equally, there are points of apparent contractual agreement – i.e. agreements made voluntarily, for exchange of value – that the law will nevertheless fail to recognise as valid. Of potential relevance in relation to public health, for example, a contract for prostitution (i.e. an agreement where one party agrees to pay a sum of money for sexual intercourse) will not be recognised at law (in technical terms, it will be *void for immorality*):[7] in this sense, a public interest limits freedom to make private agreements and arguably does so in a way that serves public health ends. And, more generally here, we might refer to the Unfair Contract Terms Act 1977 and Part 2 of the Consumer Rights Act 2015. These are of relevance in particular because they limit contracting parties' freedom to waive liability for negligently caused harm and extend protections, for example, into the contexts of consumer rights. Whilst within private law the scope for contractual obligations serving or limiting public health agendas is in itself relatively limited, contract is a crucial component of private law obligations under the heading that we

---

6 See Roger Brownsword, *Contract Law: Themes for the Twenty-First Century* (Oxford: Oxford University Press 2006).

7 See *Pearce and Another v Brooks* [1866] LR 1 Ex 213, where the owner of a carriage was unable to sue a prostitute for the value of its hire as he knew she would be using it to attract men.

are using here of 'civil obligations'. And it serves our understanding of public health law to recognise that limits exist, not just on what constitutes a formally made contract, but also on the terms that contracting parties can agree to.

As we have indicated, however, 'private law' as a term referring to civil obligations extends beyond agreements made in contract: it also embraces rights and duties found in the law of tort.[8] The term 'tort' literally means 'wrong'. Tort law sets the standards that we can expect of each other as private actors quite regardless of any private agreements. Whilst criminal law addresses 'public wrongs' – i.e. wrongs against the state (see further: Chapter 6) – tort law governs 'private wrongs' – wrongs established through law, but against parties as private individuals. Through knowledge of our obligations in tort law, we have an understanding of the standards of behaviour that are expected of us, for example, driving with due care, assuring the quality of products for consumption, or ensuring that people visiting our property are not at unreasonable risk of suffering harm.

As well as this standard-setting function, the law of tort also has a role in allowing individuals to achieve justice through legal action if their private rights are breached: tort law in this way aims both 'to right wrongs' for individuals and to provide a deterrent against wrongful actions. Moreover, obligations in tort can be seen as providing a public governance role in the sense that they lead to a form of social security – albeit not one that could perhaps strictly be labelled a 'public safety net'. In particular, if we combine the fact of legal liability for tortious harms with insurance schemes that spread the risk for guarding against and responding to harm, a mechanism develops to serve a common interest. For example, we are legally required within this jurisdiction to buy insurance to cover third-party liabilities that might arise when we are driving a motor vehicle.[9] Whilst the consequent regime operates through private arrangements between insurers and insured, in accordance with market principles, there is a clear societal benefit in this: risks are spread across a population and thus can be absorbed and redress guaranteed when harms occur.[10]

Rights and duties in tort have various foundations. Actions in tort law may therefore come under a variety of heads and lead to a range of remedies. Perhaps most familiar to non-specialists is the tort of negligence, which we explore below. But, as we will highlight, tort law also has important functions, for example, of assuring safe standards in the workplace, of governing the safety of private property, and in safeguarding people from non-consensual invasions of their person. Remedies in tort include damages to compensate for harms committed and injunctions (i.e. court orders demanding that a wrong-doing party act, or refrain from acting, in a particular way).

As noted in Chapter 3, Richard Coker and Robyn Martin, in explaining the historical development of public health law in England and Wales, find a foundation in tort law: specifically, in the law of nuisance. Nuisance serves as a means of preventing or responding to environmental harms and thus helping assure the conditions in which people can be healthy (although recall that Coker and Martin also demonstrate how nuisance suffered limitations as an overall basis for public health governance).[11] Whereas the term 'land law', and the associated area of equity and trusts, is generally taken to refer to matters regarding people's legal and beneficial interests in property (and is not the basis of questions that we consider in

---

8 See Paula Giliker, *Tort* (5th edn., London: Sweet and Maxwell 2014).

9 Road Traffic Act 1988, s. 143.

10 For a critique of tort law in this regard, and an argument for its abolition in favour a no-fault compensation scheme, see Peter Cane, *Atiyah's Accidents, Compensation and the Law* (8th edn., Cambridge: Cambridge University Press 2013).

11 Richard Coker and Robyn Martin, 'Introduction: The Importance of Law for Public Health Policy and Practice' (2006) 120 *Public Health* 2.

this book), nuisance, as a branch of tort law, governs our rights to use or enjoy land without unreasonable interference caused by pollution. English common law has doctrines of both public and private nuisance. Of relevance here is the tort of private nuisance and its relationship with different forms of statutory nuisance. (A public nuisance is a crime, representing a wrong against a community, rather than a wrong against a private individual in her own right, albeit that an individual may found a claim in tort if a public nuisance causes her 'special damage').[12]

Regarding law and public health, important provisions are found in the statutory nuisances in the Environmental Protection Act 1990 and the duties and powers that this Act gives to local authorities to inspect properties and respond to nuisances. Section 79(1) lists a wide variety of such nuisances, including:

(a)   any premises in such a state as to be prejudicial to health or a nuisance;
(b)   smoke emitted from premises so as to be prejudicial to health or a nuisance;
(c)   fumes or gases emitted from premises so as to be prejudicial to health or a nuisance;
(d)   any dust, steam, smell or other effluvia arising on industrial, trade or business premises and being prejudicial to health or a nuisance[.]

The use of the word 'or' in the above provisions ('prejudicial to health or a nuisance') has been interpreted as meaning that the word 'nuisance' refers to a common law nuisance.[13] In the limited relevant case law, it has been held that such nuisances must be understood consistently with the context of the historical public health laws (as discussed in Chapter 3). Accordingly, the Act serves to protect against disease, rather than injury.[14] However, where a nuisance does occur, under section 80 of the Act, a local authority may serve a notice ordering that it be abated or its occurrence or recurrence prohibited or restricted.

While Coker and Martin's explanation of the restrictive effect of limiting 'public health law' to protections in nuisance affords a valuable critique of the historical basis of public health laws in the UK, a wider range of actions in tort have the potential to serve public health aims and should be considered too – as well as, of course, other areas of public health governance considered elsewhere in this book.[15] In regard to alternative sorts of claim regarding land, occupiers, for example, owe duties to guard against injuries to people invited onto land,[16] including trespassers.[17] Whilst such duties would not classically be conceived as 'public health duties', they have a clear role in safeguarding health and promoting a safe environment.

In introducing the concept of tort law and its relationship with public health, beyond these discussions of torts concerning land, it is useful to exemplify how tort law operates within a distinct public health context, specifically with reference to two common law torts that determine patients' rights in the health care system. If the public health role of assuring a health care system is to work, it is insufficient for there simply to be public law obligations to provide a health service; we also require legal underpinnings to protect people from undue interference by health care practitioners and legal guarantees to assure the quality of

---

12 See further Giliker (n 8), chapter 10.
13 See Neil Parpworth, 'Public Nuisance in the Environmental Context' (2008) *Journal of Planning and Environment Law* 1526.
14 See *R v Bristol City Council, ex parte Everett* [1999] 1 WLR 1170.
15 cf also Gostin and Wiley (n 5), chapter 7.
16 Occupiers' Liability Act 1957.
17 Occupiers' Liability Act 1984.

health care that we might receive. Two areas of tort law are particularly pertinent in serving these respective requirements.

First, the tort of *battery* protects us against wrongful invasions of our bodily integrity. In the context of health care provision, this leads to rights for patients with decision-making capacity not to be treated unless they have provided consent. Although various exceptions exist,[18] generally speaking, the law of tort holds that you may not force treatment on a patient without her consent, even if this will serve her best interests or lead to some wider benefit. (It should be noted that, as well as treatment without consent constituting a private law wrong, it will also simultaneously be possible that it represents a criminal law wrong: if a doctor treats a patient without consent, she may be sued by the patient in a tort law action *and* face a public prosecution for a criminal battery.) As such, part of tort law's regulation of health care obtains in safeguarding patient autonomy, generally constraining personal or general concerns for welfare in favour of privileging individual choice.[19]

The second area of tort to consider here is found in the law of clinical negligence. Doctors are, of course, required to adhere to standards set by their statutory regulator: the General Medical Council.[20] But their activity is governed, too, at law. The law of negligence prescribes who owes a duty of care to whom, what standard of care is expected when a duty is owed, and what compensation is due when a breach of the duty of care leads to different forms of harm. Within the health care system, negligence law underpins the standards of reasonable care that are owed to patients. Where a physician practises in a way that falls short of what would be expected by a responsible body of medical practitioners, and in that failure causes harm to her patient, she may be sued.[21]

As such, we can see how the tort law system, particularly in its standard-setting function, helps to enhance the conditions in which people can be healthy. We have already seen in outline how this applies in the context of environmental protection and health care. But, to be clear, private law obligations apply against the diffuse range of private actors whose activities might impact on population health, such as restaurants, ensuring safety for consumers. They also apply against public authorities, such as councils and the NHS. Public law responsibilities, considered in Chapter 7, allow us to examine constraints on public decision-making authority. But constraints on the actions of public bodies are found also in their private law obligations.

5.3 Case studies 1 and 2: Public health and civil obligations: common law developments of negligence rules

In this section, we build on the above framing discussions by reference to two case studies in tort law. These demonstrate the potential for judges to advance health protections through arguably quite radical developments of common law rules. First, we present the case of

18 Consider e.g. Mental Health Act 1983, s. 63 (as amended); Public Health (Control of Disease) Act 1984, s. 45G (as amended); and also note the developing 'vulnerable adult' jurisdiction in the High Court, which authorises welfare decision-making for adults despite their not failing the tests for capacity in sections 2 and 3 of the Mental Capacity Act 2005: see Michael Dunn, Isabel Clare, and Anthony Holland, 'To Empower or Protect? Constructing the "Vulnerable Adult" in English Law and Public Policy' (2008) 28 *Legal Studies* 234.
19 Margaret Brazier, 'Do No Harm – Do Patients Have Responsibilities Too?' (2006) 65 *Cambridge Law Journal* 397.
20 See General Medical Council, <www.gmc-uk.org/guidance/index.asp> accessed 5 April 2016.
21 *Bolam v Friern Hospital Management Committee* [1957] 1 WLR 582; *Bolitho v City and Hackney Health Authority* [1997] 3 WLR 1151.

Donoghue v Stevenson,[22] which provided the foundations of the modern law of negligence and promoted public health ends through heightened consumer protection, and second, we look at *Fairchild v Glenhaven Funeral Services Ltd*,[23] which saw the House of Lords revise the generally understood rules of causation to allow greater legal rights to employees who had developed mesothelioma following exposure to asbestos dust at work.

5.3.1 Public health and consumer protection

In this section, we illustrate how judicial activism in relation to tort law has served to advance public health ends. Our primary focus is on the case that founded the modern law of negligence; a case that provided a solid basis for consumer protection through the law of negligence. It should be noted at the outset that negligence principles no longer apply in this area.[24] As indicated above, negligence founds liability on the basis of fault: a defendant's conduct is examined, and if she fails to exercise reasonable care, and as a consequence of this causes a person harm, she may be liable. The current law on product liability, established in Part 1 of the Consumer Protection Act 1987, is governed according to a regime of *strict liability*. This means that consumers do not have to prove fault on the part of manufacturers in order to gain redress if a product is defective: the law now focuses on the quality of the product itself, rather than how reasonable (or otherwise) the defendant may have been. In order briefly to illustrate, consider the case of *A v National Blood Authority (No. 1)*.[25] In this case, the claimants contracted Hepatitis C, having unfortunately received transfusions of contaminated blood. They thus sued the National Blood Authority, claiming for the damage that the blood – in these terms, a contaminated product – had caused. The defendants accepted that the 1987 Act imposed strict liability but argued (*inter alia*) that the infected blood should not be considered 'defective' as the risk of some of the blood being contaminated was inevitable. The court found for the claimants. The Act had been introduced to give effect to the Product Liability Directive (EEC) 85/374, and it was found that the purpose of this Directive was to enhance consumer protections. As such, it was held that it would be inconsistent for the law to be interpreted in a way that would fail to provide compensation in an instance where a person is injured by a defective product. In the current instance, the infected blood was held to be properly conceived as 'non-standard', and thus the National Blood Authority had no defence.

But, to give an indication of the radical capacity for private law to serve public health ends, let us look back to *Donoghue v Stevenson*, perhaps the most famous case in tort law. Decided in 1932, it established the basis of the contemporary principles and rules regarding negligence. The case concerned the question of what, if any, duty of care a manufacturer owes to the ultimate consumer of a product. In short, the facts were that Mrs Donoghue was bought a bottle of ginger beer, which turned out to contain the decomposing remains of a snail. She did not realise this until after consuming some of the drink, and consequently became ill. Mrs Donoghue had no relationship in contract either with the café in which the ginger beer was bought or with Stevenson, the manufacturer. Thus, the question arose whether she had any form of legal relationship with Stevenson that afforded her a right to compensation.

22 *Donoghue v Stevenson* [1932] AC 562.
23 *Fairchild v Glenhaven Funeral Services Ltd* [2002] UKHL 22.
24 For a broader analysis of the law of negligence and public health law, see Martin (n 4).
25 [2001] 3 All ER 289.

The case went to the House of Lords, where it was held that there was sufficient prox-imity between the producer and the consumer that a duty of care existed to take reasonable care not to cause her harm. Lord Atkin's speech is recognised as the most influential in the case. His Lordship sought to derive general principles of tort law from a wide survey of earlier cases in which a duty of care was established or denied. It is instructive, given the purposes of this book, to acknowledge the way in which Lord Atkin frames his opinion at its very outset:

> My Lords, the sole question for determination in this case is legal: Do the averments made by the pursuer in her pleading, if true, disclose a cause of action? I need not restate that particular facts. The question is whether the manufacturer of an article of drink sold by him to a distributor, in circumstances which prevent the distributor or the ultimate purchaser or consumer from discovering by inspection any defect, is under any legal duty to the ultimate purchaser or consumer to take reasonable care that the article is free from defect likely to cause injury to health. I do not think a more important problem has occupied your Lordships in your judicial capacity: important both because of its bearing on public health and because of the practical test which it applies to the system under which it arises.[26]

Lord Atkin goes on to expound his famous 'neighbour principle':

> The rule that you are to love your neighbour becomes in law, you must not injure your neighbour; and the lawyer's question, Who is my neighbour? receives a restricted reply. You must take reasonable care to avoid acts or omissions which you can reasonably foresee would be likely to injure your neighbour. Who, then, in law is my neighbour? The answer seems to be – persons who are so closely and directly affected by my act that I ought reasonably to have them in contemplation as being so affected when I am direct-ing my mind to the acts or omissions which are called in question.[27]

As we have indicated, Lord Atkin advances his argument in favour of this broad duty of care by reference to existing precedent in this jurisdiction. He also reflects on a comparable legal situation in the United States. We should not, however, consider his position as less than revolutionary. It provides a foundational place for private law regulation in support of public health ends. In terms familiar from Chapter 2 of this book, it is quite imaginable that the House of Lords could have taken a much more libertarian line in the case, suggesting that there was insufficient proximity between Stevenson and Donoghue and even that Mrs Donoghue anyway should accept the risk of coming to harm as a consumer of products sold freely on the open market. As it is, we arrived at the position in tort law (now overtaken by statute, as indicated above) that:

> A manufacturer of products, which he sells in such a form as to show that he intends them to reach the ultimate consumer in the form in which they left him with no reason-able possible intermediate examination, and with the knowledge that the absence of reasonable care in the preparation or putting up of the products will result in an injury

---

to the consumer's life or property, owes a duty to the consumer to take that reasonable care.[28]

Referring to this position as being 'in accordance with sound common sense', and a proposition that nobody 'who was not a lawyer would for one moment doubt',[29] the legal development born of *Donoghue v Stevenson* has led to the current law of negligence: through tort law's duty of care, we are beholden to standards in many aspects of our 'private' lives that contribute to assuring the conditions in which we can be healthy. In the decades following *Donoghue v Stevenson*, detailed rules governing negligence have emerged and their applicability refined.[30] In brief explication, a claim in negligence may be said to be founded where it is established that a party owes another a duty of care, that party breaches the duty of care, and the breach of duty causes compensable harm to the other.

Despite our observation that the House of Lords' development of common law has allowed a crucial underpinning to public health law, it should be emphasised that fulfilling the criteria for a valid negligence claim can provide a significant bar to protections of health and welfare. To hint at the challenges here, questions arise regarding the scope of matters such as establishing the existence of a duty,[31] demonstrating sufficient proximity between parties to a case,[32] establishing reasonable foreseeability,[33] proving causation,[34] and establishing which sorts of harms are compensable.[35] In the next section, we consider a more recent case where a public health end was vindicated in the face of the otherwise prohibitive rules on causation. Whilst that case serves well to demonstrate further judicial activism in this area, it should be read against a background of practical and doctrinal challenges facing litigants who would wish to advance public health missions through private law actions or the threat thereof. The short message is that private law may serve public health, and it is instructive to see how, but the capacity of tort law to serve public health is limited doctrinally, as well as by reference to real-world limitations on the impact of legal rules.

5.3.2 Public health and safety at work

The case of *Fairchild* concerned workers who had contracted mesothelioma in the course of their employment. As a point of law, there was no argument that their employers owed them a duty to guard against the risks associated with exposure to asbestos. However, mesothelioma is a condition that is contracted with a single exposure to asbestos dust: it is neither contracted on the basis of continued exposure (although one's chances of contracting it are necessarily higher the longer the exposure), nor is it made worse by ongoing exposure once the disease is present. The claimants in *Fairchild* thus faced a legal problem, which had proven fatal prior to their appeal being heard in the House of Lords:[36] whilst a duty was owed, and had been breached, the employees had each been in the service of multiple employers; as such, it was not possible to determine on the balance of probabilities which employer was causally at fault for each worker's harm. For this reason, in *Fairchild*, we find the standard

28 ibid, 599.
29 ibid.
30 See Giliker (n 8), chapters 2–6.
31 *Anns v London Borough of Merton* [1978] 1 AC 728; *Caparo v Dickman* [1990] 2 AC 605.
32 *Caparo*, ibid.
33 *Bourhill v Young* [1943] AC 92.
34 See e.g. the discussion below of *Fairchild* (n 23).
35 See Giliker (n 8), chapter 17.
36 *Fairchild* (n 23).

rules of causation within the law of negligence impeding access to damages in tort.[37] To receive protection in private law, according to generally understood legal doctrine, none of the claimants could point to a single employer and say that, but for its wrongful action, the victims would not have contracted the disease.

The judges in the House of Lords, however, considered that the law permitted that, at times, the general negligence rules on causation did not apply. *Fairchild*, they held, was such a case. In Lord Bingham's words, the court could decide 'whether in special circumstances such as those in these cases there should be any variation or relaxation of' the otherwise prohibitive rules on causation.[38] Their Lordships approached the question by considering questions of principle, legal authority, and policy. In regard to principle, there was a concern that the legal rules should not lead to an unfair result; there was a need for fairness in the rules. In regard to authority, there was a need to consider whether the case was decided in a manner consistent with English law (and this line of reasoning is complemented with a consideration of law in other jurisdictions). Regarding policy, there were two competing considerations: on the one hand, it is unjust to make a defendant liable for a harm that she did not cause; on the other, it is unjust that the claimants should suffer harm as a result of a breach of duty and not be able to receive compensation. Lord Nicholls is clear that the threshold could be changed but that the court should be explicit that such a 'balancing exercise involves a value judgment'.[39] Having established that variation of the general rules is possible, he holds:

> So long as it was not insignificant, each employer's wrongful exposure of its employee to asbestos dust, and, hence, to the risk of contracting mesothelioma, should be regarded by the law as a sufficient degree of causal connection.[40]

Similarly, Lord Hoffmann holds:

> My Lords, in my opinion the rule applied by the Court of Appeal is not a correct state-ment of the causal connection between breach of duty and damage which the law requires in a case such as this. I think it is sufficient, both on principle and authority, that the breach of duty contributed substantially to the risk that the claimant could contract the disease.[41]

In assessing the decision in *Fairchild* from a public health law perspective, it is important to remember that the decision is not just about affording compensation to the victims of mesothelioma. As Lord Hoffmann makes clear, a range of considerations are at play: the first and last in particular demonstrate the use of tort law as a component of public health law's armoury:

> What are the significant features of the present case? First, we are dealing with a duty specifically intended to protect employees against being unnecessarily exposed to the

---

37 As Tony Weir notes, in a more widely critical analysis of the House of Lords' decision, the court overlooks the claimants' entitlement to receive industrial disablement benefit: a failure to achieve compensation in tort would not have left them with nothing. See Tony Weir, 'Making It More Likely v Making It Happen' (2002) 61 *Cambridge Law Journal* 519.
38 *Fairchild* (n 23), [9].
39 ibid, [40].
40 ibid, [42].
41 ibid, [47].

risk of (among other things) a particular disease. Secondly, the duty is one intended
to create a civil right to compensation for injury relevantly connected with its breach.
Thirdly, it is established that the greater the exposure to asbestos, the greater the risk
of contracting that disease. Fourthly, except in the case in which there has been only
one significant exposure to asbestos, medical science cannot prove whose asbestos
is more likely than not to have produced the cell mutation which caused the disease.
Fifthly, the employee has contracted the disease against which he should have been
protected.[42]

And, in the circumstances, Lord Hoffmann holds that 'a rule requiring proof of a link
between the defendant's asbestos and the claimant's disease would, with the arbitrary exception of single-employer cases, empty the duty of content'.[43]

Since the case of *Fairchild*, Parliament has enacted the Compensation Act 2006, section 3
of which provides directly for compensation for mesothelioma (but only mesothelioma)
as a result of asbestos exposure in instances where it is not possible to establish that a particular tortious exposure actually caused the disease. As we have emphasised in this and the
previous section, it should not be taken from the discussion here that public health ends will
straightforwardly be served by private law obligations. However, cases such as *Fairchild*, and
consequent parliamentary activity, do indicate a willingness and capacity to address public
health problems through tort law. In the context of a study in public health law, this has
interesting implications for analysis and for practical public health strategies.

5.4 Private law as family law, and law in our domestic and private lives

As well as the concept of private law as civil obligations, we need to outline a further, conceptually, and practically distinct area of law and privacy: laws that govern our family, home,
and personal lives. These laws are a quite separate breed of 'private law', which tend to fall
under the heading 'family law',[44] but extend also to protections of rights to enjoy personal
freedoms to live in ways of our own choosing outside of the family setting. This wide concept of private law includes, for example, the basis and limitations of protections of religious
freedoms where respecting these might harm the rights-holders' health and welfare, or a
person's right to engage in unhealthy activity based on something less profound still, such
as personal preference. Necessarily, great value is placed on our freedom from interference
in the home and in our personal lives: an excess of state intrusion into our private and family lives would contravene fundamental principles of liberal democracy. However, it is also
the case that law must in various ways extend into the home. We will explain and exemplify
here and in section 5.5 how public health activity may be advanced and constrained in the
context of the scope and limits to our freedoms to make personal decisions, either for ourselves, or in the context of family life. In this part of the chapter, we present a more general
overview of the links between law, privacy, and public health.

An important point to emphasise at the outset of this is the distinction that the law
draws between personal decision-making for adults and that for children. To revisit health

---

42 ibid, [61].
43 ibid, [62].
44 Jonathan Herring, *Family Law* (7th edn., Harlow: Pearson 2015).

care choices to exemplify, adults' decision-making is governed by an evolution of common law rules and the Mental Capacity Act 2005. These offer strong protections (at least in principle)[45] of the right to consent, to choose between treatments offered, or to refuse consent to treatment even where this will lead to serious harm or death.[46] In the classic medico-legal example, these rules mean that an adult Jehovah's Witness can refuse a life-saving blood transfusion, even where no alternative exists to save her life. This right holds regardless of the implications, not just for her own health and welfare, but also consequent impacts of the decision, such as if it would leave her children without parents.[47]

Regarding decision-making for and by children, by contrast, the significant governing legislation is the Children Act 1989,[48] understood again in the wider context of common law developments. Whilst at common law a child (a 'mature minor') may be found to have requisite capacity to make decisions regarding his own health and welfare,[49] the state – through the law – places greater limitations on which such decisions will be respected. So to continue the health care example, whilst the adult Jehovah's Witness may refuse a life-saving blood transfusion, a teenage child patient who refuses consent, and does so with the full support of his parents, can find that his religious decision is overruled in favour of (what are deemed to be) his best interests.[50] The law, in other words, permits a greater lack of deference to personal values in relation to children and allows externally derived – as judges might put it, 'objective' – values to be imposed.

In the following section, we will relate this discussion to a case study in an important area of concern for public health: vaccination policy. But, in a book on public health and law, it is important to emphasise the generality of the point about the distinction that the law draws in respecting personal decision-making for children (even notwithstanding parental views) and such decision-making for adults. The difference elicited in the previous two paragraphs reflects a difference in publicly acceptable justifications: all things equal, it is easier for governments (and public health practitioners) to justify interferences with harmful personal decisions made by children than it is to overrule similar decisions made by adults.[51] This is why, for example, outright bans on selling cigarettes[52] and alcohol[53] to minors are relatively uncontroversial, whereas the institution of such restrictions on adults' choices would (at least at the time of writing) be unimaginable.[54] This principle is relevant in many potential spheres of public health activity. We can recognise the potential scope for disregarding children's and parents' decisions, for example, in relation to children's diet.[55]

---

45 See John Coggon, 'Varied and Principled Understandings of Autonomy in English Law: Justifiable Inconsistency or Blinkered Moralism?' (2007) 15 *Health Care Analysis* 235.

46 See Mental Capacity Act 2005, s. 1(4); In Re T (Adult: Refusal of Treatment) [1993] Fam 95; In Re MB (Medical treatment) [1997] 2 FLR 426. cf R (Nicklinson) v Ministry of Justice; R (AM) v Director of Public Prosecutions [2014] UKSC 38.

47 For a critical discussion of these issues, see Brazier (n 19).

48 See also Family Law Reform Act 1969, section 8, and note that the Mental Capacity Act 2005 applies (with qualifications not applicable to adults) to persons aged 16 and 17; for further detail, see Department for Constitutional Affairs, *Mental Capacity Act Code of Practice* (London: HMSO 2007), chapter 12.

49 Gillick v West Norfolk and Wisbech AHA [1986] AC 112.

50 See Re E (A minor) (Wardship: Medical treatment) [1993] 1 FLR 386. See also Margaret Brazier and Caroline Bridge, 'Coercion or Caring: Analyzing Adolescent Autonomy' (1996) 16 *Legal Studies* 84.

51 See Chapter 2 above and consider also Nuffield Council on Bioethics, *Public Health: Ethical Issues* (London: Nuffield 2007).

52 The Secretary of State has a discretion to change the age at which it is legal to buy cigarettes, but it cannot be under 16 or over 18: Health Act 2006, s. 13. The current age is 18: Children and Young Persons Act 1933, s. 7 (as amended).

53 Licensing Act 2003, s. 146.

54 This does not mean that there is no agenda to eliminate smoking over time: see the discussion of the 'end game' in section 5.5.1 below.

55 For analysis of the controversial question of childhood obesity and parental neglect, see Russell Viner, Edna Roche, Sabine Maguire, and Dasha Nicholls, 'Childhood Protection and Obesity: Framework for Practice' (2010) 341 *British Medical Journal* c3074. For an Australian perspective, see Shirley Alexander, Louise Baur, Roger Magnusson, and Bernadette

Furthermore, apparently child-focussed policies can extend to have a wider, positive public health impact. For example, a policy that would limit the sales of fast food within a given radius of schools would in practice have general public health advantages for both child and adult populations but would not usually be seen as an instance of 'nanny state paternalism' because of child-focussed justifications.[56] Thus, when considering this in the context of public health law, it is important to consider the subjects of policies – children or adults – and think about the consequent variations that exist in terms of the legitimacy (or otherwise) of respecting or overruling personal choices. Notably, such distinctions might extend, for example, to other potentially vulnerable or socially disadvantaged groups.

Family law embraces questions beyond health care and child welfare, to include matters such as divorce and marriage. But the above presents the core of family law concerns of relevance for the purposes of this book. In the current discussion, we cannot only explore the law for children and families, but must also consider individuals' personal decision-making more widely. When examining legal protections of personal decision-making, it is useful to think about how the law attaches lesser or greater value to individuals' decisions. Beyond looking at the status of the decision-maker (e.g. asking if she is an adult or a child), such decision-making can be affected in two important ways. First, the law looks at *place*: what we do in the privacy of our homes is treated as distinctly protected to what we might do in public. Second, laws governing our personal choices examine *the value of the specific, autonomous decision*. The freedom to choose to undertake activities that are fundamental or integral to us as persons receive greater legal protections than decisions regarding (what are deemed to be) trivial matters. These ideas are exemplified in a case study below regarding detained psychiatric patients' choice to smoke, but we briefly outline the conceptual distinction here.

First, contrast rights to make decisions that will potentially impact on the health of others in the home with such decisions made in public.[57] The law establishes a difference between limiting people's decision to smoke in their private home, as opposed to smoking in public places.[58] The concept of what constitutes a public place – a place that is 'fair game' for regulation – is evolving. As such, it has proven possible politically to justify restrictions on adults' rights to smoke in cars with minors present.[59] Although there has been disagreement about the acceptability of this development, it is politically more easily defended than it would be to justify restrictions on smokers' rights to smoke at home with children in the room.

Second, contrast protections of trivial *versus* more deeply held personal choices. English law distinguishes respect for personal choice in a negative sense – i.e. simple legal protections for people to be 'left alone' – and protections of particular positive choices – i.e. legal rights positively to make specific sorts of choice. In regard to the former, the law has long espoused the principle that, without examining the wisdom (or otherwise) of adults'

Tobin, 'When Does Severe Childhood Obesity Become a Child Protection Issue?' (2009) 190 *Medical Journal of Australia* 136.

56 See e.g. London Food Board and Chartered Institute of Environmental Health, *Takeaways Toolkit* (London: London Food Board 2012), which includes in its recommendations that local authorities should resist planning applications for fast food outlets within 400 metres of schools, youth-centred facilities, and park boundaries: see 30–37. This policy has been advocated additionally in the London Health Commission report *Better Health for London* (London: London Health Commission 2014). See also Public Health England, *Obesity and the Environment: Regulating the Growth of Fast Food Outlets* (London: Public Health England 2014).

57 See the reasoning (not related to a public health question) in R (*Countryside Alliance*) v AG [2007] UKHL 52.

58 See the Health Act 2006, and further discussion in section 5.5 below.

59 Health Act 2006, s. 5 (as amended); Smoke-free (Exemptions and Vehicles) Regulations 2007, SI 2007/765, regulation 11(1A). See also Children and Families Act 2014, s. 95; The Smoke-Free (Private Vehicles) Regulations 2015, SI 2015/286.

decision-making, they should not be interfered with against their will without some strong justification (say, to protect others from harm).[60] This does not, though, represent a legal endorsement of the wisdom of the choices themselves or imply that the law regards what is chosen as itself being of particular importance. In regard to stronger legal safeguards of positive choices, by contrast, the law will look to what underpins a decision – for example, how integral it is to a person's identity. Where the object of choice is considered of especial value, it receives greater protection: so if an activity is banned, and a litigant claims a right to do it, attention will be given to how valuable the activity actually is (see further: section 5.5.1 below).

The interplay between these two distinct means of understanding 'privateness' (spatial privacy and decisional privacy) can bear on how the law responds to personal decisions. All things being equal, if a decision is made in private, a person will have less cause legally to demonstrate the importance of the choice itself when claiming legal protection of it. If a decision is made in public, it is 'fairer game' for interference: part of what will determine its primacy will be how important it is. We may exemplify the principle here by reference to public health measures embodied in laws regarding road safety. Section 16(1) of the Road Traffic Act 1988 empowered the Secretary of State for the Environment, Transport and the Regions to make the Motor Cycles (Protective Helmets) Regulations 1998.[61] Regulation 4 provides that 'every person driving or riding (otherwise than in a side-car) on a motor bicycle when on a road shall wear protective headgear'. Accordingly, even a rampantly libertarian, anti-paternalist biker cannot advance reasons strong enough to avoid a legal obligation to wear a helmet whilst riding a motorcycle: personal choice here is less important than the public interest served by compulsory wearing of helmets. However, section 16(2) of the Road Traffic Act provides that a 'requirement imposed by regulations under this section shall not apply to any follower of the Sikh religion while he is wearing a turban'. The law thereby recognises one specific sort of reason that is considered of greater importance than the public health end of heightened road safety. We may consider this an example of a positive right of choice existing for a particular reason that is respected as more important than public health, whilst generally the public interest in safeguarding health is legislated for in favour of deference to personal choice.[62]

As a doctrinal legal question, these points of principle also find a crucial framing in Article 8 of the European Convention on Human Rights (ECHR). As explained in Chapter 7, by virtue of the Human Rights Act 1998, ECHR rights are enforceable against, and binding on, public authorities, including the courts in their determination of the substance of our human rights. Article 8 ECHR provides a qualified right to respect for private and family life. It bears reproducing here in full as it exemplifies, in legal terms, how tensions exist between protecting individual rights and safeguarding individual and collective goods:

Article 8: Right to respect for private and family life

1. Everyone has the right to respect for his private and family life, his home and his correspondence.
2. There shall be no interference by a public authority with the exercise of this right except such as is in accordance with the law and is necessary in a

---

60 John Stuart Mill, *On Liberty* (Edward Alexander (ed), first published 1859, Peterborough, Ontario: Broadview 1999).
61 SI 1998/1807.
62 Coggon (n 3), chapter 2.

> democratic society in the interests of national security, public safety or the eco-
> nomic wellbeing of the country, for the prevention of disorder or crime, for the
> protection of health or morals, or for the protection of the rights and freedoms
> of others.

Overall, in considering the legal situation in regard to home, family, and private life, and how this relates to public health activity, public health lawyers need to consider how laws such as those introduced in this section place limitations on personal decision-making in order to advance a public health end, as well as the limitations on public health actors to improve population health, given people's individual liberty and autonomy rights. Laws regarding personal, family, and domestic decision-making can be shown to provide a broad underpinning to a whole range of public health activities and responsibilities. Laws protecting our private lives both safeguard our welfare and health rights and guard against unjustifiable state intrusion into the private sphere.

The next part of this chapter will exemplify and expand on these points. We focus on two principal areas of public health activity: anti-smoking laws and vaccination policy. These case studies open up ideas of how public health agendas relate to law and private decision-making more generally.

5.5 Case studies 3 and 4: Public health in our home, family, and private life

In section 5.1, we referred back to Gostin's three heads of state-based public health responsibilities: a health care system, public health infrastructure, and the social determinants of health. In this part of the chapter, we build on the introductory discussion of private law governing home, family, and private life. We first examine how legal tensions can arise in regard to public health measures that interfere with (apparent) personal decision-making in the home. In doing so, we are able to demonstrate legal framings of the home itself, as well as judicial analysis of whether a choice is important enough to warrant legal protection. We then look at tensions between children's and families' health-related decision-making and public health measures. Here we examine how the law addresses tensions between deeply held values, professional perspectives on what serves children's best interests, and legal powers to mandate participation in public health practices. Finally, we provide a short conclusion on the role and limits of public health regulation in the private sphere.

5.5.1 Private rights in the home: public health and personal choice

Historically, in legal, moral, and political framings, the smoking of tobacco has been treated as a quintessentially private choice. Even when the harms of tobacco were made clear in Richard Doll's celebrated research,[63] the practice of smoking was conceived as a self-regarding activity and thus one that adults should be free to choose to engage in.[64] More recently, this paradigm has been challenged as 'denormalisation' programmes advance: public health

63 Richard Doll and A. Bradford Hill, 'The Mortality of Doctors in Relation to Their Smoking Habits' (1954) 1 (4877) *British Medical Journal* 1451.
64 Robert Goodin, 'The Ethics of Smoking' (1989) 99 *Ethics* 574.

anti-tobacco advocacy now targets an 'end game' on smoking.[65] In essence, through more recent history, we can map a progressive and multipronged approach to governance, which combines a vast array of hard legal and softer regulatory and social measures that are aimed to change smoking from an archetypically private matter to an increasingly public one[66] (on softer measures, see also Chapter 9). An examination of whether and when there is a legally protected 'right to smoke' is therefore most apt in this chapter: in essence, we might ask how much 'give' there is in a legal system to promote public health through restricting tobacco use, when smoking has long been considered a personal choice quite regardless of its negative health effects.

The most substantial legal shift on tobacco use in this jurisdiction is the Health Act 2006. Section 2 of this statute introduced smoking bans in enclosed and substantially enclosed public and work spaces. In keeping with the historical framings, its legitimacy, at least in terms presented publicly, has largely rested on prevention of harm to others: rather than relying on a paternalistic justification ('smoking is bad for you, so we will make it harder for you to do it'), the Act is premised on safeguarding third parties from the dangers of 'second-hand smoke'. In this sense, while the law clearly interferes with adults' freedom to consume a legal product, justifications associated with political liberalism are adduced in support of the interferences.[67]

Given the liberal concerns surrounding the Health Act, the drafting of the legislation reflects an acknowledgment that, in some circumstances, a ban would represent too great an interference with individual decision-making. Therefore, the statute also permits particular exemptions to the general prohibition. Section 3 creates powers to make Regulations 'providing for specified descriptions of premises, or specified areas within specified descriptions of premises, not to be smoke-free despite section 2'.

In exercise of the powers conferred by section 3, the Secretary of State for Health made the Smoke-free (Exemptions and Vehicles) Regulations 2007.[68] In keeping with the spirit implied in section 3 of the Act, which provides that exemptions may be made 'in particular, [for] any premises where a person has his home, or is living whether permanently or temporarily (including hotels, care homes, and prisons and other places where a person may be detained', they include private non-common areas of private dwellings (Regulation 3), other residential accommodation, which is listed as care homes, hospices, and prisons (Regulation 5), and offshore installations (Regulation 8). We thus see a commitment to permitting people to smoke in places where they are living, even if these may be a public place or place of work for others (e.g. prisons).[69]

Regulation 10 provided an exemption for psychiatric hospitals. When it was in effect, it permitted that a 'designated room for the use of patients aged 18 years or over in residential accommodation in a mental health unit is not smoke-free'. However, it was drafted so that it would lapse from 1 July 2008,[70] and thus any further exemption for psychiatric units would require the Secretary of State to amend the Regulations. Against expectations, no further exemption was instituted after this time. So the Health Act's ban from July 2008 reached

---

65 Ruth Malone, Patricia McDaniel and Elizabeth Smith, 'It Is Time to Plan the Tobacco Endgame' (2014) 348 British Medical Journal g1453.

66 John Coggon, 'Morality and Strategy in Politicising Tobacco Use: Criminal Law, Public Health, and Philosophy' in A.M. Viens, John Coggon and Anthony Kessel (eds), Criminal Law, Philosophy and Public Health Practice (Cambridge: Cambridge University Press 2013) 79–101.

67 Mill (n 60).

68 (n 59).

69 See also Secretary of State for Justice v Paul Black [2016] EWCA Civ 125.

70 See Regulation 10(3).

into mental health units. That result led to litigation that we will use for illustrative purposes in this chapter: was it lawful to prevent psychiatric patients from smoking in the hospitals in which they were resident? The legal position might be examined from various angles. We focus here on two.

First, we can conceive of the smoking ban within psychiatric units as a positive advance in a progressive anti-tobacco strategy: a 'next step' in a public health agenda that will serve the common good and lead ultimately to the complete eradication of tobacco use.[71] Additionally, public health advocates can point to the fact that a disproportionate number of persons with psychiatric illness are smokers, as compared with the ratio of smokers to non-smokers in populations of persons who are not diagnosed as having a mental disorder. In highlighting this distinction, they can argue that the law rightly serves a socially disadvantaged group that suffers health inequalities.[72] Accordingly, we find a position that holds that this interference with psychiatric patients' freedom to smoke, even in a place where they are resident, is justified because of the public health end that it serves.

Alternatively, we can conceive of this ban as a punitive, illiberal, and unfairly discriminatory measure that targets an already vulnerable group of persons and further limits their already heavily restricted freedoms in a place that serves as their home. Such a line of argument does not commit us to denying the physical harms of smoking tobacco. Simply, it holds that smoking is a personal choice for adult psychiatric patients just as it is for every other adult and should be protected as such – especially in their home. The failure to provide an exemption infantilises the patients and unfairly picks them out as a class that should be treated differentially against their will.[73]

In ethical terms (see further: Chapter 2), the pro-ban argument here rests on utilitarian claims about improved population health outcomes, supplemented with claims rooted in a prioritarian theory of social justice. The state has a mandate to advance a non-smoking law in psychiatric units: first, because it has a role in protecting and promoting public health and, second, because it has duties to attend especially to the otherwise neglected interests or rights of disadvantaged groups. The anti-ban argument, by contrast, may be said to rest on libertarian concerns for adults' rights to make choices, holding that personal decisions – including harmful ones – should not be interfered with even where public benefits can be identified, especially where they entail interference with decisions made in the home.

Having seen this legal background, and the framing of alternative ethico-political arguments for and against the ban as it relates to psychiatric hospitals, let us consider in more depth how privacy law has practically functioned in relation to the anti-tobacco public health agenda. The Health Act might be considered objectionable by some libertarian critics,[74] but the doctrine of *Parliamentary Sovereignty* means that the statute itself cannot be subject to direct legal challenge as to its validity. However, under section 6 of the Human Rights Act 1998 (see further: Chapter 7), it is possible to challenge the lawfulness of a public authority's decision-making in its generation of *secondary legislation*, i.e. instruments such as the Regulations, which are created through delegated powers. So the question we explore here is whether the

---

71 See Malone et al (n 65).
72 cf Deborah Arnott and Simon Wessely, 'Should Psychiatric Hospitals Completely Ban Smoking? – Yes' (2015) 351 *British Medical Journal* h5654.
73 cf Michael Fitzpatrick, 'Should Psychiatric Hospitals Completely Ban Smoking? – No' (2015) 351 *British Medical Journal* h5654.
74 Consider e.g. Michael Fitzpatrick's criticisms of arguments regarding the harms of second-hand smoke: Michael Fitzpatrick, *The Tyranny of Health – Doctors and the Regulation of Lifestyle* (Abingdon: Routledge 2001).

Secretary of State's failure to provide an exemption, and thus the extension of the smoking ban into psychiatric units, represents an unacceptable public health policy that should be constrained against to protect individual rights of personal decision-making. In the case of *R (on the application of G) v Nottinghamshire Healthcare NHS Trust*, both the Regulations and the NHS Trust's independently devised no-smoking policy were challenged by detainees at Rampton Secure Psychiatric Hospital. As Rampton is a place of work, and as the patients were unable to go outside and it would now be unlawful for them to smoke inside, they were not permitted to smoke at all. Their legal challenge was heard first in the Divisional Court, where it failed,[75] and then went to the Court of Appeal.[76]

The Rampton smokers' argument was framed primarily around their autonomy rights – smoking was an important personal choice of each patient, that choice deserved legal protection, and their rights not to be interfered with in their home – on average, patients would be resident in Rampton for eight years. Their claims were based on Article 8 ECHR, which we have seen in section 5.4 provides for a right to respect for one's private and family life and home and correspondence. The patients' legal challenge was supplemented, furthermore, with a claim under Article 14 ECHR. This requires that members of groups not suffer undue discrimination in their enjoyment of ECHR rights. It was unfair, the smokers' argument went, that the Regulations should permit a comparable group, prisoners, to smoke, while they – a group identifiable as detained psychiatric patients – could not.

The Court of Appeal upheld the first instance decision by a majority of two to one. Keene LJ provided a dissenting judgment,[77] explaining that he would have allowed the appeal against the Secretary of State. His reasoning, which interestingly includes a statement that he is a non-smoker, is premised on the idea that paternalist reasons would be insufficient to justify the ban: harm to others through second-hand smoke would be the only legitimate basis for the non-exemption in psychiatric units. And, given the practical possibility to make safe arrangements to allow detainees at Rampton to smoke, Keene LJ found that the ban was disproportionate. By his reasoning, through Article 8, a great primacy is placed on individual autonomy and privacy, and this extends to rights to choose to smoke tobacco. The judge notes how some people find smoking to be an important and highly valued activity. Given the importance that might attach to it, he finds that it should fall within rights protected under Article 8. This finding is underscored, in his view, by an acceptance of the discrimination argument: detained psychiatric patients were a group that could suffer discrimination under Article 14.

In a shared judgment by Lord Clarke MR and Moses LJ, the majority treats as one the questions of the patients' autonomy rights and whether Rampton is their home:

> We do not think . . . that the issue as to the scope of article 8 can or should be answered by considering simply whether smoking is an activity integral to a person's identify, or is an aspect of social interaction or whether Rampton is to be regarded as a patient's home within the meaning of article 8. Rather, a conclusion can only be reached by considerations of all those factors.[78]

75 [2008] EWHC 1096 (Admin).
76 [2009] EWCA Civ 795.
77 ibid, [92]–[112].
78 ibid, [37].

In addressing the different components of this, the judges find that, although the patients are resident at Rampton, it is a *public* institution. As such, protections of decision-making within this sort of home are less strong because it is a less private home. The judges state:

> No patient can choose freely what he eats or drinks. That is not simply because restrictions can be justified, but more fundamentally because of the nature of the institution in which he eats and drinks. Even if . . . [as is anyway not the case at law] a person may do as he pleases in his own home, no-one can expect such freedom when detained in a secure hospital.[79]

Regarding the process of evaluating the choice to smoke, their Lordships state, 'Any conclusion which depends on a court's assessment of the importance of a particular activity is open to substantial dispute'.[80] However, they go on to hold that the 'less the appellant can rely upon the nature of the place in which the activity is pursued, the more he must rely upon the proximity of the activity to his personal identity or physical and moral integrity'.[81] Having acknowledged the controversy of judges making such a determination, they hold that smoking is not an activity that is protected by Article 8; it is of insufficient importance.[82]

Although such reasoning was adequate to dispense with the appeal, it is interesting in particular to note the judicial comments, made *obiter*, regarding the possible justification of the regulations under Article 8(2) had Article 8 been engaged. Had it been necessary to consider justification, the judges are clear that the overall purpose of the ban is in accordance with law. And, in relation to the specific case, attention was given to the appellants' being detained *mental health* patients: this imposed special obligations to protect their health, which did not arise outside of a health care context. Their Lordships also note that Article 8(2) permits interferences with autonomous decisions for the 'protection of health'; implicit in this, they hold, is acceptance of paternalistic interference, as the provision just says 'health', rather than 'health *of others*'. Further potential rationales for the ban are considered too, such as the idea of smoking as self-harm, the democratic legitimacy of the Regulations, and the feasibility of the ban in hospitals as compared with prisons.

In conclusion, the Rampton smokers' case allows us to see how ECHR rights, and their qualifications, may serve rather than limit public health agendas (see further: Chapter 7). However, they also expose the controversy of value-laden decision-making here and perhaps cause us to question the suitability of judges to make such determinations. Their role, of course, requires them to reach a decision. But the process is necessarily impressionistic. Rather than rely on clear rules or obviously applicable precedents, understanding the scope and reach of Article 8 requires an examination of principle and an attribution and weighing of values. Critics might ask how satisfactory it is for judges to be declaring the substance and relative worth of values such as health and privacy, especially given how contestable the meanings of these matters are. Nevertheless, in the instance of the Rampton smokers' case, privacy laws have been interpreted to protect a public health agenda. But, on examining the reasoning of the three Court of Appeal judges, we can suppose that the outcome could as easily – at least as a matter of legal determination – have been decided in the alternative.

79　ibid, [44].
80　ibid, [45].
81　ibid, [49].
82　ibid.

5.5.2 Rights in family life: population health and individual choice

Vaccinations are one of the triumphs of public health practice. From Edward Jenner's famous success in developing protection against smallpox, through to contemporary efforts to eradicate polio, vaccines have served individual health ends by defending the vaccinated person from harm and have served population health ends by helping achieve herd immunity against disease threats. As preventive measures, the capacity for vaccines to stop instances of ill health arising in the first place represents a clear public health advantage: rather than suffer and then try to respond to disease, we have the ability to forestall its onset in the first place. From a population perspective, there seems little but sense in vaccination programmes.

However, vaccination programmes give rise to considerable concerns and controversies (see also Chapter 3).[83] These fall under various headings. In particular, we might note the following three. First, recall Geoffrey Rose's 'prevention paradox', which we discussed in Chapter 1.[84] For conditions against which herd immunity might be achieved – i.e. against which whole populations might be defended – there is little benefit to any individual in participating. If you live in a society where a disease is eradicated because your fellow citizens are immune to it, although by being vaccinated yourself you contribute to the strength of the herd immunity, your own interests are served little, if at all, by participating. Second, sometimes, as part of the population paradox, comes not just the small likelihood of individual benefit but the potential for individual harm. We may know, for example, that a particular disease will be eradicated if sufficient people participate in a vaccination programme. We may also know, though, that any individual suffers a 1 in 1,000 chance of suffering serious harm from receiving the vaccine. From a population perspective, we might say the risk is clearly worth taking: the harm that will ensue is less than the harms that follow from not having the vaccination programme. But the individual might not want to submit to the risk where it is for the general, rather than the individual, good. Finally, as already indicated above, we live in a political system that recognises and aims to respect a diversity of views and values. For any number of reasons, people may on principled grounds decide that they do not wish to participate in a vaccination programme. Their decision may, for example, be based on questions of scientific understanding: if there is conflicting expert opinion on the benefits and harms of a vaccine, why should people be expected to participate in a programme? Or, even if the science underpinning a vaccine is accepted, people may have alternative principled objections: for example, a person might object to the use of a vaccine whose manufacture breaches 'animal rights'.

As a question of public health ethics, therefore, we find tensions between views holding that vaccination programmes underpinned by sufficient evidence are a general good that should be instituted as a matter of policy and views holding that the combination of controversies means that participation in vaccination schemes should be a matter of individual choice. Moving to English public health law, in contrast with the law in some jurisdictions,[85]

83 Angus Dawson, 'Vaccination Ethics' in Angus Dawson (ed), *Public Health Ethics – Key Concepts and Issues in Policy and Practice* (Cambridge: Cambridge University Press 2011) 143–153. In relation to philosophical and ethical questions in regard to the vaccine discussed in this section, see also Tom Sorell, 'Parental Choice and Expert Knowledge in the Debate about MMR and Autism' in Angus Dawson and Marcel Verweij (eds), *Ethics, Prevention, and Public Health* (Oxford: Oxford University Press 2007) 95–110; Stephen John, 'Expert Testimony and Epistemological Free-Riding: The MMR Controversy' (2011) 61 *The Philosophical Quarterly* 496.
84 Geoffrey Rose, 'Sick Individuals and Sick Populations' (1985) 14 *International Journal of Epidemiology* 32.
85 Daniel Salmon, Stephen Teret, Raina MacIntyre, David Salisbury, Margaret Burgess, and Neal Halsey, 'Compulsory Vaccination and Conscientious or Philosophical Exemptions: Past, Present, and Future' (2006) 367 (9508) *The Lancet* 436.

there is no legal obligation to participate in vaccination programmes. Policies that fall short of being 'hard law' exist to encourage participation (for a discussion of softer modes of regulation, see further: Chapter 9), but the law does not force people generally, through weight of legal obligation, to serve their and the population's health by being vaccinated against diseases (cf also Chapter 3). Rather, it is a matter of parental or individual choice.

Having considered above how personal decision-making might or might not be protected, and having noted the different place of children and adults in public health law, the second case study we look at here concerns judicial determinations on whether individual children might be compelled to receive the measles, mumps, and rubella (MMR) vaccine. This vaccine, which is designed to provide individual immunity against the three conditions, as well as conferring a population-level benefit where sufficient children are immunised, was the source of considerable controversy. Andrew Wakefield's studies, since discredited and formally retracted, but at the time highly publicised, linking the MMR vaccine to autism led many parents to the view that they would not expose their children to a risk of serious harm, notwithstanding the consequent susceptibility to contracting measles, mumps, and rubella.

Official advice holds that the vaccine is safe.[86] Yet, based on the latent distrust that endures following Wakefield, there are still those who doubt the advice that their children should be immunised. As a matter of general policy, it could not be the case – politically, and until such time as Parliament might act, legally – that a compulsory regime be instituted in relation to MMR. However, the controversy around Wakefield has led to a situation where rates of disease have increased.[87] As noted above, decision-making for children is governed by the Children Act 1989. Section 1 of this Act provides that, in decision-making for a child, her welfare is 'the court's paramount consideration'. There is, in English law, a considerable respect for a plurality of different views on what serves people's best interests and a general understanding that parents will understand and serve their children's best interests. However, at times, the courts will impose a decision in a child's best interests, even where she is a 'mature minor' and where she has parental support for a view that contrasts with that of the court. The specific legal question we look at here is whether the courts will compel the non-consensual provision of the MMR vaccine.

It is important to stress that any given family law case, based as it is on a particular child's best interests, will necessarily be decided on its own merits. As such, we cannot say (as a legal proposition) that 'It will *always* . . .' or 'It will *never* be in the child's best interests to make her take the MMR vaccine'. However, a small series of decided cases indicates the courts' willingness to make individual determinations that at least hint at a generalisable legal position on this question. Although it would be going too far to suggest that a commonly held legal obligation now exists, consideration of case law here hints to some interesting points in public health law. To exemplify, we will explore in a little depth the most recent of three MMR cases: F v F.[88]

In F, a father sought a declaration that his two daughters, a 15- and an 11-year-old, who for the purposes of the litigation were known, respectively, as L and M, should be given the MMR vaccine. The girls and their mother, with whom they lived, were opposed to this. In her judgment, Theis J describes L and M as 'charming, intelligent, articulate and thoughtful' and

---

86 See NHS, <www.nhs.uk/conditions/vaccinations/pages/mmr-vaccine.aspx> accessed 5 April 2016.
87 Fiona Godlee, Jane Smith and Harvey Marcovitch, 'Wakefield's Article Linking MMR Vaccine and Autism Was Fraudulent' (2011) 342 *British Medical Journal* c7452.
88 [2013] EWHC 2683 (Fam).

characterises their asking of questions as 'perceptive and well targeted'.[89] Having noted that her paramount consideration must be the girls' welfare and that, in two previous cases, the court had determined that the vaccination should be given,[90] the judge says:

> The mother's opposition to L and M receiving these vaccinations can be summarised as follows:
>
> (1) She questions the benefits of the vaccine and remains concerned about any possible side effects;
> (2) She questions the father's change in position bearing in mind what she considered was the parties' agreement that the girls should not be vaccinated; [when the parents had been together, and in light of the Wakefield studies, they had both agreed at that stage not to vaccinate];
> (3) She is concerned about the impact of the vaccination being undertaken against the girls' wishes, in particular L who has had psychological problems including anxiety issues that she has received counselling for;
> (4) L is a vegan and part of her objection is based on the content of the vaccine, which includes animal based ingredients (e.g. gelatine).[91]

In assessing the evidence, Theis J makes repeated reference to points that we might relate to the quality of the decision-making capacity supporting refusal. In particular, questions are raised both about the bare rationality of a refusal and about the strength of the girls' knowledge and understanding of relevant points. There are also questions raised in the evidence about the girls having been influenced in their decisions by their mother.[92]

To reach her legal determination that the vaccine should be given, the judge stresses the imperative 'to carefully consider and weigh up L and M's expressed wishes'.[93] Explaining that her reasons apply just to the case in front of her, considered on the basis of the evidence she had heard and the specific facts, Theis J holds, at paragraph 22:

(1) Whilst I am acutely aware of both L and M's wishes and feelings in relation to this issue, as described in detail in both of Ms Vivian's [i.e. the expert's] reports, I consider their views have inevitably been influenced by a number of factors which affects the weight that should be attached to those wishes and feelings. . . .

(2) Whilst the welfare considerations for each child must be considered separately Ms Vivian did not consider the court should treat them differently. L may be better informed and have a better understanding as she is older, but Ms Vivian considered her views were naïve; she considered neither L or M were [sic] able to give a balanced view and felt they had become over-focussed on the ingredients without being able to balance that with other considerations. I agree. . . .

(3) [Although the decision would impact on the girls emotionally, this was not sufficient reason not to provide the vaccine if it would be in their best interests.]

(4) [The decision goes against the girls' wishes, which is] an important factor, particularly bearing in mind their ages but the court also has to consider their level of understanding

---

89 ibid, [6].
90 B (Child) [2003] EWCA Civ 1148; LCC v A, B, C & D (Minors by Their Children's Guardian), K, and S [2011] EWHC 4033 (Fam).
91 F (n 88), [10].
92 See ibid, [11]–[15].
93 ibid, [18].

of the issues involved and what factors have influenced their views. In this case I do not consider there is a balanced level of understanding by them of the issues involved, the focus has been on the negative aspects in a somewhat unfocussed way.

(5)   The medical advice is for children to receive the vaccine even though it is accepted that there are risks of side effects of the vaccine. The health risk of getting any of the diseases the vaccine prevents is clear. They are serious diseases that could have long-term health consequences. . . .

(6)   Whilst I have carefully considered the effect on them of making a decision that does not accord with their wishes and feelings I am clear that the combination of the secure relationship they have with each parent and the responsibility on these parents to exercise their parental responsibility in the light of the court's decision will ensure that the consequences of the court's decision will be managed in a responsible way. As Ms Vivian said, that is what parenting is about.

In concluding this section, we may note a further couple of points raised by the case of F. Albeit that the case is based on a different legal regime, there are concerns comparable with those raised in the Rampton smokers' case. We again see how apparent privacy rights might be set aside in favour of the public health agenda, in a situation where both individual and general health benefits may be seen to arise. An additional comparison is the complexity of this area of law in terms of legal rules and common law precedent. Although a legal frame-work exists, it is clear that the sorts of personal rights at play might well have lent themselves to a contrary legal determination. The cases that we have highlighted in relation to family, domestic, and personal life thus allow us to see the tensions between private choice and public health and also the scope for law in this area to advance a public health agenda. Whilst such scope exists, it should be stressed how controversial and contestable the above decisions are and how open the surrounding legal doctrine is to differing interpretations.

Chapter 5: Summary

- 'Private law' may be taken as a term to refer to:

  o   Laws that define our civil obligations, particularly in relation to legal contracts and torts, and
  o   Laws that govern our home, family, and personal lives.

- Legal rights in relation to civil obligations set standards and help advance public health agendas, for example, by:

  o   Assuring environmental protections and
  o   Defining the standards of care that we owe to each other.

- Such rights apply, not just against individuals and private corporations, but also against public authorities.
- Legal rights in regard to home, family, and personal lives can help advance public health agendas, for example, by:

  o   Explicitly allowing that concerns for health might justify interferences with private and family life and
  o   Ensuring children are treated in their best interests.

- However, the different areas of private law also place constraints on public health agendas, for example, because of protections of individual freedoms to make unhealthy decisions.

5.7 Further readings

Roger Brownsword, 'Public Health, Private Right, and the Common Law' (2006) 120 *Public Health* 42.

Paula Giliker, *Tort* (5th edn., London: Sweet and Maxwell 2014).

Lawrence Gostin and Lindsay Wiley, *Public Health Law: Power, Duty, Restraint* (3rd edn., University of California Press 2016), chapter 7.

Jonathan Herring, *Family Law* (7th edn., Harlow: Pearson 2015).

Robyn Martin, 'Public Health and the Scope of the Potential Liability in Tort' (2005) 21 *Professional Negligence* 39.

Chapter 6

Criminal law and public health

6.1 Criminal regulation and public health: competing or shared agendas?

There are different social problems that we seek to mitigate or resolve for which there are different kinds of approaches we can select from. Of all the different areas of law, criminal law as an approach to social problems is likely the most familiar to people without legal training or experience. From daily news stories of criminality to popular television crime dramas to seeing police officers on duty on the street, we are often exposed to different examples of criminal law and criminal justice functioning within society. Both criminal regulation and public health policy should be understood as particular approaches to social problems, insofar as each have their own mission, objectives, and methods in relation to mitigating or resolving social problems. There are many areas where criminal regulation and public health activity overlap and interact with each other – most prominently in higher-risk behaviours related to sex, alcohol, and illicit psychoactive substances, but increasingly in relation to bioterrorism,[1] occupational health and safety,[2] and environmental public health issues.[3]

Given the respective missions, objectives, and methods of criminal regulation and public health policy, it is worth comparing these approaches – including where they might have shared agendas, as well as how they often provide inherently conflicting perspectives from which to approach social issues. For instance, from a regulatory point of view, addressing drug use from a criminal law perspective will end up looking very different than approaching it from a public health perspective.[4] A public health approach to drugs, such as the 'four pillars' model focussing on prevention, treatment, enforcement, and harm reduction

---

1 Biological Weapons Act 1974, ss. 1(1), 2; Anti-Terrorism Crime and Security Act 2001, Part 6.
2 Health and Safety at Work Act 1974; Health and Safety (Offences) Act 2008. Also see e.g. Diana Kloss, *Occupational Health Law* (5th edn., Oxford: Wiley 2010), section 2.2 and chapter 5.
3 Environmental Protection Act 1990, ss. 33, 79(1); Water Resources Act 1991, s. 85. Also see e.g., Elizabeth Fisher, Bettina Lange and Eloise Scotford, *Environmental Law: Text, Cases & Materials* (Oxford: Oxford University Press 2013), chapter 8; Robert Lee and Mark Stallworthy, 'From the Criminal to the Consensual: The Shifting Mechanisms of Environmental Regulation' in A.M. Viens, John Coggon and Anthony Kessel (eds), *Criminal Law, Philosophy and Public Health Practice* (Cambridge: Cambridge University Press 2013) 214–236.
4 See e.g. Donald MacPherson, *A Framework for Action – A Four-Pillar Approach to Drug Problems in Vancouver* (Vancouver: City of Vancouver 2001); Alex Stevens, *Drugs, Crime and Public Health: The Political Economy of Drug Policy* (London: Routledge-Cavendish 2011); Doug Husak, 'Drugs, Crime and Public Health: A Lesson from Criminology', in Viens, Coggon, and Kessel (eds) 42–61, and Tom Walker, 'Criminal Law, Drugs and Harm Reduction', in Viens, Coggon, and Kessel (eds) 62–78 (n 3).

strategies, focuses on health, safety, and empowerment as dominant values, while a criminal law approach traditionally focuses on drug consumption as harmful behaviour undertaken by weak-willed or morally flawed individuals deserving punishment. Sometimes we do see models that are a mixture of criminal law and public health approaches, such as the use of drug courts that act as alternatives to traditional criminal justice models and that suspend criminal sanctions for successful completion of drug treatment and rehabilitation programmes.[5]

The scope and basis of what specifically constitute legitimate public health agendas may be contested, but the ways such agendas are designed and constrained rely on claims about what is legitimate: what public health actors and agencies may, must, and ought to do. The aims of criminal justice systems have perhaps more overtly moralised objectives still: as Andrew Ashworth and Jeremy Horder say, 'Criminal liability is the strongest formal censure that society can inflict, and it may also result in a sentence that amounts to a severe deprivation of the ordinary liberties of the offender'.[6] Both public health and criminal law, furthermore, may at an abstract level be said to share a common goal of protecting public goods or values. Nevertheless, it might be argued that, even if criminal law and public health both represent moral agendas, these agendas are not always compatible. For principled reasons, the argument might go, criminal law is simply too moralistic and too heavy a tool for public health agendas, which fall outside the scope of criminal justice concerns. However, at least intuitively, some will reject the notion that criminal law should serve as a tool of public health, beyond, perhaps, the tightly circumscribed 'police powers' that might be exercised to control serious infectious diseases.[7]

While the underlying theme of this book is to consider the various ways in which the law can successfully function as a tool for both the promotion and limitation of public health measures, the relationship between criminal regulation and public health policy in particular provides one of the starkest areas of tension between law and public health. In examining their respective aims and justifications, as well as how criminal law has been used in relation to public health policy, it is clear why questions are raised about whether criminal regulation and public health have competing or shared agendas and whether criminalising behaviour that negatively impacts on public health is always a sensible approach. For this reason, it is important to evaluate the extent to which criminal law should be thought to offer an appropriate form of governance for public health policy and practice. With this chapter, we therefore explore and expand upon these themes and show how, in various ways, the criminal law does offer an approach within public health regulation with particular advantages and disadvantages. We also consider how public health approaches may serve the criminal justice system.

The chapter is divided into three further sections. First, in section 6.2, we explain what criminal law entails, both conceptually and practically. This allows an introduction to the field itself as well as critical reflections on the synergies and tensions found in criminal justice and public health agendas. Following this, the chapter moves to specific examples

---

5 Peggy Fulton Hora, William Schma and John Rosenthal, 'Therapeutic Jurisprudence and the Drug Treatment Court Movement: Revolutionizing the Criminal Justice System's Response to Drug Abuse and Crime in America' (1999) 74 *Notre Dame Law Review* 439; Gill McIvor, 'Drug Courts: Lessons from the UK and Beyond' and Alex Stevens, 'Treatment Sentences for Drug Users: Context, Mechanisms and Outcomes' in Anthea Hucklesby and Emma Wincup (eds), *Drug Interventions in Criminal Justice* (Maidenhead: Open University Press 2010) 135–160.

6 Andrew Ashworth and Jeremy Horder, *Principles of Criminal Law* (7th edn., Oxford: Oxford University Press 2013) 1.

7 See e.g. Mark Rothstein, 'Rethinking the Meaning of Public Health' (2002) 30 *Journal of Law, Medicine & Ethics* 144; Richard Epstein, 'In Defense of the "Old" Public Health: The Legal Framework for the Regulation of Public Health' (2004) 69 *Brooklyn Law Review* 1421; and further the discussion in Chapter 7 below.

outlining how criminal measures protect people from harms by third parties and exemplifies the significance of this in relation to public health case studies in relation to the transmission of disease. Then, in section 6.3, the chapter moves to what is seen as generally more controversial territory: the use of criminal law's coercive measures to force individuals to protect their own health. Finally, in section 6.4, the chapter moves from considering how criminal law may serve as a tool for public health practice to explain how public health also may serve criminal justice aims, with a primary focus on forensic epidemiology.

6.2 Criminal law: aims, agendas, and relationship with public health

Compared with some areas of law, people might think they are generally quite familiar with the idea of criminal law, its function, and its purpose. However, in reality, there are significant philosophical and political divides on whether, when, and why criminalisation may be appropriate.[8] Although some of the distinct rationales for criminal law measures can be mutually compatible, they at times vary. It is helpful to understand the basic aims, scope, and values criminal law seeks to promote in itself, as well as in comparison to public health as a means of evaluating the relationship between both approaches.

6.2.1 Liability for wrongful and harmful behaviour

Crimes are kinds of conduct that are defined by criminal law as wrong. In emphasising wrongful conduct, this is not to say that criminal law is not concerned with harmful conduct. Quite to the contrary, much of criminal law is concerned with harm, but it is particularly concerned with the wrongfulness of that harmful conduct.[9] While the moralistic undertones of criminal law will be evident in many areas, this is also not to say that criminal regulation is solely concerned with conduct that is necessarily morally wrong: criminal regulation involves prohibition of conduct that is wrong in itself (*malum in se*) as well as conduct that is wrong only in virtue of it being declared so by law (*malum prohibitum*).

Paradigmatically, crimes are *public wrongs* (contrast the discussion of tort law and private wrongs in Chapter 5). As Duff notes:

> We should interpret a 'public' wrong, not as a wrong that injures the public, but as one that properly concerns the public, i.e. the polity as a whole. . . . A public wrong is thus a wrong against the polity as a whole, not just against the individual victim: given our identification with the victim as a fellow citizen, and our shared commitment to the values that the [criminal] violates, we must see the victim's wrong as also being our wrong.[10]

---

8 See e.g. Patrick Devlin, *The Enforcement of Morals* (Oxford: Oxford University Press 1965); Joel Feinberg, *Harm to Others: The Moral Limits of the Criminal Law*, Volume 1 (Oxford: Oxford University Press 1984); Grant Lamond, 'What Is a Crime?' (2007) 27 *Oxford Journal of Legal Studies* 609; Douglas Husak, *Overcriminalization: The Limits of the Criminal Law* (Oxford: Oxford University Press 2008); Andrew Simester and Andreas von Hirsch, *Crimes, Harms, and Wrongs: On the Principles of Criminalisation* (Oxford: Hart Publishing 2011).

9 While criminal law is primarily concerned with harmful wrongdoing, there are also areas that still concern harmless wrongdoing. For more on the latter category of conduct, see Joel Feinberg, *Harmless Wrongdoing: The Moral Limits of the Criminal Law*, Volume 4 (Oxford: Oxford University Press 1990).

10 Antony Duff, *Answering for Crime: Responsibility and Liability in the Criminal Law* (Oxford: Hart Publishing 2007) 141–142.

We might draw some contrasts here with public health. While the latter is not concerned with public wrongs, the notion of 'public' here resonates with aspects of the public health enterprise. Both criminal law and public health are concerned with actions or phenomena that not only set back individual interests but collective interests, as well as seeking to uphold shared values that make us individually and collectively better off. Moreover, both criminal law and public health – given the very nature of the publicity of the wrongfulness or harmfulness of the behaviour that they are concerned with – take on roles of responsibility in relation to these behaviours. While criminal regulation takes on responsibility for punishing public wrongs, public health policy takes on the responsibility for preventing harms to public health.[11] This also can provide a further point of contrast. While criminal law's focus on punitive sanctions for wrongdoing tends to makes its approach reactive, public health predominately takes a preventative approach.[12]

Criminal regulation concerns not only identifying which forms of conduct constitute public wrongs and enforcing rules that prohibit such forms of conduct but also punishing those individuals who fail to comply with these rules. It is the criminal conduct that violates important collectively held values that allows for these public wrongs to be deserving of blame and punishment by the state (contrast the remedies for private wrongs, described in Chapter 5). Perhaps the two most prominent reasons for having criminal sanctions are to *deter* wrongful activity in the first place and to provide *retribution* for wrongful activity that is committed. Furthermore, many scholars contrast the idea of criminal laws, which provide for different offences, and the function of the *criminal justice system*, which may serve further purposes still, for example, to encourage rehabilitation of offenders and to allow reintegration following a punitive sentence. As such, different justifications for the legitimacy of criminal sanctions may align closer to the aims and role of public health than others.

The wrongdoing that criminal law is concerned with includes both *fault-based* offences and *strict liability* offences. Fault-based offences are concerned with action (or inaction) that is blameworthy – e.g. recklessness or gross negligence – and it is this blameworthiness that makes someone deserving of punitive sanctions. Fault-based offences have a mental element (*mens rea*) included as part of the offence. This means that, as well as looking at the criminal act (*actus reus*), a prosecution relies on proving that a defendant acted with criminal intention: for example, to convict someone of the common law crime of murder, the defendant must be shown to have intended to kill.[13] Strict liability offences are punishable, however, merely in virtue of undertaking a punishable offence.[14] That is, there are some forms of wrongful

---

11 Wrongdoing has a central role within criminal regulation that is unlike public health. While public health is primarily concerned with harm (broadly understood), we are beginning to see increasing aspects of public health policy – especially in relation to health promotion – focussing on considerations of personal responsibility and blaming individuals for being in poor states of health. See, e.g. Daniel Wikler, 'Personal and Social Responsibility for Health' (2002) 16 *Ethics and International Affairs* 47; M. Marchman Andersen, S. Oksbjerg Dalton, J. Lynch, C. Johansen, and N. Holtug, 'Social Inequality in Health, Responsibility and Egalitarian Justice' (2013) 35 *Journal of Public Health* 4; Eli Feiring, 'Lifestyle, Responsibility and Justice' (2008) 34 *Journal of Medical Ethics* 33; Rebecca Brown, 'Moral Responsibility for (Un)healthy Behaviour' (2013) 38 *Journal of Medical Ethics* 695.
12 Though this is starting to change with the so-called 'preventative turn' in criminal law. See e.g. Andrew Ashworth, Lucia Zedner and Patrick Tomlin (eds), *Prevention and the Limits of Criminal Law* (Oxford: Oxford University Press 2013); Andrew Ashworth and Lucia Zedner, *Preventative Justice* (Oxford: Oxford University Press 2014).
13 The meaning of 'intention' can itself be subject to considerable legal nuance: e.g. in murder, intention includes foresight as a virtual certainty. Equally, other concepts such as recklessness and gross negligence can fulfil the *mens rea* component of an offence, e.g. in gross negligence manslaughter.
14 Famously, Lord Diplock maintained, in *Sweet v Parsley* [1970] AC 132 at 163, 'where the subject-matter of a statute is the regulation of a particular activity involving potential danger to public health, safety or morals, in which citizens have a choice whether they participate or not, the court may feel driven to infer an intention of Parliament to impose, by penal sanctions, a higher duty of care on those who choose to participate and to place on them an obligation to take whatever measures may be necessary to prevent the prohibited act, without regard to those considerations of cost or business practicability'.

conduct that cause harm (or have a sufficiently high risk of expected harm) that they deserve punishment, independent of your knowledge or intentions in relation to the behaviour. There are a number of strict liability criminal offences related to public health concerning the regulation of food,[15] licit and illicit drugs,[16] weapons,[17] drinking water and sanitation,[18] air quality,[19] waste management,[20] and pollution,[21] amongst others.[22]

Looking again at a general level, we tend to think of criminal law as a necessarily 'heavy' mode of regulation. By deeming something to be criminal, we are condemning it morally, and criminal sanction leads to clear, public stigmatisation: think, for example, of serious violent and sexual offences. However, it is important not to treat the idea of criminal law or regulation simplistically. In reality, there are criminal sanctions (rightly or wrongly) that do not attract great levels of stigma: think, for example, of 'lesser' driving offences. Equally, there are legal and regulatory interventions that are not criminal but which generate a great deal of stigma: think, for example, of anti-social behaviour orders. The choice to criminalise an activity for the purpose of promoting public health will involve an evaluation of the values at stake and whether those values can justify the use of such coercive methods.[23]

6.2.2 Criminalisation, values, and harm

Another point of contrast between criminal law and public health concerns which values inform these approaches. These values not only provide direction as to what social issues these approaches seek to govern, but they also contribute to justifying state interference in our lives in order to protect or promote those values. Both criminal law and public health, albeit in different ways, are concerned with protecting the conditions in which people can lead good lives. While public health agendas will be based on the idea that health is constitutive of the good life, criminal law is informed by other values. Nevertheless, it is also possible to see how the values that inform criminal law can be conducive to the promotion of health as well (e.g. peace, order, and safety). As noted in the previous section, both criminal law and public health concern themselves with protecting citizens from harm. While the prevention and/or reduction of harm can be seen as a shared aim, the values underpinning this agenda can differ and the resultant balancing of these values can conflict. Moreover, there are also other areas where there is much less overlap in values. For example, the increasing focus of public health actors' on values of equality and equity (see e.g. the discussion of the Faculty of Public Health in Chapter 1) has not been much taken up within criminal regulation.

---

15 *Callow v Tillstone* [1900] 64 JP 823; Food Safety and Hygiene (England) Regulations 2013, SI 2013/2996, reg. 19 and Schedule 2.
16 Medicines Act 1968; Misuse of Drugs Act 1971; Misuse of Drugs Regulations 1985, SI 1985/2066; *PSGB v Storkwain Ltd* [1986] 2 All ER 635.
17 Firearms Act 1967, s. 5; *R v Howells* [1977] 3 All ER 417; *R v Deyemi* [2007] EWCA Crim 2060.
18 Water Industry Act 1991, s. 70.
19 Clean Air Act 1991, ss. 1, 2.
20 Environmental Protection Act 1990, s. 33; *Ezeemo & Ors v R* [2012] EWCA Crim 2064.
21 *Alphacell Ltd v Woodward* [1972] AC 824; Water Resources Act 1991, section 85; Environmental Permitting (England and Wales) Regulations 2010, SI 2010/675, regs. 12, 38.
22 There were also other strict liability offences related to public health that no longer exist, as a result of statutory amendments. For example, the sale of tobacco to persons under 16 (Children and Young Persons (Protection from Tobacco) Act 1991, s. 1[3]) and the sale of knives to persons under 18 (Criminal Justice Act 1988, s. 141A[4]).
23 See e.g. Ronald Bayer and Jennifer Stuber, 'Tobacco Control, Stigma, and Public Health: Rethinking the Relations' (2006) 96 *American Journal of Public Health* 47; Ronald Bayer, 'Stigma and the Ethics of Public Health: Not Can We but Should We' (2008) 67 *Social Science & Medicine* 463; Laura Williamson, Betsy Thom, Gerry Stimson, and Alfred Uhl, 'Stigma as a Public Health Tool: Implications for Health Promotion and Citizen Involvement' (2014) 25 *International Journal of Drug Policy* 333.

One condition that needs to be in place to live the good life is a sufficient level of autonomy or liberty. This liberty can be understood in a negative sense: a good life is one where persons are free from, for instance, physical attacks that cause injuries and ill health. Liberty can also be understood in a positive sense: a good life is one where persons are provided the opportunity to pursue important goals and projects. In both senses, while criminal prohibitions seek to restrict the liberty of some (i.e. criminals) they are justified interventions in virtue of the way in which these restrictions actually promote the freedom and rights of others. Another condition that needs to be in place to live the good life is a sufficient level of wellbeing. Wellbeing, both individual and collective, of which health will be a central component, is also essential to allowing individuals to pursue the goals, projects, and relationships that make their lives valuable. Similarly, the use of criminal regulation – indeed, this is true with other forms of non-criminal regulation as well – is not merely about creating a sphere of protection for individuals through prohibitions, it also about using the law to create the conditions that allow one to maintain, amongst other things, good health. Thus, criminal prohibitions can be used, not only as a practical means of harm reduction, but also as a way of promoting other valuable ends, such as autonomy and wellbeing, or the conditions necessary for allowing people to achieve those ends. On such a view, we would be justified in using criminal law as an intrusive measure when it provides a reasonable and proportionate way of protecting what is valuable within society.

This is exemplified in John Stuart Mill's famous harm principle – a principle governing the justified use of the coercive interventions of the state. According to Mill, 'the only purpose for which power can be rightfully exercised over any member of a civilised community against his will is to prevent harm to others'.[24] On this view, values such as autonomy need to be balanced against individual and community wellbeing, and in cases where behaviour causes harm to others, it becomes legitimate for the state to use its powers to mitigate or prevent such behaviour. The state is justified in restricting the choices that constitute public wrongs so as to allow others the freedom to live lives free of other-regarding behaviours that place them at risk of harm. As we shall see in the subsequent case studies, the balance between values such as autonomy and wellbeing not only can be undertaken differently between criminal law and public health, but can also differ within these approaches themselves. For example, it is generally easier to justify state interference to protect wellbeing and limit autonomy in the case of infectious disease transmission than it is in the case of health promotion activities. In each instance, competing values will need to be reconciled within our regulatory policies. In what follows below, we touch on different forms of criminal regulation that will emphasise different values, and it is worth keeping in mind how this compares to the values involved in selecting other modes of regulation (see, for instance, the discussion of the intervention ladder in Chapters 2, 3, and 9).

6.2.3 Why criminalise behaviours that harm the public's health?

Having considered the idea of criminal law generally, we have seen that it is a subtler concept than might at first appear. It seeks to balance different values that allow different means of controlling and responding to different modes of behaviour. As such, we come to a position that suggests that there may well be a place for criminal regulation of questions relevant to

---

24 John Stuart Mill, *On Liberty* (Edward Alexander (ed), first published 1859, Peterborough, Ontario: Broadview 1999). For more on the application of Mill's harm principle to public health, see, for instance, Madison Powers, Ruth Faden, and Yashar Saghai, 'Liberty, Mill and the Framework of Public Health Ethics' (2012) 5 *Public Health Ethics* 6; Lawrence Gostin and Kieran Gostin, 'A Broader Liberty: J.S. Mill, Paternalism, and the Public's Health' (2009) 123 *Public Health* 214.

public health. As ever, these may relate to controls of individuals as well as groups and institutions. We might, for example, use criminal measures to defend against interpersonal violence. Equally, it may be that criminal measures are appropriate to govern manufacturers of producers such as medicines, to ensure that sufficient attention is given to regulatory compliance. We may look to criminal measures serving public health agendas (as per examples such as those just given). But consider also that criminal law measures might limit public health goals: for example, a person's rights to bodily integrity include the bases of criminal liabilities that defend against third-party interference, even for her own (health) good.

Public health laws in the UK remain, in many parts, rooted in Victorian philosophies (see Chapter 3).[25] A great part of criminal law is also governed by an Act from this period: the Offences Against the Person Act 1861: a multifaceted and archaic statute with provisions originally including criminal offences for bigamy, sodomy, and obstructing clergymen from discharging their duties. Whilst scholars and others criticise this legislation for being outdated and inappropriate, its provisions continue to define wrongful conduct and prescribe standards of acceptable behaviour through threat of severe sanction.[26] Although it has been extensively amended over the years, modern criminal justice practice primarily focuses on just a few sections of the 1861 Act and the substantial body of case law that been developed around it. In particular, sections 18 (wounding with intent to do grievous bodily harm), 20 (inflecting bodily injury, with or without a weapon), and 47 (assault occasioning actual bodily harm) of the Act criminalise different levels of harm that may be committed. Through these provisions themselves, and judicial interpretation of them, an understanding has developed of which harms should be criminalised and what exceptions there should be to criminal prohibitions. For example, whilst it is a crime to commit grievous bodily harm, it is in the public interest to allow such conduct in the course of proper medical or surgical treatment.[27] Similarly, and as explored in the next case study, judges have developed the rules and principles regarding what sorts of harms are covered by the provisions in the Act, including health harms.

Before looking at some specific examples of criminal regulation in public health, however, it is important to consider an idea from regulatory theory.[28] It is orthodox to consider means of regulation as having the potential to be 'escalated'. This means that, if a 'softer' method of control fails to work, a 'harder' one might be applied. Criminalisation and the regulation of actors within the criminal justice system are often seen as the highest point of escalation within such a framework. As one of the most coercive forms of regulation available to the state, the use of criminal law is often seen as a last resort. This point bears specific emphasis because, in regard to criminal law and public health, criminal law actually has a

---

25 Victorian social policy, especially in public health, had a strong emphasis on social control and morality – on securing public order, ensuring cleanliness, and reforming immoral character traits. See e.g. Martin Wiener, *Reconstructing the Criminal: Culture, Law, and Policy in England, 1830–1914* (Cambridge: Cambridge University Press 1994); David Taylor, *Crime, Policing and Punishment in England, 1750–1914* (Basingstoke: Macmillan 1998); John Carter Wood, *Violence and Crime in Nineteenth Century England: The Shadow of Our Refinement* (London: Routledge 2004).

26 John Cyril Smith, 'Case Commentary on Parmenter' (1991) *Criminal Law Review* 43, called the Act 'a ragbag of offences brought together from a wide variety of sources with no attempt, as the draftsman frankly acknowledged, to introduce consistency as to substance or as to form'. See also Law Commission, *Reform of Offences against the Person* (Law Com No 361, 2015).

27 See, for example, Andrew Ashworth, 'Criminal Liability in a Medical Context: The Treatment of Good Intentions', in Andrew Simester and Tony Smith (eds), *Harm and Culpability* (Oxford: Oxford University Press 1996) 173–193; Margaret Brazier and Sara Fovargue, 'Transforming Wrong into Right: What Is "Proper Medical Treatment"?' in Sara Fovargue and Alexandra Mullock (eds), *The Legitimacy of Medical Treatment: What Role for the Medical Exception?* (London: Routledge 2016) 12–31.

28 Ian Ayres and John Braithwaite, *Responsive Regulation: Transcending the Deregulation Debate* (Oxford: Oxford University Press 1995). And, on regulation more generally, see Chapter 9.

very expansive reach as an ultimate threat in support of laws that help assure the conditions in which people can be healthy. Failure to comply with the laws considered in the previous chapter, such as those concerning statutory nuisance, road traffic safety, or smoking tobacco in proscribed places, may all result in criminal sanction. This is equally so in relation to the more central examples of public health laws, such as measures in the Public Health (Control of Disease) Act 1984 (as amended) and the Civil Contingencies Act 2004 (examined in this regard in section 6.3.3, and see also Chapters 3 and 7).

As such, whilst instinctively people might reject the idea that criminal regulation has a place in public health law, most people will in reality find this ultimate threat to be pragmatically sound and politically acceptable provided the specific aims of the laws are valid.[29] More controversially, but still generally accepted, most people accept the legitimacy of criminal liability supporting measures that protect a person's own health and safety in the case of seatbelt and motorcycle helmet laws (see section 6.3.2). As such, it is not hard to make a case for the overlapping agendas, and complementarity, of criminal justice and public health. The key, however, lies in being able to identify those issues where the complementarity of aims and agendas is mutually supporting and establishing which particular criminal regulatory interventions can be shown to be, on balance, advantageous.

6.2.4 Case study 1: Criminalising contagion: risk, harm, and sexually transmitted infections

There has been considerable academic and policy discussion of the justifiability of criminal regulation being applied in cases of non-disclosure, exposure, and transmission of disease – especially sexually transmitted infections such as HIV[30] but also in the case of notifiable diseases.[31] Such criminal offences can be seen to mirror the moral obligation we have to disclose our infectious status and not to infect others.[32] For over a century, it had been understood as a point of legal principle that, if a person consented to sex, her partner had committed no wrong if he transmitted an infection through sexual intercourse.[33] However, in recent years, section 20 of the Offences Against the Person Act 1861 has been used to prosecute reckless transmission of HIV on the basis that the negative consequences of the infection on a person's health amounts to grievous bodily harm.[34] There have been two central cases involving the criminalisation of

---

29 See e.g. Grant Lamond, 'Coercion and the Nature of Law' (2001) 7 *Legal Theory* 35. It is also important to recognise the difference between what criminal regulations exist on the books and those that are actually legally enforced in practice. The issue of selective enforcement of the criminal law also has relevance for public health more generally, as selective enforcement tends to disproportionately disadvantage more vulnerable or marginalised groups in society contributing to densely woven, systematic patterns of disadvantage.

30 See e.g. UNAIDS, *Criminal Law, Public Health and HIV Transmission: A Policy Options Paper* (Geneva: Joint United Nations Programme on HIV/AIDS 2002); Robert Klitzman, Sheri Kirshenbaum, Lauren Kittel, Stephen Morin, Shaira Daya, Maddalena Mastrogiacomo, and Mary Jane Rotheram-Borus, 'Naming Names: Perceptions of Name-Based Reporting, Partner Notification and Criminalisation of Non-Disclosure among Persons Living with HIV' (2004) 1 *Sexuality Research and Social Policy* 38; Matthew Weait, *Intimacy and Responsibility: The Criminalisation of HIV Transmission* (Abingdon: Routledge-Cavendish 2007); James Chalmers, *Legal Responses to HIV and AIDS* (Oxford: Hart Publishing 2008).

31 See e.g. Public Health (Control of Disease) Act 1984, s. 11(4).

32 See e.g. John Harris and Soren Holm, 'Is There a Moral Obligation Not to Infect Others?' (1995) 311 *British Medical Journal* 1215; Margaret Brazier and John Harris, 'Public Health and Private Lives' (1996) 4 *Medical Law Review* 171; Rebecca Bennett, Heather Draper and Lucy Frith, 'Ignorance Is Bliss? HIV and Moral Duties and Legal Duties to Forewarn' (2000) 26 *Journal of Medical Ethics* 9; Marcel Verweij, 'Obligatory Precautions against Infection' (2005) 19 *Bioethics* 323; Margaret Battin, Leslie Francis, Jay Jacobson, and Charles Smith, *The Patient as Victim and Vector: Ethics and Infectious Disease* (Oxford: Oxford University Press 2009) part IV.

33 *R v Clarence* [1886–90] 16 Cox CC 511.

34 The transmission of other sexually transmitted infectious diseases, such as hepatitis and herpes, has also been prosecuted under the 1861 Act.

HIV transmission that are worth briefly examining, in which convictions under the 1861 Act were appealed – though, ultimately, both appeals were lost and both men were imprisoned.[35]

In the case of R v Dica,[36] the Court of Appeal ruled that a person was guilty of recklessly transmitting HIV if he, knowing he was HIV positive, transmitted the virus to another person through sexual intercourse and did not tell the sexual partner of his HIV status. It was the defendant's failure to disclose his HIV-positive status and the subsequent HIV transmission that constituted the criminal act of harming.[37] In the case of R v Konzani,[38] the issue concerned, in relation to the trial judge's instructions to the jury, whether consent could be used as a defence against the offence of HIV transmission if there was prior disclosure of the defendant's known HIV-positive status. The Court of Appeal ruled that, in cases where someone is charged with recklessly transmitting HIV, the defence could only be raised where the consent was 'willing' or 'conscious'. In distinguishing between 'willingly running the risk of transmission' and 'willingly consenting to the risk of transmission', the Court argued that, since the defendant did not disclose his HIV status, there was no way for his partner to consent to the risk.[39] Here, again, in both cases, we see the interplay between values such as autonomy and wellbeing – with the importance accorded to disclosure and willing consent to the risk of HIV transmission – and how the interpretation of concepts such as recklessness can modify (and complicate) how we understand harm to others.

As noted earlier, one characteristic of criminal law is its tendency to be a blunt and oppressive regulatory instrument. This has been readily demonstrated in the case of the criminalisation of HIV transmission. Given the generality of criminal laws and how infrequently they are revised, many of the criminal prohibitions do not reflect current scientific evidence and knowledge on HIV prevention, transmission, and treatment.[40] A consequence of these prohibitions has also been a great deal of fear, stigma, and discrimination.[41] This stigma can also serve to discourage people from being tested for HIV in the first place, for fear of what comes with being labelled as HIV positive. As a result, such criminalisation actually has an undermining effect on HIV prevention and treatment efforts – both in terms of maintaining successful adherence with treatment, as well as reducing the number of people being tested.[42] There are also questions of justice that arise in relation to the prosecution

---

35 To date, there have been 29 prosecutions – 27 males and 2 females – with a majority of the cases ending in guilty verdicts and appeals of those cases dismissed: see National AIDS Trust, *Table of Cases of People Charged with Grievous Bodily Harm Under Section 20 of the Offences against the Person Act 1861, for Reckless Sexual Transmission of Serious Infections in England and Wales* (London: NAT 2016). There have been no convictions for HIV transmission under section 18 (intentional transmission), but a handful of cases were subsequently dropped where individuals were initially charged under the section.

36 [2004] EWCA Crim 1103.

37 This case has been subject to much critical discussion. See, e.g. Matthew Weait, 'Criminal Law and the Sexual Transmission of HIV: R v Dica' (2005) 68 *Modern Law Review* 121.

38 [2005] EWCA Crim 706.

39 This case has also been subject to critical discussion. See, e.g. Matthew Weait, 'Knowledge, Autonomy and Consent: R v Konzani' (2005) *Criminal Law Review* 763.

40 Harlon Dalton, 'Shaping Responsible Behavior: Lesson from the AIDS Front' (1999) 56 *Washington and Lee Law Review* 931; Scott Burris, Leo Beletsky, Joseph Burleson, Patricia Case, and Zita Lazzarini, 'Do Criminal Laws Influence HIV Risk Behaviour? An Empirical Trial' (2007) 39 *Arizona State Law Journal* 467.

41 Norbert Gilmore and Margaret Somerville, 'Stigmatization, Scapegoating and Discrimination in Sexually Transmitted Diseases: Overcoming "Them" and "Us"' (1994) 39 *Social Science & Medicine* 1339; Peter Aggleton, Kate Wood, Anne Malcolm, and Richard Parker, *HIV-Related Stigma, Discrimination and Human Rights Violations: Case Studies of Successful Programmes* (Geneva: UNAIDS 2005); Anish Mahajan, Jennifer Sayles, Vishal Patel, Robert Remien, Daniel Ortiz, Greg Szekeres, and Thomas Coates, 'Stigma in the HIV/AIDS Epidemic: A Review of the Literature and Recommendations for the Way Forward' (2008) 22 *AIDS* S67.

42 See e.g. Carol Galletly and Steven Pinkerton, 'Conflicting Messages: How Criminal HIV Disclosure Laws Undermine Public Health Efforts to Control the Spread of HIV' (2006) 10 *AIDS and Behavior* 451; Ingrid Katz, Annemarie Ryu, Afiachukwu Onuegbu, Christina Psaros, Sheri Weiser, David Bangsberg, and Alexander Tsai, 'Impact of HIV-Related Stigma on Treatment Adherence: Systematic Review and Meta-Synthesis' (2013) 16 *Journal of the International AIDS Society* 18640.

of these offences. Particular marginal or vulnerable groups may be disproportionally susceptible to negative treatment (e.g. women and sex workers at greater risk of gender-based violence related to a positive HIV status) as well as the risk of selective prosecution in cases where judgments of culpability could be influenced by a moralism about how people were infected (e.g. intravenous drug users) or groups that have a high prevalence (e.g. the framing of HIV as a 'gay' or 'African' disease).[43]

Recall earlier, there were two justifications for criminal sanctions discussed: retribution and deterrence. According to a retributivist account of punishment, we are justified in criminalising HIV transmission because those who intentionally or recklessly infect others *deserve* to be punished. As we saw in the cases of *Dica* and *Konzani*, much of that basis for desert was based on autonomy-based considerations and how non-disclosure of HIV status played a central role in the wrongness of the harm incurred. Such a retributivist focus does not align closely with how public health operates. According to a deterrence account of punishment, we are justified in criminalising HIV transmission because it will prevent others from engaging in similar behaviour for fear of being subject to criminal sanctions. Nevertheless, the available evidence indicates that criminalisation is not successful in changing sexual behaviour or reducing the spread of HIV.[44] In both instances, we have very good reasons for questioning whether the criminalisation of HIV transmission is itself justified and whether it is an effective and ethical public health measure.[45]

6.2.5 Case study 2: Criminal sanctions in support of disease control measures

Both criminal law and public health employ forms of social control. There are a number of compulsory preventative and restrictive measures involving intervening with, and sometimes into, the human body that can be used by public health practitioners for the purposes of disease control, such as testing, treatment, vaccination, quarantine, isolation, and social distancing. These public health measures can either sometimes resemble criminal law methods (e.g. restricting people's movement through temporary detention, as in the case of quarantine and isolation) or sometimes can be carried out with the assistance of criminal justice officials (e.g. applying to a justice of the peace for a compulsory isolation order or using police officers to enforce a social distancing order). For these reasons, people often associate these disease control measures as forms of criminal regulation.

Strictly speaking, however, these control measures are not themselves part of the criminal law but arise from 'police powers', which refer to the state's civil authority to regulate non-criminal behaviour in order to promote or protect the health, safety, and morals of the public. This can involve, within the bounds of constitutional and statutory constraints,

---

43 See also Jonathan Montgomery, 'Medicalizing Crime – Criminalizing Health?' in Charles Erin and Suzanne Ost (eds), *The Criminal Justice System and Health Care* (Oxford: Oxford University Press 2007) 257–272.

44 See e.g. Burris et al (n 40).

45 We also have good reasons, given the state of legislation such as the Offences Against the Person Act 1861 and the rapid pace of development of scientific evidence on issues relating to HIV, to question whether the criminal courts are best placed to be making these calls. From a public health perspective, there are other appropriate regulatory strategies that could be put in place that focus on HIV education, prevention, treatment, care, and support as primary aims, which have been shown to be successful. See e.g. Wayne Johnson, David Robert Holtgrave, William McClellan, and Michael Goodman, 'HIV Intervention Research for Men Who Have Sex with Men: A 7-Year Update' (2005) 17 *AIDS Education and Prevention* 568; Edward Green, Daniel Halperin, Vinand Nantulya, and Janice Hogle, 'Uganda's HIV Prevention Success: The Role of Sexual Behaviour Change in the National Response' (2006) 10 *AIDS and Behavior* 335.

the restriction of private interests for the benefit of the community. Even though the term 'police' is used, the notion of police powers is not synonymous with criminal regulation. Many police powers have been used to authorise the state to use its coercive powers to protect public health in the context of preventing the spread of infectious diseases through inspection powers, compelling treatment, and the use of restrictive measures. While, historically, the use of public health police powers received strong support and were upheld by the courts, in more recent years, some scholars have questioned these powers and even sought to restrict their use in order to prevent violations of individual rights (e.g. rights to due process) and to reduce the potential for abuse, such as in contexts of epidemics or pandemics.[46]

The explicit power to quarantine individuals involuntarily and without due process was repealed with the enactment of the Public Health Act 1896. Nevertheless, in the case of notifiable diseases,[47] authorities do have the power to obtain quarantine and isolation orders,[48] as well as orders for physical examination, movement restrictions, and protecting clothing/equipment.[49] In the context of disease control measures, there is a strong emphasis on protecting the population from potential harm, thus placing limits on values such as liberty and autonomy.

Not only has criminal law been used as a response to disease transmission, as we saw in section 6.2.4, it has also been used as a means to try to prevent disease transmission. In the case of *Enhorn v Sweden*,[50] the legality of using the state's coercive powers to detain an HIV-positive person for the purposes of limiting disease transmission was challenged on the grounds that it violated his Article 5 right under the European Convention on Human Rights (ECHR) – the right to liberty and security of person. Public health authorities in Sweden sought to use their statutory powers to impose a compulsory isolation order for a period of seven years, which was found to violate Enhorn's Article 5 right because 'the authorities failed to strike a fair balance between the need to ensure that the HIV virus did not spread and the applicant's right to liberty'.[51] While his detention was found to be unlawful for violating his human rights, it is important to see that it was the disproportionate burden of the detention that was problematic. The ECHR, as do all human rights instruments, allow for limitations in liberty for legitimate purposes (such as disease control), but they must be done in a way that strives for a fair balance of benefits and burdens.[52] We discuss this case – and in particular, the 'proportionality' dimension of it – at greater length in the next chapter of this book.

---

46 See e.g. Michelle Daubert, 'Pandemic Fears and Contemporary Quarantine: Protecting Liberty through a Continuum of Due Process Rights' (2007) 54 *Buffalo Law Review* 1299; Wendy Parmet, 'J.S. Mill and the American Law of Quarantine' (2008) 1 *Public Health Ethics* 210. Restrictive measures also raise important ethical issues; see e.g. Daniel Markovits, 'Quarantines and Distributive Justice' (2005) 33 *Journal of Law, Medicine & Ethics* 323; A.M. Viens, Cécile Bensimon and Ross Upshur, 'Your Liberty or Your Life: Reciprocity in the Use of Restrictive Measures in Contexts of Contagion' (2009) 6 *Journal of Bioethical Inquiry* 207.

47 Public Health (Control of Disease) Act 1984 s. 10; Health Protection (Notification) Regulations 2010, SI 2010/659, Schedule 1; Health Protection (Part 2A Orders) Regulations 2010, SI 2010/658.

48 Public Health (Control of Disease) Act 1984, ss. 35–37; Public Health (Infectious Disease) Regulations 1988, SI 1998/1546; Civil Contingencies Act 2004, s. 21(3); Health and Social Care Act 2008, ss. 45, 129; Health Protection (Part 2A Orders) Regulations 2010, reg. 9.

49 Health and Social Care Act 2008, s. 129, inserting s. 45G into Public Health (Control of Disease) Act 1984. Also cf the Immigration Act 1971 on physical examination.

50 [2005] 41 EHRR 633.

51 ibid, [55].

52 For commentary on this case, see Robyn Martin, 'The Exercise of Public Health Powers in Cases of Infectious Disease: Human Rights Implications' (2006) 14 *Medical Law Review* 132.

6.3 Ensuring responsibility for one's own health

Much of the regulatory focus on criminal law in general and its application to public health in particular has concerned how its prohibitions seek to reduce harm to others. The reason why we can justify the use of the criminal law to advance public health goals is largely understood in relation to limiting the effects of other-regarding behaviour that harms individuals and groups. What about self-regarding behaviour? Is it justified to use the criminal law to limit behaviours that, primarily, result in self-inflicted harm? Should criminal regulation be concerned with promoting the health and wellbeing of the very people being targeted by the criminal laws themselves, and does this prioritisation of wellbeing over autonomy raise ethical and legal questions about the legitimacy of such measures? As we see in Chapter 9, in the discussion of the NHS Constitution, generally English law and policy-makers avoid imposing 'hard' responsibilities on people to safeguard their own wellbeing. However, it is important to examine how at times the weight of the criminal law does impose duties on people to protect their own health.

6.3.1 Hard paternalism and public health

We all have good reasons to promote and protect our own health – reasons that hold us responsible for our state of health, even acknowledging the social and structural determinants that contribute to our health status. We are all aware, as well, of the diversions and impediments that can get in the way of fulfilling our personal health responsibilities. In these contexts, where we fail to use our autonomy and liberty to promote our own health, is it justifiable to paternalise people in order to ensure they are taking responsibility for their own health?

Paternalism involves interfering or limiting a person's autonomy in order to promote her wellbeing. Kalle Grill provides a helpful summary of the conditions that are typically included in definitions of paternalism:[53]

1)   an interference condition that delimits the kind of action that may be paternalistic, most often excluding non-intrusive actions;
2)   a consent condition that limits paternalistic actions to such actions as have not been consented to – excluding actions that are performed in response to explicit consent and possibly also tacit and inferred consent; and
3)   a benevolence condition that limits paternalistic actions to such actions as are motivated, and perhaps also justified, by the good of the person(s) interfered with.

Very often, there is also:

4)   a superiority condition that restricts paternalism to such actions as are performed by an agent who considers herself in some way superior to the person(s) interfered with.

Thus, public health measures are paternalist when they interfere in some way with a person's choice or behaviour in order to benefit their health or wellbeing, and it is done either without their consent or, perhaps, sometimes even against their consent. Public health officials

---

53   Kalle Grill, 'Paternalism' in Ruth Chadwick (ed), *Encyclopedia of Applied Ethics* (2nd edn., San Diego: Academic Press 2012) 359–369.

are almost always going to be in a position of epistemic superiority – given their expertise and access to specialist data, they will have superior understanding and knowledge about what would be better for health compared to the targets of their interventions.[54] There will be many public health measures that will satisfy these paternalistic conditions. While we often worry about paternalism as being a distinctive way of wronging someone – and so it provides us with a prima facie reason to avoid such conduct – is important to recognise that the existence of paternalism does not end the debate as to whether some intervention is justified or not. There may be contexts in which public health interventions are ultimately justified even if they are paternalistic.[55]

We can distinguish between two kinds of paternalism – hard and soft paternalism – on the basis of whether the person's autonomy we are limiting in order to promote their well-being is acting in a voluntary and knowledgeable way. According to Feinberg:

> Hard paternalism will accept as a reason for criminal legislation that it is necessary to protect competent adults, against their will, from the harmful consequences even of their fully voluntary choices and undertakings. . . . Soft paternalism holds that the state has the right to prevent self-regarding harmful conduct . . . when, but only when, that conduct is substantially nonvoluntary, or when temporary intervention is necessary to establish whether it is voluntary or not.[56]

Just as it is necessary to justify using the state's powers to coercively limit the liberty of individuals in order to promote the health of the community, we also require a justification for the moral and legal permissibility of using liberty-limiting interventions to promote an individual's own health. It is more difficult to justify criminal regulation on the basis of hard paternalism, as it involves disregarding individual preferences or desires as expressions of their autonomy or liberty in favour of protecting or promoting their wellbeing.

Furthermore, there will also be contexts where it will not be so easy to separate the self-regarding and other-regarding aspects of a public health measure. Take, for instance, public health policy regarding alcohol consumption. Some public health measures will be directed at reducing self-inflicted harms from alcohol as well as the harms to others that result from misuse of alcohol, such as road traffic and pedestrian accidents from drunk driving, inter-personal violence, and foetal alcohol syndrome. In such cases, it can become difficult to dis-entangle the paternalistic component of the measure from the non-paternalistic component, and this raises questions as to whether the partially paternalistic aspect of the measure should be thought sufficient to make all of it morally or legally problematic.

6.3.2 Case study 3: Road safety laws

Injuries and deaths due to road traffic accidents for drivers, passengers, and pedestrians are a major public health problem.[57] In regulating how we can use vehicles, the state enacts rules that seek to protect us from our own choices and behaviours that result in our

---

54 However, defining what health is and whether experts should always be thought to be in a better epistemic position than the people whose health status is in question has been contentious. See, e.g. John Coggon, *What Makes Health Public? A Critical Evaluation of Moral, Legal, and Political Claims in Public Health* (Cambridge: Cambridge University Press 2012), chapter 1.
55 For more on paternalism and public health, see e.g. Thomas Nys, 'Paternalism in Public Health Care' (2008) 1 *Public Health Ethics* 64; James Wilson, 'Why It's Time to Stop Worrying about Paternalism in Health Policy' (2011) 4 *Public Health Ethics* 269; Tom Walker, 'Paternalism and Populations' (2016) 9 *Public Health Ethics* 46.
56 Joel Feinberg, *Harm to Self: The Moral Limits of the Criminal Law* (Oxford: Oxford University Press, 1986) p. 12.
57 World Health Organization, *Global Status Report on Road Safety* (Geneva: WHO 2015); Public Health England, *Reducing Unintentional Injuries on the Roads among Children and Young People under 25 Years* (London: Public Health England 2014).

own mortality and morbidity. Road safety laws – such as speed limits,[58] seatbelts and child restraint requirements,[59] motorcycle helmet requirements,[60] or hand-held mobile phone and distracting technology use bans[61] – with criminal sanctions associated with non-compliance, provide numerous examples of paternalistic criminal regulation that are directed at reducing associated health burdens. To be sure, these self-inflicted harms also have a significant impact on others, such as the friends and family of the accident victims and via the medical costs associated with treating such victims within the publically funded health service. As with so many other areas of public health policy, the individual and social costs of an activity can be difficult to separate, which results in making the justification for the regulation of such activities more complex. Nevertheless, let us proceed on the basis that one of the primary justifications for such road safety laws is focussed on preventing harm to the drivers themselves.[62]

As we saw before with Mill's articulation of the harm principle, the use of criminal regulation can be justified in cases where it could be used to mitigate harm to others. However, Mill appears to be firmly anti-paternalist, since he thought an individual's own good alone could not justify state intervention when it comes to informed and voluntary activities. Would this mean that the only justified use of criminal regulation to advance public health goals would be restricted to activities protecting harm to others, or will there be instances where both soft and hard paternalistic criminal prohibitions could be justified? Much of the recent work on the application of the harm principle to public health suggests that – with examples such as road safety, given the minimal level of restrictions, how unimportant these restrictions are to wider goals and projects and the resultant individual (and collective) benefit – many of these measures can be accommodated within a generally, though not absolute, anti-paternalist approach to public health.[63]

While paternalistic criminal prohibitions strongly encourage, and sometimes force, people to act in ways conductive to promoting their health and wellbeing in ways they are not likely to select themselves, we should also not discount the wider long-term contributions they can make to shifting cultural attitudes in relation to the activity they are regulating. When first introduced, for instance, mandatory seatbelt laws were viewed as an unwanted and heavy-handed intrusion into our private lives, but now opposition to such measures is extremely low, and most of us comply with wearing seatbelts automatically and unthinkingly.[64] When considering the extent to which paternalism should be thought to be morally or legally problematic, we should consider both the intent and the effect of the criminal regulation as an aspect of public health policy.

---

58 Road Traffic Regulation Act 1984, ss. 17, 86. 89.
59 Road Traffic Act 1988, ss. 14, 15; Motor Vehicles (Wearing of Seat Belts) Regulations 1993, SI 1993/176; Motor Vehicles (Wearing of Seat Belts by Children in Front Seats) Regulations 1993, SI 1993/31; Motor Vehicles (Wearing of Seat Belts) (Amendment) Regulations 2006, SI 2006/1892.
60 Road Traffic Act 1988, ss. 16, 17; Motor Cycles (Protective Helmets) Regulations 1998, SI 1998/1807, reg. 4.
61 Road Traffic Act 1988, ss. 2, 3; Road Vehicles (Construction and Use) Regulations 1986, SI 1986/1078, reg. 110, inserted by Road Vehicles (Construction and Use) (Amendment) (No. 4) Regulations 2003, SI 2003/2695 reg. 2.
62 Jessica Nihlén Fahlquist, 'Saving Lives in Road Traffic – Ethical Aspects' (2009) 17 Journal of Public Health 385.
63 For more on the extent to which Mill's harm principle may admit of paternalistic interventions, see e.g. Joel Feinberg, 'Legal Paternalism' (1971) 1 Canadian Journal of Philosophy 105; Richard Arneson, 'Mill versus Paternalism' (1980) 90 Ethics 470; Sven Hansson, 'Extended Antipaternalism' (2005) 31 Journal of Medical Ethics 970; Raphael Cohen-Almagor, 'Between Autonomy and State Regulation: J.S. Mill's Elastic Paternalism' (2012) 87 Philosophy 557; Ben Saunders, 'Reformulating Mill's Harm Principle,' (2016) 125 Mind 1005.
64 See, for instance, Jerome Legge, Traffic Safety Reform in the United States and Great Britain (Pittsburgh: University of Pittsburgh Press 1991), chapters 2 and 4; Department of Transport, Seat Belt and Mobile Phone Use Surveys: England and Scotland, 2014 (London: Department of Transport 2015).

6.4 Public health as a tool for criminal justice

We often think about people such as police officers, prison guards, criminal court judges and members of the Crown Prosecution Service (CPS) as exhausting the list of criminal justice officials, but there are also different regulatory authorities that are charged with monitoring, investigating, and, in some cases, bringing a prosecution in conjunction with the CPS. Prominent examples include the Health and Safety Executive and the Department for Environment, Food and Rural Affairs (DEFRA) and its associated bodies (e.g. Animal and Plant Health Agency, Environment Agency, Drinking Water Inspectorate).

There has also been a growing trend for public health practitioners – via their data collection and investigative methods and epidemiological expertise – to become more involved with the criminal justice process. While this chapter has primarily focussed on criminal law as a tool for public health, it is important also to briefly explore how public health can be used as a tool for criminal justice. This integration of law enforcement and public health is known as forensic epidemiology. The idea of forensic epidemiology is quite broad, with scholars and practitioners using it to cover everything from the use of epidemiological evidence and epidemiologists as expert witnesses in civil litigation, to investigating potential criminal sources of disease outbreaks.[65] As the area has developed, we have seen it cover a multitude of areas – including searches, inspections and embargoes, mental health, terrorism, food-borne illness, violence, and environmental concerns.[66]

While the reciprocal use of criminal law and public health tools can further speak to the compatibility or shared agendas and values of both approaches, there is still a need to consider the wider implications of integrating these. Using public health expertise to advance criminal justice aims involves wider social and political considerations that should be kept in mind. In particular, it is important to consider how such collaboration may negatively affect the public perception of the public health enterprise and the trust the public places in its officials.[67]

6.4.1 Case study 4: Bioterrorism and forensic epidemiology

Terrorism using biological agents as weapons is, of course, a criminal offence[68] and can have a negative impact on public heath through direct contact with pathogens or their contamination of the food and water supplies. It was with the 2001 anthrax attacks in the United States that we began to see an increased awareness of how public health could be used to support criminal justice efforts in relation to bioterrorism. In particular, epidemiological investigation can be used to help detect disease outbreaks, discover the source of the outbreak, and determine whether disease outbreaks might have a criminal origin.[69] Through the use of monitoring and surveillance systems and developing an epidemic curve in relation to an outbreak, it is possible to detect

---

65 Sana Loue, *Forensic Epidemiology: A Comprehensive Guide for Legal and Epidemiology Professionals* (Carbondale, IL: Southern Illinois University Press 1999); Ken Alibek and Stephen Hadelman, *Biohazard* (New York: Random House 1999); Richard Goodman, Judith Munson, Kim Dammers, Zita Lazzarini, and John Barkley, 'Forensic Epidemiology: Law at the Intersection of Public Health and Criminal Investigations' (2003) 31 *Journal of Law, Medicine and Ethics* 684.

66 See e.g. Sana Loue, *Case Studies in Forensic Epidemiology* (New York: Kluwer 2002); Sana Loue, *Forensic Epidemiology: Integrating Public Health and Law Enforcement* (London: Jones and Bartlett 2010); Sana Loue (ed), *Forensic Epidemiology in the Global Context* (New York: Springer 2013).

67 See especially, Zita Lazzarini, 'Forensic Epidemiology: Strange Bedfellows or the Perfect Match? Can Public Health and Criminal Law Work Together without Losing Their Souls?' in Viens, Coggon and Kessel (eds) (n 3).

68 See e.g. Biological Weapons Act 1974.

69 Daniel Jernigan et al, 'Investigation of Bioterrorism-Related Anthrax, United States, 2001: Epidemiologic Findings' (2002) 8 *Emerging Infectious Disease* 1019.

and respond to serious bioterrorist threats to public health – as well as using such infrastructure for non-terrorist outbreaks, such as unintentional bacterial contamination within a food supply chain. This epidemiological knowledge can also contribute to informing government officials as to whether restrictive measures, such as quarantine or isolation, should be employed in relation to exposure to a suspected bioterrorist pathogen.[70] These kinds of methods and expertise are not generally available with officials within the criminal justice system and represent a massive contribution to the investigation and potential prevention of bioterrorist attacks.

Chapter 6: Summary

- Criminal regulation and public health policy have aims and justifications that can sometimes be shared and sometimes come into tension.
- Criminal regulation involves prohibition of conduct that is a public wrong, either in itself (*malum in se*) or in virtue of it being declared so by law (*malum prohibitum*).
- Criminal regulation also concerns punishing those individuals who fail to comply with criminal rules prohibiting these public wrongs. Criminal law contains both *fault-based* offences (for acts that are punishable for blameworthy behaviour) and *strict liability* offences (for acts that are punishable for committing prohibited behaviour).
- Criminal regulation is primarily concerned with public wrongs that consist in harmful behaviour – both behaviours that result in harm to self as well as harm to others.
- While criminal regulation has traditionally been used as a public health tool, public health methods are increasingly being used as a tool for criminal justice.
- The tendency for criminal regulation to be a blunt and oppressive tool, as well as one with a legacy of moralism, can make it problematic for public health.

6.5 Further readings

Timothy Akers, Roberto Potter, and Carl Hill, *Epidemiological Criminology: A Public Health Approach to Crime and Violence* (Oxford: Wiley 2012).
Jonathan Herring, *Criminal Law: The Basics* (London: Routledge 2009).
Douglas Husak, *Overcriminalization: The Limits of the Criminal Law* (Oxford: Oxford University Press 2008).
Zita Lazzarini, Richard Goodman, and Kim Dammers, 'Criminal Law and Public Health Practice' in Richard Goodman, Richard Hoffman, Wilfredo Lopez, Gene Matthews, Mark Rothstein, and Karen Foster (eds), *Law in Public Health Practice* (Oxford University Press 2007) 136–167.
Sana Loue, *Forensic Epidemiology: Integrating Public Health and Law Enforcement* (London: Jones and Bartlett 2010).
Catherine Stanton and Hannah Quirk (eds), *Criminalising Contagion: Legal and Ethical Challenges of Disease Transmission and the Criminal Law* (Cambridge: Cambridge University Press 2016).
A.M. Viens, John Coggon, and Anthony Kessel (eds), *Criminal Law, Philosophy and Public Health Practice* (Cambridge: Cambridge University Press 2013).

---

70 Joseph Barbera, Anthony Macintyre, Lawrence Gostin, Tom Inglesby, Tara O'Toole, Craig DeAtley, Kevin Tonat, and Marci Layton, 'Large-Scale Quarantine Following Biological Terrorism in the United States: Scientific Examination, Logistic and Legal Limits, and Possible Consequences' (2001) 286 *Journal of the American Medical Association* 2711.

Chapter 7

Public law and public health

7.1 Introduction to public law

In Chapter 5, we addressed the apparent paradox that forms of law that relate to the rights and duties we owe to each other as *private* citizens might nonetheless have value in pursuit of the ends of *public* health. By contrast, here we focus on that area of law that delineates the powers and responsibilities, and restricts the activities, of that which Gostin and Wiley have described as 'the public entity that acts on behalf of the people . . . to protect or promote the population's health':[1] that is, government.

Public law has been at the heart of public health law in the United Kingdom at least since the Public Health Act 1848, which, as discussed in Chapter 3, allocated responsibilities to local authorities and provided an institutional framework through which public health activity could be undertaken. But the Victorian era also demonstrates – notably in the context of vaccination legislation – that tensions may arise between the exercise of public responsibilities and personal autonomy. Public law thus has two functions, which will be analysed in depth below: it *facilitates* governmental activity but also *constrains* such activity in situations where it is deemed to infringe individual rights.

7.1.1 Nature and forms of public law

In one sense, virtually all law, at least as it is popularly understood, is public law. Although legal scholars have long understood that private organisations possess the capacity to make and enforce binding rules[2] – in some cases, rules that apply within the public sector as well[3] – by far the greater part of the analysis of legal principles, processes, and institutions is concerned with laws made by the legislature (primary legislation), executive (delegated or secondary legislation) and/or judiciary (case law): institutions, making up the three branches of government, that might properly be described as 'public'. However, the distinction that is normally drawn between 'public' and 'private' law does not rest upon the identity of the law-maker: for example, both legislature and judiciary can, and do, make laws that govern contractual relations, which are viewed as 'private law' . Rather, it turns upon

---

1 Lawrence Gostin and Lindsay Wiley, *Public Health Law: Power, Duty, Restraint* (3rd edn., Berkeley: University of California Press 2016) 6.
2 See e.g. Louis Jaffe, 'Law-Making by Private Groups' (1937) 51 *Harvard Law Review* 201.
3 See Colin Scott, 'Private Regulation of the Public Sector: A Neglected Facet of Contemporary Governance' (2002) 29 *Journal of Law and Society* 56.

the identities of the parties – thus, private law is concerned with legal relationships between individuals, or between private corporate entities (or any combination thereof) – and, perhaps less straightforwardly, the range of effects produced by the law – thus, the impact of public law cases tends to be more wide-ranging than that of private law cases that, read very narrowly, impact only upon the parties to the case in question.[4]

Thus, while the distinction between 'public' and 'private' law in the UK is far from watertight, in part because the absence of a codified constitution has meant that there has been no need to develop a theory or taxonomy that identifies that which falls within the remit of the state and that which does not, and in part because a historically dominant strand of British constitutional jurisprudence has regarded government officials as subject to the same 'ordinary' law as the rest of the populace,[5] we might define this area of law in the manner adopted elsewhere by one of the present authors:

> Public law is concerned with three matters which are fundamental to the operation of any modern state. First, it entails study of the institutional structure of government and of the rules which underpin this structure. Secondly, and relatedly, it sets out the relationships which the various institutions of government have with each other and the limits beyond which they may not lawfully act. Thirdly, it is concerned with the relationship between the individual and the state.[6]

The last of these elements warrants some expansion. It might be argued that criminal law is 'concerned with the relationship between the individual and the state', insofar as a governmental entity (usually, Parliament) proscribes certain conduct that is considered to represent a threat to the safety and welfare of the public at large, and the state then prosecutes failure to comply with the law in question. However, given the scope and complexity of criminal law and the specificity of its mode of enforcement, it is best considered as an entirely discrete category of law, and this is the approach taken in Chapter 6 of this text.

Public law is also sometimes known as 'constitutional and administrative law', which provides further insight into its subject-matter. 'Constitutional law' might be understood as a field in which the focus of attention lies with governmental arrangements and powers and with the limitations to those powers, both in respect of relations between different government bodies, and vis-a-vis individual citizens. In the UK, which is lacking a 'higher-order' constitutional law comparable to that which exists in almost all other states, limitations to powers have traditionally been manifest primarily through political mechanisms – such as the media, elections, and ministerial accountability to Parliament – rather than through legal principles enunciated by courts. However, this pattern has changed somewhat over recent decades, as legal processes such as judicial review of administrative action and the Human Rights Act 1998 (discussed below) have provided an alternative, and sometimes more effective, means of ensuring that government acts within its allotted powers.[7]

---

4   This seems to understate the impact that legal decisions have beyond the immediate parties to the case in hand, for discussion of which see e.g. Marc Galanter, 'The Radiating Effects of Courts' in Keith Boyum and Lynn Mather (eds), *Empirical Theories about Courts* (New York: Longman 1983) 117.
5   See Martin Loughlin, *Public Law and Political Theory* (Oxford: Clarendon Press 1992), especially chapter 5.
6   Keith Syrett, *The Foundations of Public Law* (2nd edn., Basingstoke: Palgrave Macmillan 2014) 1.
7   See ibid, 11–16.

'Administrative law' often has a somewhat more workaday character, being concerned with disputes that arise in respect of the powers and duties exercised by the state in relation to the individual (or collective entities, such as NGOs or corporate bodies).[8] This having been said, this form of law is often deployed as a means of placing pressure upon government to adopt, drop, or change a policy or decision, hence forming part of a wider political campaign.[9] It also forms a mechanism through which the allocation of resources by government can be legally scrutinised. The most prominent mechanism for resolving disputes of this type is the process of judicial review of administrative action, in which senior courts assess whether executive actions and decisions are lawful by reference to certain 'grounds' that have been articulated by the judiciary. These seek to assess whether the governmental body in question has lawful authority to act in such a way, whether its decision is one that has been rationally reached, and whether it has acted in a procedurally fair manner. However, institutions other than courts are more frequently engaged in such matters: these include tribunals, ombudsmen, and inquiries.[10]

A third area that falls under the umbrella of public law, and that sits somewhere between the two categories previously outlined, is human rights law. Until recently, legal protection for interests that individuals might hold against the British state – such as the rights to liberty, freedom of association, and freedom of expression – primarily took the form of negative 'civil liberties': freedoms were residual in that it was permissible for a person to do anything that was not proscribed by common law or statute. The enactment of the Human Rights Act 1998 affords positive protection to the rights accorded by the European Convention on Human Rights to individuals. This means that, where a 'victim' alleges that a protected right has been violated by the state, the burden of justification lies upon the body in question to show that the measures taken are prescribed by law, that they pursue at least one of a range of objectives that are in the interests of the community as a whole, and that they are no more intrusive toward the individual than is necessary to achieve the specified objective(s). It should be noted that the future of the Act is uncertain, with the Conservative Government elected in 2015 pledged to repeal it, albeit that it is likely to be replaced by a comparable, if somewhat weaker, piece of legislation.[11]

The European Convention on Human Rights, which is given domestic effect by the 1998 Act, is a product of the Council of Europe, a regional intergovernmental organisation whose aim is 'to achieve a greater unity between its members for the purpose of safeguarding and realising the ideals and principles which are their common heritage and facilitating their economic and social progress', to which end its members commit to acceptance of the principles of the rule of law and to accord enjoyment to persons of human rights and fundamental freedoms.[12] The better-known European regional organisation is, of course, the European Union (EU). This source of public health law warrants special consideration, even though much of that law might also be described as 'public' in that it concerns relations

---

8   It should be noted that there are some variations in the principles, processes, and institutions of administrative law in the three legal systems operating in England and Wales, Scotland, and Northern Ireland.

9   See Carol Harlow and Richard Rawlings, *Pressure Through Law* (Abingdon: Routledge 1992).

10 As illustrations of the activities of such institutions and processes that are at least somewhat germane to the public health arena, see e.g. the Diffuse Mesothelioma Payment Scheme Regulations 2014, SI 2014/916, reg. 25 (right of appeal to First-Tier Tribunal where unsuccessful application for compensation has been reviewed and applicant remains unsatisfied); Parliamentary and Health Service Ombudsman, *Dying without Dignity* (London: The Stationery Office 2015); *The BSE Inquiry* (London: The Stationery Office 2000).

11 See Conservative Party, *Protecting Human Rights in the UK* (London: Conservative Party 2014).

12 Statute of the Council of Europe, ETS 1 (1949), Articles 1 and 3.

between governmental institutions (both within the Union and between the Union and Member States) and between such institutions and citizens, as well as the legal regulation of activities of public interest.[13] It is discussed in the next chapter of this book.[14]

7.1.2 Functions of public law

Since public law is fundamentally concerned with the exercise of power by governmental institutions – both in relation to other such institutions and to the individual – it possesses a profoundly political character: indeed, it has been said that 'public law is simply a sophisticated form of political discourse'.[15] Accordingly, we may identify certain distinct roles performed by legal norms, processes, and institutions in this context, which are reflective of differing perspectives on the appropriate role for the state within society. As public health is also a profoundly political activity,[16] an awareness of these approaches is vital to development of a proper understanding of the nature and function of public health law.

Broadly speaking, we may discern two main perspectives on the role of public law from the academic literature. By far the dominant strand conceives of the role of law primarily as a means of controlling the activities of government, with a view to preserving a sphere of individual autonomy undisturbed from state 'intervention'. Such a view is thus premised upon a minimal role for the state: government should be kept within its bounds or, as one standard textbook on English administrative law somewhat portentously phrases matters, 'the powerful engines of authority must be prevented from running amok'.[17] Law (and in this instance, the focus lies largely upon law as articulated by courts rather than other mechanisms of adjudication or scrutiny) operates as an external checking mechanism – seeking, fundamentally, to ensure the *accountability* of government – and provides a 'retrospective form of redress for those who are harmed by actions or decisions that exceed the legal authority that a particular institution has been allocated'.[18] The emphasis of this approach is well captured by the 'red light' traffic light metaphor adopted by Carol Harlow and Rick Rawlings.[19]

The alternative tradition, which Harlow and Rawlings christen the 'green light' view,[20] regards law (here, understood more broadly to comprise a variety of mechanisms, both judicial and non-judicial) as complementary to, rather than antagonistic towards, the work of government. Proponents of this approach point to 'a new relationship between the courts and those who derive their authority from the public law, one of a partnership based on a common aim, namely the maintenance of the highest standards of public administration'.[21] Thus, law facilitates good government, operating instrumentally (and, preferably, prospectively)

---

13 See Patrick Birkinshaw, *European Public Law* (London: Butterworths 2003).
14 It should be noted that, while the EU is not primarily a human rights organisation, its engagement with human rights norms has increased significantly over time. Rights guaranteed by the European Convention on Human Rights are stated to constitute general principles of EU law under Article 6(3) of the Treaty on European Union (TEU), and the Treaty also provides for the EU to accede to the Convention: Article 6(2) TEU. Additionally, the Union has its own Charter of Fundamental Rights and Freedoms, drawn up at the turn of the twenty-first century, which now has the same legal value as other EU Treaty provisions: Article 6(1) TEU. The latter is considered briefly in Chapter 8; Convention law, which is given domestic legal effect in the UK by the Human Rights Act 1998, is addressed in this chapter.
15 Loughlin (n 5), 4.
16 See e.g. John Coggon, *What Makes Health Public? A Critical Evaluation of Moral, Legal and Political Claims in Public Health* (Cambridge: Cambridge University Press 2012) 48–61; Daniel Goldberg, 'Against the Very Idea of the Politicization of Public Health Policy' (2012) 102 *American Journal of Public Health* 44.
17 William Wade and Christopher Forsyth, *Administrative Law* (11th edn., Oxford: Oxford University Press 2014) 4.
18 Syrett (n 6), 5.
19 Carol Harlow and Richard Rawlings, *Law and Administration* (3rd edn., Cambridge: Cambridge University Press, 2009) 1.
20 ibid.
21 *R v Lancashire County Council, ex parte Huddleston* [1986] 2 All ER 941, 945 (Sir John Donaldson MR).

as a tool that assists decision-makers in discharging their functions in a manner that is conducive to the interests of the community that they serve. This perspective clearly takes a much more positive standpoint on the role of the state in modern society, consonant with a broadly social democratic position, although it does not necessarily entail outright refutation of the value of individual autonomy.

While these two approaches possess considerable explanatory value as accounts of the work that law might do, the practice of public law, perhaps unsurprisingly, is more nuanced than the theory. This is reflected in the process through which an application for judicial review of administrative action (such as that brought by the Rampton smokers, discussed in Chapter 5) is brought in England and Wales. The process contains both 'green light' elements designed to afford a degree of protection to governmental bodies seeking to work in the public interest (such as a short time limit for lodging the application and a preliminary filtering stage designed to weed out unmeritorious claims) and 'red light' components that assist in ensuring that unlawful actions do not go unchecked (in particular, a generous approach to the question of who has 'standing' to challenge a public body). At risk of belabouring the 'traffic light' metaphor, much of the practice of contemporary public law might therefore best be described as 'amber light' in character. Tomkins summarises this approach as premised upon the belief 'that the state can successfully be limited by law, although that law ought properly to allow for the administration to enjoy a degree – albeit a controlled degree – of discretionary authority',[22] and notes that 'the goal of this project is to safeguard a particular vision of human rights'.[23]

7.1.3 Structure of this chapter

The remainder of this chapter considers public law in its various forms – constitutional law, administrative law, and human rights law – and the differing approaches taken to its function in the public health context. As with other chapters of this book, the intention is not to present an exhaustive account of all instances in which norms or standards derived from public law impact upon public health, but rather to illustrate to the reader that knowledge of public law can significantly enhance our understanding of how law operates to serve and constrain public health aims and agendas.

7.2 Constitutional and administrative law and public health

7.2.1 Case study 1: 'Capacity-building': functions, institutions, accountability, and mission

As explained in the opening section of this chapter, a central function of public law is to establish institutions of government and to confer powers and duties upon them. In Magnusson's terms,[24] we might view this as the 'capacity-building' aspect of law: the creation of agencies to pursue public health goals, the allocation of authority, and the establishment of mandates. This role is well illustrated by the statute that set outs the organisational structure of the NHS

---

22 Adam Tomkins, 'In Defence of the Political Constitution' (2002) 22 *Oxford Journal of Legal Studies* 157, 160.
23 ibid.
24 Roger Magnusson, 'Mapping the Scope and Opportunities for Public Health Law in Liberal Democracies' (2007) 35 *Journal of Law, Medicine and Ethics* 571, 576. See further: Chapter 3.

in England, the National Health Service Act 2006, particularly in light of its very substantial amendment by the Health and Social Care Act 2012, which engaged with public health in a much more thoroughgoing manner than previous legislation relating to the NHS.[25]

Section 2A of the 2006 Act imposes a duty upon the Secretary of State for Health to 'take such steps as [s/he] considers appropriate for the purpose of protecting the public in England from disease or other dangers to health',[26] while Section 2B imposes duties upon a local authority and the Secretary of State to 'take such steps as [it or s/he] considers appropriate for improving the health of', respectively, 'the people in its area' and 'the people of England'.[27] The section therefore allocates public health responsibility to both central and local government, but divides it such that *health protection* functions fall to the minister,[28] while *health promotion* functions fall to both. The legislation further specifies certain measures that may be taken in fulfilment of both duties, although the lists are not intended to be exhaustive: thus, protection may be achieved through conduct of research; provision of microbiological services; provision of vaccination, immunisation, and screening services; provision of information and advice, etc.[29] Similarly, promotion may be accomplished by means of provision of information and advice, provision of 'services or facilities designed to promote healthy living (whether by helping individuals to address behaviour that is detrimental to health or in any other way)',[30] provision of financial incentives to encourage adoption of healthier lifestyles, etc.[31] It should be noted that, while the protection and promotion functions are expressed in mandatory language as duties ('must take such steps'), considerable discretion is vested in central and local government as to the extent and manner in which the obligations are discharged ('such steps as . . . considers appropriate'). The permissive manner in which the duties are phrased is likely to render them relatively immune from challenge in court;[32] hence, arguments that insufficient attention is being accorded to discharge of public health functions under the Act appear more likely to be successfully articulated in political forums (see further: Chapter 9).

In addition to setting out public health functions, legislation also allocates those functions to specified individuals or bodies. In this respect, the picture is somewhat more complicated than the preceding outline would suggest. The Act provides scope for the Secretary of State to delegate health protection and promotion functions to other bodies (the NHS Commissioning Board, Clinical Commissioning Groups, and local authorities).[33] In practice, those functions that are not delegated to others are exercised by an executive agency of the Department of Health, Public Health England, which carries them out on the minister's behalf.[34] The Act also makes provision for appointment of Directors of Public Health as lead

25 This is a reflection of the Conservative–Liberal Democrat Coalition Government's professed ambition to 'create a public health service, not just a national sickness service': HM Government, *Healthy Lives, Healthy People: Our Strategy for Public Health in England* (CM 7985 2010) [1.5]. See further the discussion in Chapter 3 above, n.79 and accompanying text.

26 Inserted by Health and Social Care Act 2012, s. 11.

27 ibid, s. 12.

28 But note that 'the Government sees local authorities having a critical role at the local level in ensuring that all relevant organisations are putting plans in place to protect the population against the range of threats and hazards': Department of Health, *The New Public Health Role of Local Government* (London: Department of Health 2012) 5. This is expressed to 'link to, but be different from' the statutory role in respect of planning for public health emergencies, for which see below, nn.88–92 and accompanying text. On the distinction between promotion and protection and division of responsibilities, see *National Aids Trust v National Health Service Commissioning Board* [2016] EWHC 2005 (Admin).

29 National Health Service Act, s. 2A(2), inserted by Health and Social Care Act 2012, s. 11.

30 For example, establishment of smoking cessation clinics.

31 National Health Service Act, s. 2B(3), inserted by Health and Social Care Act 2012, s. 11.

32 See the discussion in section 7.2.2 below, especially n.62 and accompanying text.

33 National Health Service Act 2006, s. 7A, inserted by Health and Social Care Act 2012, s. 22.

34 See Department of Health/Public Health England, *Framework Agreement between the Department of Health and Public Health England* (London: Public Health England 2013).

officers for the public health functions allocated to local government; this appointment is made jointly by the Secretary of State and local councils, and the appointee is an employee of the local authority.[35] Government has stated that Directors 'will need to have specialist public health expertise, and access to specialist resources, spanning the three domains of public health, health improvement, health protection, and health care public health (i.e. the population health aspects of NHS-funded clinical services)'.[36]

A 'capacity-building' role for public law may extend beyond mere allocation of tasks to specified individuals and institutions, to encompass facilitation of a particular manner of carrying out those tasks. Notable in this regard is the establishment in every upper-tier local authority of a Health and Wellbeing Board, whose membership is specified to include the Director of Public Health.[37] As observed in Chapter 3, this development appears to fit within a 'New Public Health' paradigm, insofar as it offers an institutional means of pursuing an integrative approach to addressing public health issues, which spans various areas of government and engages with civil society. To this end, the Board's membership may consist of 'such other persons, or representatives of such other persons, as the local authority thinks appropriate' (which might include, for example, representatives of voluntary organisations).[38] More directly, section 195 of the 2012 Act imposes a duty upon the Board to encourage integrated working, including with those who arrange for the provision of 'services that may have an effect on the health of individuals but are not health services'.[39] Furthermore, the Board is responsible for production of Joint Strategic Needs Assessments and Joint Health and Wellbeing Strategies under section 116 of the Local Government and Public Involvement in Health Act 2007;[40] these are, respectively, assessments of the current and future health and social care needs of the local community and strategies for meeting those needs. Statutory guidance on this process notes that 'the policy intention is for Health and Wellbeing Boards to also consider wider factors that impact on their communities' health and wellbeing, and local assets that can help to improve outcomes and reduce inequalities';[41] the Government has added that it expects Directors of Public Health who are engaged in this activity to 'ensure a rigorous focus on local priorities and action across the life course to ensure a preventive approach is embedded in the local system'.[42]

Consistently with public law's function in ensuring that public institutions and officials are accountable for their actions and decisions, the legislation also provides mechanisms for the monitoring and control of the discharge of public health functions by local authorities. Thus, sections 73B(5) and (6) of the National Health Service Act 2006 respectively require the Director of Public Health to prepare, and the local authority to publish, an annual report,[43] while sections 73A(3) and (4) enable the Secretary of State to direct the local authority to review the discharge of responsibilities by the Director, to investigate failures in that regard, and to take steps specified in the Direction[44] – however, only the local authority can dismiss the Director (following consultation with the Secretary of State).[45] A further

---

35 National Health Service Act 2006, s. 73A, inserted by Health and Social Care Act 2012, s. 30.
36 Department of Health (n 28), 4.
37 Health and Social Care Act 2012, s. 194(2)(d).
38 ibid, s. 194(2)(g).
39 ibid, ss. 195(4), (6).
40 As inserted by Health and Social Care Act 2012, ss. 192–193.
41 Department of Health, *Statutory Guidance on Joint Strategic Needs Assessments and Joint Health and Wellbeing Strategies* (London: Department of Health 2013) [3.2].
42 Department of Health (n 28), 2.
43 Inserted by Health and Social Care Act 2012, s. 31.
44 ibid, s. 30.
45 National Health Service Act 2006, ss. 73A(5), (6), inserted by Health and Social Care Act 2012, s. 30.

accountability mechanism is provided in section 73C, which enables the Secretary of State to make Regulations to establish procedures for dealing with complaints about the exercise of public health functions by local authorities.[46]

The preceding discussion has centred upon conferral of power to individuals or institutions that then undertake functions connected to public health. As a matter of constitutional law, this may be understood as Parliament authorising the executive (notably, the Secretary of State, who then further delegates power, and local authorities) to act in this field, albeit that this picture is complicated by the fact that much of the detail of the primary legislation is fleshed out by further legislation that is classified as secondary (such as Regulations) or tertiary (such as Directions and statutory guidance) in character,[47] made in each case by the executive branch.

However, conferral of legal authority within the British constitution also now occurs between the UK legislature – Westminster – and the legislative bodies in Scotland, Wales, and Northern Ireland, following the devolution legislation enacted initially in 1998.[48] Each of these bodies has legislative powers in respect of health, including public health, subject to certain reservations, and as noted in Chapter 3,[49] each of the national legislative assemblies has acted in this area.[50] There is growing disparity between the approaches taken in the constituent parts of the United Kingdom, a matter that warrants a degree of further investigation and analysis that cannot be attempted in a book of this length or scope.

Nonetheless, one aspect of the devolved legislation is worthy of brief consideration here for the additional light that it casts upon the 'capacity-building' role performed by public law. The Well-being of Future Generations (Wales) Act 2015 (which, as previously noted, takes a broad approach to the concept of wellbeing, extending significantly beyond health to encompass matters such as prosperity, equality and vibrancy of culture) contains a set of goals in section 4, which include 'a healthier Wales', described as 'a society in which people's physical and mental well-being is maximised and in which choices and behaviours that benefit future health are understood'. These goals have a particular function insofar as public bodies are placed under a duty to set, to publish, and to take reasonable steps to meet objectives that will contribute to their achievement;[51] there will be measurement of performance in this regard through publication of indicators and annual reporting.[52] More broadly, the goals 'collectively, express a vision for the long-term economic, environmental, social and cultural well-being of Wales'.[53] Here, therefore, may be seen the function of public law in establishing a mission (or more accurately, in the case of the 2015 Act, missions) for the state, something that Gostin considers to be a vital component of any modern public health statute.[54] As he notes, such provisions have political, as well as legal, impact; they are likely to inform the terms of debate within political institutions and civil society and to provide

46 Inserted by Health and Social Care Act 2012, s. 32. See the NHS Bodies and Local Authorities (Partnership Arrangements, Care Trusts, Public Health and Local Healthwatch) Regulations 2012, SI 2012/3054, Part 5.
47 For the distinction between secondary and tertiary legislation, see James Holland and Julian Webb, *Learning Legal Rules: A Students' Guide to Legal Method and Reasoning* (8th edn., Oxford: Oxford University Press 2013) 11–13.
48 Northern Ireland Act 1998, Scotland Act 1998, Government of Wales Act 1998.
49 See Chapter 3 above, nn.123–127 and accompanying text.
50 In the case of Northern Ireland, legislative activity on public health has to date been minimal, but see now Department of Health, Social Services and Public Safety, *Review of the Public Health (Northern Ireland) Act 1967: Final Report* (Belfast: DHSSPS 2016).
51 s. 3.
52 ss. 10–13.
53 Explanatory Notes to the Well-being of Future Generations (Wales) Act 2015, [19].
54 Lawrence Gostin, *Public Health Law: Power, Duty, Restraint* (2nd edn., Berkeley: University of California Press 2008) 25.

justification for decisions and actions taken, in addition to structuring the legal duties that are imposed upon public bodies.

7.2.2 Case study 2: Public law as a framework for the allocation of resources

It is a fundamental principle of constitutional law, articulated in Article 4 of the Bill of Rights 1689, that government must seek authorisation for the raising of resources from Parliament. This is done through the annual Finance Acts, which set out taxes, excise duties, exemptions, and reliefs; these are preceded by a Budget statement given by the Chancellor of the Exchequer, which sets out the fiscal proposals that are subsequently given legislative form. While such legislation is clearly not oriented primarily at public health, it may nonetheless contain measures that seek to address public health objectives. Most notably, excise duties are charged on purchase of tobacco products and alcoholic liquors; the 2016 Budget statement also saw the announcement of a 'sugar tax', to be levied on soft drinks manufacturers from 2018.

Monitoring and control of government expenditure is also a key function of the legislature, although one that is often regarded as inadequately performed.[55] In practice, decisions on how much money should be allocated to government departments (such as the Department of Health) and, within those departments, to particular areas of activity (such as public health) are political decisions taken by ministers, with the Chancellor of the Exchequer being the key actor.[56] While constitutional lawyers will be alert to the need to analyse and critique the processes that exist for holding choices on expenditure to account, such decisions will, in practice, be immune to challenge through the administrative law process of judicial review: they will be regarded by courts as falling within the 'macro-political field'[57] in that they involve 'questions of general policy affecting the public at large or a significant section of it (including interests not represented before the court)'.[58] Courts will refuse to intervene because to do so would entail 'donning the garb of policy-maker, which they cannot wear'[59] – that is, it would be a violation of the principle of the separation of powers.

Challenge by way of judicial review would appear to be much more plausible at a 'meso-level' of resource allocation, where decisions on which public health services are funded, and to what extent, are taken. For example, a court might be asked to adjudicate upon the lawfulness of decisions such as those to cease or reduce funding for a form of screening, for smoking cessation clinics, or for public health educational or informational activities. Here, it is important to note that, were a challenge of this type to succeed, the outcome will not necessarily be reinstatement of funding. Judicial review is not an appeal process, and courts are not empowered to substitute their view of the 'correct' decision for that of the original decision-maker. Rather, the decision is remitted to the decision-maker, which may reach the same conclusion again, although, in so doing, it must act in accordance with the law (including, but not restricted to, any norms and principles articulated by the

---

55 See Syrett (n 6), 86.
56 See e.g. HM Treasury, *Spending Review and Autumn Statement 2015* (Cm 9162 2015).
57 *R v Secretary of State for Education and Employment, ex parte Begbie* [1999] EWCA Civ 2100, [82] (Laws LJ).
58 ibid, [80].
59 ibid.

court in the original hearing).[60] Nonetheless, the mere threat of judicial review may often suffice to persuade a public body to reverse its original decision.[61]

There is, in fact, limited legal precedent in this field. Almost all cases in which allocation of resources for health is the subject of adjudication concern *health care*, as distinct from population health interventions; put differently, challenges are to the 'micro-level' decision of *whether a particular patient is entitled to access a specific treatment or service*.[62] Of course, such litigation has implications for the health of populations, not least because, given finite resources, allocation of funds for a particular treatment or service gives rise to opportunity costs elsewhere in the community for which the decision-maker has responsibility. Nonetheless, the focus of judicial consideration lies with individual and curative, rather than collective and preventive, health measures. One might surmise that the paucity of case law concerning funding for public health is a reflection of its historical subservience to medicine in the UK, at least since the founding of the NHS, coupled with a (surely accurate) perception that 'public health law and policy is inescapably political and politicised'[63] and, as such, not amenable to adjudication.

However, from a consideration of analogous situations, we may make some predictions as to the manner in which the courts might proceed if called upon to adjudicate upon in the types of scenario outlined above. One possible response would be to regard such matters as, in essence, *non-justiciable*, that is, inappropriate for resolution in court, with the consequence that there will be judicial refusal to intervene in the choice made by the allocative decision-maker. Authority for this approach can be derived from the earlier cases on allocation of health care resources and, especially, R v Secretary of State for Social Services, ex p Hincks,[64] which concerned a refusal to fund *services for a community* (in this case, orthopaedic facilities at a hospital) as distinct from a particular treatment for an individual patient. Lord Denning MR held that the duty to provide hospital accommodation and medical services under section 3 of the National Health Service Act 1977 was not absolute but was subject to availability of resources. On this reading, he was not prepared to call into question whether the Secretary of State was 'doing the best he can with the financial resources available to him'. Bridge LJ expressed sympathy for the applicants who had had to wait for surgery but concluded that he: 'hope[d] that they have not been encouraged to think that these proceedings offered any real prospects that this court could enhance the standards of the National Health Service, because any such encouragement would be based upon manifest illusion'.

The case law on health care resource allocation has developed significantly since this case was decided in 1980 and courts are now considerably more willing to scrutinise decisions and to declare them unlawful, especially for failure to comply with procedural standards such as provision of reasons for decisions and provision for consideration of exceptional cases.[65] A line of authority that may be apposite to the funding of public health is that which considers the lawfulness of processes for consultation in relation to reorganisation of public services, including those in health. In certain instances, such decisions have been held to be

60 See Syrett (n 6), 186–187.
61 See Harlow and Rawlings (n 9).
62 For discussion of these cases, see Judith Laing and Jean McHale (eds), *Principles of Medical Law* (4th edn., Oxford: Oxford University Press 2017), chapter 7; Christopher Newdick, *Who Should We Treat?* (2nd edn., Oxford: Oxford University Press 2005), chapter 5.
63 Goldberg (n 16), 46.
64 [1980] 1 BMLR 93.
65 See Laing and McHale (eds) (n 62); Newdick (n 62).

unlawful,[66] although the outcome will turn upon the precise nature of the statutory provision in question (if one exists)[67] and upon the steps taken by the public body during the consultation process.[68] A further possibility is that withdrawal or restriction of funding for public health services might amount to a breach of public sector duties under equalities legislation, especially those arising under the Equalities Act 2010. Here, too, much will depend upon the particular facts, especially the rigour with which the public body approaches the assessment of the impact of its decision.[69]

Given the context-specific nature of these cases, it is, therefore, difficult to draw generalisable conclusions as to the manner in which public law will operate in this context. However, it is certainly plausible to envisage that courts will carefully scrutinise the process by which decisions on funding of public health services and interventions are reached in order to ensure that there is compliance with standards of 'good administration' in the manner that a 'green light' approach to public law would prescribe.

7.2.3 Case study 3: Communicable disease legislation: 'red', 'green', and 'amber' light approaches to public law

Analysis of the legislation currently governing control of communicable disease in England and Wales – both as it was initially drafted and in its subsequent amended form – enables us to discern differing approaches to the role of public law, as outlined in section 7.1.2. The original Public Health (Control of Disease) Act 1984 can be considered to fit within a 'red light' paradigm. The powers that it confers and the duties that it imposes are highly specific – indeed, they have been described as 'inflexible'[70] – and contain a number of safeguards to guard against the abuse of power. For example, an order made under section 16, which enables a local authority to direct that diseases additional to the limited range specified in the Act or in regulations made thereunder[71] shall be 'notifiable diseases' (thereby triggering application of the remaining provisions of the Act), requires approval by the Secretary of State for Health, must be advertised 'in a local newspaper circulating in the district and in such other manner as [the local authority] think[s] sufficient for informing persons interested', must be sent to 'each registered medical practitioner who after due inquiry is ascertained to be practising in [the] district', and cannot come into operation until at least a week has elapsed after the advertisement.[72] Similar specificity is evident in secondary legislation made under the Act: thus, the Public Health (Infectious Diseases) Regulations 1988 contain a measure obliging local authorities or port health authorities to report to the Chief Medical Officer instances where they 'have reason to believe that rats in their district or port health

---

66 See e.g. *Smith v North Eastern Derbyshire Primary Care Trust* [2006] EWCA Civ 1291; *R (on the application of Morris) v Trafford Health Care NHS Trust* [2006] EWHC 2334 (Admin).

67 Even where there is no statutory requirement to consult, common law nonetheless establishes certain minimum standards of fairness, breach of which may give rise to a finding of unlawfulness: see *R (on the application of Coughlan) v North & East Devon Health Authority* [1999] EWCA Civ 1871, [108] (Lord Woolf MR).

68 Thus, compare to the cases cited in n.66 above, *R (on the application of F) v Healthy Futures Joint Committee of Primary Care Trusts* [2007] EWHC 1611 (Admin); *R (on the application of Fudge) v South West Strategic Health Authority* [2007] EWCA Civ 803.

69 See e.g. *R (on the application of Green) v Gloucestershire County Council* [2011] EWHC 2687 (Admin) (closure of libraries).

70 Robyn Martin, 'The Limits of Law in the Protection of Public Health and the Role of Public Health Ethics' (2006) 120 (Supplement 1) *Public Health* 71, 74.

71 See ss. 10, 13, respectively.

72 ss. 16(2), (3). Where the local authority considers the situation to be an emergency, it may make an order without prior approval by the Secretary of State, but in this instance, a copy of the order must be transmitted to the Secretary of State immediately, and it lapses after a maximum of one month unless the Secretary of State has approved it in advance; ss. 16(4), (5).

district are threatened by or infected with plague, or are dying in unusual numbers' and, in such cases, to 'take measures for destroying all rats in the district or port health district and for preventing rats from gaining entry to buildings'.[73]

The narrowness of these provisions is reflective of the Victorian origins of the legislative framework relating to communicable disease.[74] They are framed as focussed powers and duties that afford little scope for flexibility or discretion to public authorities (such as local government bodies) in the manner in which they are exercised. Furthermore, they are supplemented by a range of equally specific measures whose objective is to control the spread of disease through criminal sanctions that may be visited upon particular individuals such as those having care of children;[75] letting premises;[76] owning, driving, or conducting public conveyances;[77] keeping lodging houses;[78] or taking part in wakes.[79] The Act may therefore be characterised as a form of 'command and control' regulation, a mode in which the state yields authoritative power, often of a criminal law character (see further: Chapter 6), in order to achieve specified goals: 'the force of law is used to prohibit certain forms of conduct [and] to demand some positive actions'.[80]

This is entirely in line with the dominant understanding of public law that itself emanates from the Victorian era and which is most famously articulated in the work of Albert Venn Dicey.[81] Dicey's model of the rule of law, in which the 'red light' approach described above is rooted, expresses preference for rules over discretion and seeks (albeit in a somewhat implicit manner) to minimise governmental intervention so as to maximise individual autonomy. The measures set out in the 1984 Act are justifiable – even on Dicey's liberal, individualist conception of state and society – as means to limit harm to others, but the powers conferred are confined as narrowly as possible and are subject to safeguards so as to prevent their abuse by public bodies whose activities ought (on a Diceyan reading) to be regarded with suspicion by the law. This serves, wherever possible, to preserve individual freedoms against the state. That said, and as will be noted in the next section of this chapter, certain of the measures do appear to infringe individual liberties in a manner that might have caused Dicey some alarm. For example, while there is no power to compulsorily treat someone suffering from one of the diseases specified as notifiable under the Act and its associated Regulations, the Act sets out no time limits for detention in cases where a person has been removed to hospital to prevent the spread of disease and where no suitable alternative accommodation (i.e. that in which adequate precautions can be taken to prevent further spreading of disease) would be available in the event of departure from hospital.[82]

As noted in Chapter 3, the 1984 Act was substantially amended by Part 3 of the Health and Social Care Act 2008, primarily to bring English law in line with the International Health Regulations of 2005 (discussed in the next chapter). Here, we can detect a move away from a 'red light' model towards a more facilitative function for law. In effect, the statute provides a 'toolkit' of powers to enable the state to address the threats presented by communicable

---

73 SI 1988/1546, reg. 11.
74 See further the discussion in Chapter 3 above, n. 95–101 and accompanying text.
75 Public Health (Control of Disease) Act 1984, s. 21.
76 ibid, s. 29.
77 ibid, s. 34.
78 ibid, s. 39.
79 ibid, s. 45.
80 Robert Baldwin, Martin Cave and Martin Lodge, *Understanding Regulation: Theory, Strategy and Practice* (2nd edn., Oxford: Oxford University Press 2012) 106.
81 Originally published 1885: see now Albert Venn Dicey, *The Law of the Constitution* (John Allison (ed), Oxford: Oxford University Press 2013). For an introduction to Dicey's conception of the rule of law, see Syrett (n 6), 40–49.
82 Public Health (Control of Disease) Act 1984, s. 38(2).

disease in whichever manner it considers is likely to be most effective. It does so in two respects.

First, in line with the 'all hazards' approach prescribed by the 2005 Regulations, the statute does not restrict the powers that are exercisable under it to specified diseases; instead, they are available much more flexibly to enable the state to respond to any 'infection or contamination which presents or could present a significant harm to human health'.[83] Second, the powers themselves are much more liberally worded than those contained in the previous legislation. For example, a Minister has broad powers to make Regulations[84] 'for the purpose of preventing, protecting against, controlling or providing a public health response to the incidence or spread of infection or contamination in England and Wales (whether from risks originating there or elsewhere)', both in respect of a particular form of infection or contamination or generally and 'so as to make provision of a general nature, to make contingent provision or to make specific provision in response to a particular set of circumstances'.[85] Such 'health protection regulations' may operate in a number of ways, including conferral of functions on local authorities and other persons; creation of offences; permission or prohibition of the levy of charges; and permission or requirement of the payment of incentive payments, compensation, and expenses – it is notable here that a wider range of interventions is envisaged than the imposition of criminal sanctions. Broad powers are also conferred upon magistrates to order measures in relation to persons, things, or premises:[86] the statute provides that orders so made shall relate to a range of specific restrictions or requirements (such as quarantining, disinfection or decontamination, health monitoring, and restrictions on travel or contact), but it also confers supplementary powers upon magistrates to order 'such other restrictions or requirements as [s/he] considers necessary for the purpose of reducing or removing the risk in question'.[87]

The breadth of the powers conferred by the 2008 Act would be a matter of concern for those advocating a 'red light' approach to the function of public law. From such a perspective, it might be argued that they are open to abuse by state authorities – especially that they might be used in a manner that amounts to an unjustifiable infringement of individual autonomy. To guard against the latter possibility, there are certain 'amber light' protections contained within the legislation that are intended to ensure compatibility with principles of human rights. Thus – and in contrast to the position under the previous legislation – a magistrate's order, which requires detention in hospital, isolation, or quarantine, can last only for 28 days.[88] In addition, restrictions or requirements contained in 'health protection regulations', and decisions to impose such restrictions or requirements, are only lawful where they are 'proportionate to what is sought to be achieved' in response to a threat to public health.[89] This provision effects a balancing between what is needed in the interests of population health and the autonomy of individuals in a manner that is characteristic of human rights law, as the next section of this chapter will discuss (see also Chapter 2).

---

83 Health and Social Care Act 2008, s. 129, inserting s. 45A into Public Health (Control of Disease) Act 1984.
84 Secondary legislation of this sort is often viewed with concern (especially by adherents to a more 'red light' perspective) because it confers powers upon the executive to make legislation with minimal parliamentary scrutiny. In this instance, with certain exceptions, the Regulations are subject only to the 'negative resolution' procedure, i.e. they will come into effect unless Parliament (or the National Assembly of Wales) passes a resolution to annul them: see ibid, s. 129, inserting s.45Q into Public Health (Control of Disease) Act 1984. For a brief outline of this form of legislation, see Syrett (n 6), 85.
85 Health and Social Care Act 2008, s. 129, inserting ss. 45C(i) and (ii) into Public Health (Control of Disease) Act 1984.
86 ibid, s. 129, inserting ss. 45G, H and I into Public Health (Control of Disease) Act 1984.
87 ibid, s. 129, inserting s. 45K(2) into Public Health (Control of Disease) Act 1984.
88 ibid, s. 129, inserting s. 45L(3) into Public Health (Control of Disease) Act 1984.
89 ibid, s. 129, inserting ss. 45D(1), (2) into Public Health (Control of Disease) Act 1984.

While not solely concerned with communicable disease – or, indeed, with public health – a further piece of legislation is worthy of brief consideration here, as an additional illustration of the more flexible, facilitative legal framework that now governs public health in the twenty-first century. The Civil Contingencies Act 2004 imposes duties upon local bodies to assess the risk of an 'emergency' occurring and to maintain plans for responding to such emergencies, with further duties of cooperation and provision of information placed upon other bodies.[90] It also confers powers on government to make regulations to respond to emergencies and contains certain safeguards in respect of their use.[91] 'Emergency' is defined broadly by the Act[92] but would clearly include a pandemic or epidemic or chemical contamination. The NHS, which is a 'Category 1 responder' under the Act,[93] uses the term 'major incident' in this context and defines this as 'any occurrence that presents serious threat to the health of the community or causes such numbers or types of casualties, as to require special arrangements to be implemented'.[94]

7.3 Human rights law and public health

7.3.1 Case study 4: Negative obligations – public health measures as restrictions on rights

Discussions in earlier parts of this book – particularly in Chapter 2 – have made clear that there is a fundamental tension at the heart of public health, between individual autonomy and collective responsibility. As Gostin puts it:

> Public health regulation is designed to monitor health threats and intervene to reduce risk or ameliorate harm within the population. At the same time, public health powers encroach on fundamental civil liberties such as privacy, bodily integrity, and freedom of movement, association, or religion.[95]

This is very familiar territory for those working within the subcategory of public law that concerns human rights. Indeed, it speaks to a central question in rights analysis and jurisprudence – the traditional classification of rights as either negative (rights that 'are fulfilled when all members of a community exercise restraint from doing anything that might violate the freedom of others')[96] or positive (those that 'require others to provide the material means of life to those unable to provide for themselves').[97] The civil and political rights enumerated by Gostin fall squarely within the first category, and it is rights of this type that have traditionally enjoyed by far the greatest level of protection within legal systems, particularly in Western democracies: that is, there has been a dominant 'liberal consensus on human rights . . . which has succeeded in establishing the language of civil and political rights as the

---

90 Part 1 of the Act.
91 Part 2 of the Act.
92 See ss. 1, 19.
93 See Schedule 1.
94 NHS England, *NHS England Emergency Preparedness, Resilience and Response Framework* (Leeds: NHS England 2013) [6.5.3].
95 Gostin (n 54), 43. See also Krebs: 'the central ethical dilemma, therefore, in public health, is to balance respect for individual freedom and liberty with the responsibility of governments to provide their citizens with some degree of protection in relation to health': John Krebs, 'The Importance of Public Health Ethics' (2008) 86 *Bulletin of the World Health Organization* 579, 579.
96 Tony Evans, 'A Human Right to Health?' (2002) 75 *Third World Quarterly* 197, 200.
97 ibid.

acceptable voice . . . of human rights talk'.[98] The hegemonic status enjoyed by such rights, underpinned by familiar and potent ethical propositions such as Mill's 'harm principle', is such that any measure that might interfere with their enjoyment presumptively constitutes an unacceptable – in many cases, an unlawful – act, such that rights of this nature appear to function as 'trumps', both legally and discursively.[99] By contrast, positive (social, economic, and cultural) rights – which include a right to health, though much less clearly a right to *public health*[100] – 'may conflict with negative freedoms, particularly those associated with economic activity including free market practices and the freedom to own and dispose of property'.[101] This is because realisation of such rights, which 'are often more likely to entail the expenditure of resources than efforts to assure civil and political rights',[102] is likely to necessitate an 'attempt to impose a duty on the wealthy to fulfil them',[103] albeit indirectly, for example, through redistributive taxation policies that might fund social welfare programmes in housing, health, or education.

However, it is important to note that human rights law seeks (albeit, not always successfully) to *manage* the tension between autonomy and collective responsibility rather than operating in such a manner that the former will inevitably hold sway: for this reason, the claim that rights act as 'trumps over some background justification that states a goal for the community as a whole' is apt to be somewhat misleading.[104] Rather, it might more accurately be stated that 'rights trump a collective goal that lacks sufficient justification'.[105] This formulation draws our attention to the fact that rights adjudication imposes a *justificatory obligation* upon the party whose actions constitute an interference with an individual's autonomy.

This approach to public law differs in an important respect from that described in the preceding section, especially that of a 'command and control' character. There, 'the legitimacy and legality of governmental action is derived from the fact that the actor is authorised to act. Thus, public law, under this conception, focuses on delimiting the borders of public action and on ensuring that decisions are made by those authorised to make them'.[106] By contrast, in rights adjudication, a 'claim to legitimate authority is plausible only if the law [or decision, policy or action] is demonstrably justifiable to those burdened by it in terms that free and equals can accept'.[107] Under this approach, the role of law is to function as a framework for scrutiny of the justifications that have been advanced for a decision or action and to establish that these are intended to pursue objectives, and are grounded in values, which command broad acceptance within the political community (even if the affected individual does not accept that they should have been invoked in his/her particular case). This enables a comparison to be drawn between the importance of the (collective) goals pursued by

98 ibid, 201.
99 See Ronald Dworkin, 'Rights as Trumps' in Jeremy Waldron (ed), *Theories of Rights* (New York: Oxford University Press 1985) 153–167.
100 Aoife Nolan, *Children's Socio-Economic Rights, Democracy and the Courts* (Oxford: Hart Publishing 2011) 31.
101 Evans (n 96), 200.
102 This right is stated in Article 5(e)(iv) of the International Convention on the Elimination of all Forms of Racial Discrimination (1965), but the right to health specified in Article 12 of the International Covenant on Economic, Social and Cultural Rights (1966) refers instead to public health measures as being 'steps to be taken . . . to achieve the full realisation of the right', as distinct from public health being a right in itself.
103 Evans (n 96), 200.
104 Dworkin (n 99). For critical analysis of the 'trumps' metaphor as deployed by Dworkin, see Paul Yowell, 'A Critical Examination of Dworkin's Theory of Rights' (2007) 52 *American Journal of Jurisprudence* 93.
105 Yowell, ibid, 95.
106 Moshe Cohen-Eliya and Iddo Porat, *Proportionality and Constitutional Culture* (Cambridge: Cambridge University Press 2013) 122.
107 Mattias Kumm, 'The Idea of Socratic Contestation and the Right to Justification: The Point of Rights-Based Proportionality Review' (2010) 4 *Law and Ethics of Human Rights* 142, 143.

the state and the burden imposed on the (individual) interest. Thus, properly understood, 'rights represent a balance between potentially conflicting interests, some individual, some social'.[108]

These points are well illustrated in the public health context by the case of *Enhorn v Sweden*.[109] Here, the applicant, a 56 year-old man who was HIV positive and who had transmitted the virus to a 19 year-old, was made subject to a compulsory isolation order issued by the County Administrative Court, under the (Swedish) Infectious Diseases Act 1988, following failure to comply with instructions issued by the county medical officer. He absconded frequently from the hospital, and in consequence, the order for his detention was renewed on several occasions over a period of more than six years until the medical officer finally determined that there were no grounds for his further involuntary placement in isolation. The applicant alleged that he had been unlawfully deprived of his liberty contrary to Article 5 of the European Convention on Human Rights. He failed to persuade the European Court of Human Rights that the deprivation of liberty had been inadequately 'prescribed by law' (in particular, that the procedures and criteria for detention were not sufficiently precise), but he did succeed in demonstrating that the detention was not *proportionate*.

In order to understand this dimension of the ruling, it is important to appreciate that Article 5 of the Convention sets out a right ('Everyone has the right to liberty and security of the person') but subsequently sets out a series of situations in which this right may lawfully be curtailed or removed, which includes subparagraph (e) ('the lawful detention of persons for the prevention of the spreading of infectious diseases'). Hence, a public health rationale was proffered by the state as justification for interference with the right to liberty. However, the Court was clear that the actions taken would only be lawful if

> the spreading of the infectious disease is dangerous to public health or safety, and . . . detention of the person infected is the last resort in order to prevent the spreading of the disease, because less severe measures have been considered and found to be insufficient to safeguard the public interest'.[110]

This formulation allowed the Court to 'weigh' the individual's right against the interests of the community, but also to assess whether detention was in the individual's best interests, e.g. for the provision of medical treatment. In this instance, the Swedish government had failed to demonstrate that it had given consideration to measures that would intrude less severely upon the applicant's right to liberty than those that had been taken. Moreover, in view of the fact that, despite his periods of absence from hospital, the applicant had not infected any other sexual partners with HIV, it could not be said that detention was a 'last resort' measure. Accordingly, the state authorities had failed to strike a fair balance between the need to ensure that the HIV virus did not spread and the applicant's right to liberty.

The United Kingdom is a party to the European Convention on Human Rights and the Convention has, in effect, been 'incorporated' into domestic law by means of the Human Rights Act 1998, section 2 of which obliges courts to take into account the jurisprudence

---

108   David Feldman, *Civil Liberties and Human Rights in England and Wales* (2nd edn., Oxford: Oxford University Press 2002) 6.

109   [2005] 41 EHRR 633.

110   ibid, [44]. It should be noted that articulation of the proportionality test in terms of whether the measure taken was the 'last resort' differs from the manner in which the test is usually formulated, where the assessment is more usually one of whether the detriment to the individual as a result of imposition of the measure is excessive in relation to the benefits that might be gained from it. The stricter standard applied in *Enhorn* would appear to reflect the weight that is accorded to the right to liberty under the Convention.

of the European Court of Human Rights. The reasoning in *Enhorn* would therefore apply to an analogous situation arising in the UK. Indeed, Martin uses the case to argue for reform of the Public Health (Control of Disease) Act 1984, contending that 'any doubt as to the implications of the Human Rights Act 1998 for the Public Health Act 1984 must now have been settled by the decision in *Enhorn*'.[111] As noted in Chapter 3 and in the preceding discussion in this chapter, such reform, has, of course, now taken place, although the primary driver for this lies in the need to comply with the International Health Regulations (considered in Chapter 8), rather than human rights law.

However – and consistently with the notion of 'balance' analysed above and explicitly invoked by the European Court of Human Rights in the case itself – it should not be assumed that the outcome in *Enhorn* is indicative that human rights adjudication will *necessarily* result in a privileging of individual autonomy vis-a-vis the community interest in all cases addressing public health (see also the discussion of the Rampton smokers' case in Chapter 5). Indeed, in the relatively few cases in which matters that might be considered to fall within this category (as distinct from individual medical treatment) have fallen for determination in the European Court of Human Rights, the tendency is rather to accord a significant degree of discretion to governmental authorities to take such actions as they consider necessary to protect or ameliorate the health of the population. For example, in *Laskey v United Kingdom*, the criminal prosecution of a number of individuals who had participated in consensual acts of a sado-masochistic nature was held by the European Court of Human Rights not to amount to a violation of Article 8 of the Convention (the right to respect for private and family life, home, and correspondence). The argument put by the UK Government – that the prosecutions sought to deter certain forms of behaviour on public health grounds and were thus a justifiable interference with the exercise of the right under paragraph (2) of Article 8 – was accepted, the Court holding that:

> The determination of the level of harm that should be tolerated by the law in situations where the victim consents is in the first instance a matter for the state concerned since what is at stake is related, on the one hand, to public health considerations and to the general deterrent effect of the criminal law, and, on the other, to the personal autonomy of the individual.[112]

The measures taken thus fell within the 'margin of appreciation' – the discretionary area of judgment – accorded by the Court to governmental authorities in Member states. Similar conclusions have been reached by the European Court of Human Rights in cases concerning resource allocation within health systems.[113] The Court has noted that satisfaction of a claim to access a particular treatment or service 'amounts to a call on public funds which, in view of the scarce resources, would have to be diverted from other worthy needs funded by the taxpayer'[114] and that 'the allocation of public funds in the area of health care, which is a fervently debated issue in a number of European states, is not a matter on which the Court should take a stand':[115] rather, the assessment of whether demands for particular

111 Robyn Martin, 'The Exercise of Public Health Powers in Cases of Infectious Disease: Human Rights Implications' (2006) 14 *Medical Law Review* 132, 143.
112 [1997] 24 EHRR 39, [44].
113 For further discussion, see Keith Syrett, 'Healthcare Rationing and the Law', in Andre den Exter and Martin Buijsen (eds), *The Compendium of European Health Law* (Antwerp: Maklu-Uitgevers 2017).
114 *Pentiacova v Moldova*, App no 14462/03 (ECtHR, 4 January 2005).
115 *Wiater v Poland*, App no 42290/08 (ECtHR, 15 May 2012), [39].

interventions can be met, given the need for husbandry of scarce resources in the interests of the wider population, is a matter for national authorities to determine.[116] Within a domestic context, this non-interventionist jurisprudential stance is mirrored by reluctance to permit the Human Rights Act 1998 to form the basis of a claim in judicial review. For example, in Condliff,[117] the Court of Appeal cited with approval the European Court of Human Rights' observation that 'regard must be had to the fair balance that has to be struck between the competing interests of the individual and of the community as a whole',[118] in support of its conclusion that a Primary Care Trust that had refused to provide funding for laparoscopic gastric bypass surgery for patients under a particular body mass index level had reached a rational (and therefore, lawful) decision, and had not violated the applicant's rights under Article 8.

It should also be noted that, while the preceding cases concern the balance between the *autonomy of the individual* and collective public health interests, norms of human rights law may additionally be invoked by *corporations* seeking to oppose public health measures. A notable recent instance in which this has occurred is in relation to legislation that requires warnings to be placed on cigarette packs and/or plain packaging. Opposition to such laws in Europe has, to date, predominantly occurred through the avenues of intellectual property and free trade (for the impact of which upon public health, see further: Chapter 8).[119] However, elsewhere, the right to freedom of speech, enshrined in the First Amendment to the US Constitution, formed the basis of successful legal challenge to graphic warnings issued by the federal Food and Drug Administration;[120] while in New Zealand, the Government has taken legal advice on the consistency of its plain packaging legislation with section 14 of the New Zealand Bill of Rights Act 1990 (which protects freedom of expression)[121] in light of previous arguments made by tobacco companies in respect of pictorial warnings.[122] Since case law of the European Court of Human Rights establishes that the right to freedom of expression contained in Article 10 of the Convention extends to 'commercial speech' and covers messages conveyed on product packaging,[123] and since the same Article guarantees the 'right to receive and impart information . . . without interference by public authorities', it is not implausible to envisage comparable challenges being mounted in the UK under the Human Rights Act 1998.[124] However, since 'the protection of health' is an objective that may justify interference with this right under paragraph (2) of Article 10, a court that was called upon to adjudicate such a matter might very well consider such measures to be lawful, assuming always that they meet the standard of proportionality.

---

116 See *Sentges v Netherlands*, App no 27677/02 (ECtHR, 16 July 2002).
117 [2011] EWCA Civ 910.
118 In *Sentges* (n 116).
119 See Alberto Alemanno and Enrico Bonadio, 'Plain Packaging of Cigarettes under EU Law' in Tania Voon, Andrew Mitchell, and Jonathan Liberman (eds), *Public Health and Plain Packaging of Cigarettes: Legal Issues* (Cheltenham: Edward Elgar 2012) 214–237.
120 R.J. *Reynolds Tobacco Co. v. FDA*, 696 F.3d 1205 (D.C. Cir. 2012). For discussion, see David Orentlicher, 'The FDA's Graphic Tobacco Warnings and the First Amendment' (2013) 369 *New England Journal of Medicine* 204.
121 New Zealand Ministry of Justice, 'Legal Advice: Smoke-Free Environments (Tobacco Plain Packaging) Amendment Bill: Consistency with New Zealand Bill of Rights 1990' (6 December 2013), <www.justice.govt.nz/policy/constitutional-law-and-human-rights/human-rights/bill-of-rights/smoke-free-environments-tobacco-plain-packaging-amendment-bill> accessed 5 April 2016.
122 See Janet Hoek, Nick Wilson, Matthew Allen, Richard Edwards, George Thomson, and Judy Li, 'Lessons from New Zealand's Introduction of Pictorial Health Warnings on Tobacco Packaging' (2010) 88 *Bulletin of the World Health Organization* 861.
123 See e.g. *Casado Coca v Spain* [1994] 18 EHRR 1.
124 For example, to the Standardised Packaging of Tobacco Products Regulations 2015, SI 2015/829. These Regulations were unsuccessfully challenged in R (*British American Tobacco*) and *others v Secretary of State for Health* [2016] EWHC 1169 (Admin), but on the basis of an alleged violation of Article 1, Protocol 1 ECHR (right to peaceful enjoyment of possessions).

7.3.2 Case study 5: Positive obligations – rights as the basis of public health interventions

The discussion to date has focussed on rights as a basis for an obligation of non-interference on the part of the state. But, as previously noted, rights may also give rise to positive obligations, that is, those whose 'key characteristic is the duty upon states to undertake specific affirmative tasks' to uphold them.[125] The distinction between the types of obligation is frequently captured in a now familiar tripartite division between duties to respect (abstain from interfering with), protect (prevent third parties from violating) and fulfil (take measures to ensure the enjoyment of) human rights.[126] The latter two categories – and particularly, the obligation to fulfil – require the state to take action, in contradistinction to the negative obligation to respect, which underpins the situations analysed in the preceding section.

As an instrument that enshrines rights of a civil and political nature, the European Convention on Human Rights does not contain a right to health, so positive obligations to take steps to promote population health must be derived from other rights. The most pertinent are likely to be Article 2 (the right to life); Article 3 (prohibition of torture and inhuman and degrading treatment and punishment); and Article 8 (right to respect for private and family life, home, and correspondence).

A developing line of jurisprudence of the European Court of Human Rights with relevance to public health concerns a right to live in a healthy environment.[127] Illustrative of this development is *Tătar v Romania*,[128] where it was alleged that the state had failed to take adequate steps to regulate gold mining activity, which had resulted in the contamination of water supply with sodium cyanide. Although in this instance the Court did not consider that a causal link between exposure to the substance and the asthma suffered by the applicant's son had been established, it did hold that suitable measures had not been taken to protect the right to enjoy a healthy environment, which it regarded as a dimension of the right to respect for private life and home under Article 8. Similarly, in *Di Sarno v Italy*,[129] a violation of Article 8 was also made out where there had been a failure to collect, treat, and dispose of waste. As in *Tătar*, the Court did not feel able conclusively to determine that that the health of the local population had been adversely affected, but nonetheless considered that the state had failed in its duty to adopt reasonable and appropriate measures to safeguard the right of the local population to live in a safe and healthy environment.

In these cases, the extent of the impact upon population health was uncertain. However, in other cases in which adverse effects upon health were clear, violations of Convention rights have been successfully argued on the basis that the state failed to comply with a positive obligation. Thus, in *Elefteriadis v Romania*,[130] a violation of Article 3 was found to have occurred where a previously fit prisoner contracted pulmonary fibrosis and chronic obstructive bronchopneumopathy having shared cells and court waiting rooms with smokers; the European Court of Human Rights held that the state had failed to take adequate measures to protect his health, such as responding to his requests to be moved to a non-smoking cell.

---

125 Alastair Mowbray, *The Development of Positive Obligations under the European Convention on Human Rights by the European Court of Human Rights* (Oxford: Hart Publishing 2004) 2.
126 For an early statement of this typology, see UN Special Rapporteur for the Right to Food, *The Right to Adequate Food as a Human Right: Final Report Submitted by Asbjørn Eide*, UN Doc E/CN.4/Sub.2/1987/23 (1987) [67]–[69].
127 See Council of Europe, *Manual on Human Rights and the Environment* (2nd edn., Strasbourg: Council of Europe Publishing 2013).
128 App no 67021/01 (ECtHR, 27 January 2009).
129 App no 30765/08 (ECtHR, 10 January 2012).
130 App no 38427/05 (ECtHR, 25 January 2011).

And, in *Brincat v Malta*,[131] the Court held that there had been a violation of Articles 2 and 8 in cases of exposure to asbestos: the government had failed to satisfy its positive obligations to legislate or take other practical measures to ensure that shipyard workers were adequately informed of and protected from the risks to their health.

Also worthy of note in this regard is the European Social Charter, which supplements the Convention by setting out a series of economic and social rights, amongst which is Article 11, which requires states:

> to take appropriate measures designed inter alia to remove as far as possible the causes of ill health; to provide advisory and educational facilities for the promotion of health and the encouragement of individual responsibility in matters of health; and to prevent as far as possible epidemic, endemic and other diseases.

This has been viewed as imposing a wide range of positive obligations upon states. These include implementation of measures to reduce risks arising from asbestos, water, and noise pollution; adoption of food hygiene standards; imposition of restrictions on the supply of tobacco; operation of widely accessible immunisation programmes; taking steps to prevent accidents; provision of health education and information; provision of counselling and screening (especially for children and pregnant women); and provision of a framework of regulation covering matters such as health and safety at work, and women's, children's, and elderly persons' rights to health.[132] Illustrative of the Article's reach is the case of *Marangopoulos Foundation for Human Rights v Greece*,[133] in which the state was held in violation, among other matters, for its failure to educate a local population on the health risks associated with lignite mining and for failure to implement sufficient epidemiological monitoring of those living in the vicinity.

As for the UK, it has ratified the Charter and accepted Article 11. However, by contrast with the European Convention on Human Rights, no legislation has been enacted to give domestic effect to its provisions; thus, since the UK is a dualist state,[134] obligations under the instrument sound only in international law. Furthermore, the UK has not acceded to the system of collective complaints that was used in the *Marangopoulos Foundation* case. Accordingly, the impact of the Charter on public health law in the UK is minimal; it functions, if at all, primarily as a means by which NGOs and other actors might exert political pressure on government to take action on population health issues.

Chapter 7: Summary

- Public law is concerned with the rules governing the institutional structure of government, the relations between different parts of government, and the relationship between the individual and the state. It is usually divided into *constitutional law*, *administrative law*, and *human rights law*.
- Public law provides an avenue through which the mission of government in respect of public health may be articulated, a means of establishing institutions to address public

---

131 [2014] ECHR 836.
132 See Secretariat of the European Social Charter, *The Right to Health and the European Social Charter* (Strasbourg: Council of Europe 2009).
133 Complaint No. 30/2005 (European Committee of Social Rights, 6 December 2006).
134 See further: Chapter 8.

health goals (and to hold such institutions to account), and a framework for the allocation of resources to actors and activities within the public health domain.

- The dominant approach to public law sees its role as one of *control*, with a particular view to the protection of individual autonomy. However, a subsidiary, more recent perspective regards public law as a means to *facilitate* the undertaking of tasks by the state, including those relating to protection or promotion of population health.
- Human rights law can act as a constraint upon the state's activities in relation to public health by prioritising individual over collective interests; however, rights jurisprudence requires courts to strike a *balance* between individual interests and collective goals, meaning that the former are not always preferred.
- Human rights law may require the state to take certain steps to secure population health, especially in the environmental context. This is a developing area of law and its impact upon the UK is, as yet, unclear.

7.4 Further readings

Department of Health, *The New Public Health Role of Local Government* (London: Department of Health 2012).

Enhorn v Sweden (2005) 41 EHRR 633.

Health and Social Care Act 2012, ss. 11–12, 22, 30–32, 192–193.

Judith Laing and Jean McHale (eds), *Principles of Medical Law* (4th edn., Oxford: Oxford University Press 2017), chapter 7.

Robyn Martin, 'The Exercise of Public Health Powers in Cases of Infectious Disease Human Rights Implications' (2006) 14 *Medical Law Review* 132.

Public Health (Control of Disease) Act 1984, as amended by Health and Social Care Act 2008, Part 3.

Keith Syrett, *The Foundations of Public Law* (2nd edn., Basingstoke: Palgrave Macmillan 2014).

Well-being of Future Generations (Wales) Act 2015.

Chapter 8

European Union law, international law, and public health

While this book concerns public health law as it operates in the United Kingdom – and, particularly, in the legal jurisdiction of England and Wales – it would be incomplete without an analysis of laws that emanate from regional and international levels of governance. This is so for two reasons.

First, from a *legal* perspective, such laws either form a further component of the 'internal' regulatory framework within which population health issues are addressed in this country (this is the case as regards European Union law from the accession of the UK to the then European Economic Community on 1 January 1973 to date, and also as regards international treaties that have been given effect by domestic legislation), or they impose obligations and restrictions upon the UK 'externally', as an actor in the international arena. Second, from a *public health* standpoint, 'the determinants of health . . . do not originate solely within national borders'.[1] This has been true for centuries – consider, for example, the spread of bubonic plague in the medieval era – but it is a matter of growing importance as a consequence of globalisation.

In addition to its role in offering an account of the nature of the laws of the European Union and those that derive from international treaties, together with the impact that these might have upon the regulation of population health in this country, this chapter will fulfil a further goal. It serves to underline the point we have made elsewhere in this book, especially in Chapters 1, 3, 4, and 9, that it is impossible to develop an understanding of contemporary public health law by reference only to the powers and responsibilities of government within the UK (whether national, devolved, or local). Rather, a broad reading of the subject-matter, such as the one we adopt in this book, behoves us to consider the contribution of non-governmental actors and that made at *multiple layers of governance* – in this instance, those which exist 'above' the level of the nation state.

8.1 Introduction to European Union law

As an entity, the European Union (EU) is extremely difficult to categorise. It has some characteristics of an international organisation, but it is perhaps better regarded as 'a multi-level system of governance in which norms are promulgated through interactions between

---

1 Lawrence Gostin, *Global Health Law* (Cambridge, MA: Harvard University Press 2014) 32.

subnational, national, EU and transnational institutions and actors'.[2] In particular, its legal order has a unique character that is distinct from that of international law examined in the second part of this chapter. This was articulated in an early judgment of the European Court of Justice (now the Court of Justice of the European Union), as follows:

> By contrast with ordinary international treaties, the EEC Treaty[3] has created its own legal system which, on the entry into force of the Treaty, became an integral part of the legal systems of the Member States and which their courts are bound to apply. By creating a Community of unlimited duration, having its own institutions, its own personality, its own legal capacity and capacity of representation on the international plane and, more particularly, real powers stemming from a limitation of sovereignty or a transfer of powers from the States to the Community, the Member States have limited their sovereign rights, albeit within limited fields, and have thus created a body of law which binds both their nationals and themselves.[4]

In the United Kingdom, the European Communities Act 1972 defined the relationship between national and (what is now) EU law. Under section 2(1), provisions of EU law that are 'directly applicable' – those arising from the Treaties themselves and Regulations made by EU institutions – were to be automatically incorporated into national law without any further action on the part of governmental bodies in the UK. Those EU laws that are not directly applicable – the most important being Directives – are the subject of section 2(2), which conferred power on the executive to make secondary legislation to give effect to such laws: 'this has been the usual manner in which EU law obligations have been brought into effect in the UK as a matter of national law'.[5]

EU law may also have 'direct effect', as the European Court of Justice outlined in 1963:

> The objective of the EEC Treaty . . . implies that the Treaty is more than an agreement which merely creates mutual obligations between the contracting states . . . the Community constitutes a new legal order of international law for the benefit of which the states have limited their sovereign rights, albeit within limited fields, and the subjects of which comprise not only Member States but also their nationals. Independently of the legislation of Member States, Community law therefore not only imposes obligations on individuals but is also intended to confer upon them rights which become part of their legal heritage.[6]

This means that EU law can be privately enforced[7] – that is, that individuals can rely upon its provisions in national courts against state officials or institutions and private entities or individuals (albeit not in the latter case in respect of EU Directives, since these are only 'vertically' directly effective *against the state* when they have not been implemented via domestic legislation). Moreover, as provided for in the UK by section 2(4) of the European Communities

---

2 Tamara Hervey and Jean McHale, *Health Law and the European Union* (Cambridge: Cambridge University Press 2004) 34.
3 This refers to the founding Treaty of Rome, [1957], which created the original European Economic Community, which later became the European Community and, finally, the European Union.
4 *Costa v ENEL* (C-6/64) [1964] ECR 585.
5 Aidan O'Neill, *EU Law for UK Lawyers* (2nd edn., Oxford: Hart Publishing 2011) 56.
6 *NV Algemene Transporten Expeditie Onderneming van Gend en Loos v Nederlandse Administratie der Belastingen* (C-26/62) [1963] ECR 1.
7 See Paul Craig and Grainne de Búrca, *EU Law: Text, Cases and Materials* (6th edn., Oxford: Oxford University Press 2015) 185.

Act, EU law takes precedence over conflicting norms of domestic law, whether these are established previously or subsequently, since:

> Recourse to the legal rules or concepts of national law in order to judge the validity of measures adopted by the institutions of the Community would have an adverse effect on the uniformity and efficacy of Community law . . . the law stemming from the Treaty, an independent source of law, cannot because of its very nature be overridden by rules of national law, however framed, without being deprived of its character as Community law and without the legal basis of the Community itself being called into question.[8]

A wide variety of institutions and agencies operating at EU level may have a role in the shaping of public health laws.[9] In general, the Council of Ministers (which consists of the ministers of Member State governments responsible for the subject area under discussion) and the European Parliament jointly decide upon legislative proposals that are advanced by the European Commission; the latter has both legislative and executive functions. An especially important player in the public health arena is the Commission's Directorate General for Health and Food Safety (DG Santé, formerly known as DG SANCO), whose aims include the protection and improvement of public health in the Union. This goal is pursued by policies and actions under a number of headings, including 'steering EU public health', 'ensuring health security', 'taking action against diseases', 'health in society', and 'fostering good health'.[10]

The future place of these laws as a component of the patchwork of regulation of public health in the United Kingdom is now highly uncertain. As this book goes to press, a majority of those voting in the June 2016 referendum on the UK's continued membership of the Union expressed a desire to leave. It is important to recognise that, irrespective of how this situation plays out within domestic politics (and it should be noted that, as a matter of law, the referendum is advisory only: the Westminster Parliament retains sovereignty to act in whatsoever manner it chooses, including ignoring the outcome), the UK remains, for the time being, bound by EU treaties and the obligations that arise thereunder. Article 50 of the Treaty on European Union, which is triggered by way of notification to the European Council by the Member State of its intention, provides for a process of negotiated withdrawal over a period of up to two years (which can be extended by unanimous approval of the Council with the agreement of the Member State concerned). Once a deal is struck (or if the negotiation period elapses without any such agreement being concluded), EU law will cease to apply. However, it does not follow that all laws relating to public health emanating from the EU that have infiltrated the domestic legal system during the period of the UK's membership will be repealed: the Government has indicated that EU laws taking effect through the 1972 Act will initially be retained and subsequently reviewed. The picture is therefore a highly complex one but, for the time being at least, the European Union remains an important source of domestic public health law, which is worthy of extended consideration.

---

8 *Internationale Handelsgesellschaft mbH v Einfhur – und Vorratsstelle für Getreide und Futtermittel* (C-11/70) [1970] ECR 1125.
9 See Tamara Hervey and Jean McHale, *European Union Health Law: Themes and Implications* (Cambridge: Cambridge University Press 2015) 63–69.
10 European Commission, <www.ec.europa.eu/health/index_en.htm> accessed 5 April 2016.

8.2 European Union law and public health

As the leading text on health law in the EU notes, a very wide range of laws made by EU institutions impact upon public health; those relating to the environment and health and safety at work are particularly important examples.[11] There is insufficient scope in a book of this length to explore these in full, but illustrative examples will be provided of such action in the fields of communicable disease (pandemic planning and preparedness) and in relation to two important vectors for non-communicable disease, alcohol and food.

These will be preceded by an exploration of the source of lawful authority for action at EU level on matters of public health and the allocation of legal responsibilities between EU and Member State institutions. While such matters fall particularly within the compass of public law, as noted in Chapter 7, they are of wider importance since they speak to a question identified by Gostin and Wiley as being both fundamentally important and profoundly contentious in the context of public health law (albeit, in the United States): 'which government is to act?'.[12]

8.2.1 EU public health competence

In order to comprehend the nature and scope of the EU's role in public health law, it is necessary first to understand how legal authority is allocated between the institutions of the EU and those of Member States. A central concept here is the distribution of *competences* between the two levels. In a general sense, 'competence' may be understood as 'the possibility to change legal positions by performing a special kind of act',[13] and it is thus related to the question of legal validity: in the absence of competence, acts are not legally valid. The term is not one that is much deployed within UK domestic public law discourse, but it might broadly be seen as referring 'both to the issue of jurisdiction (the scope of action) and to the issue of powers (the means and instruments for action)'.[14]

'The general principle is, and always has been, that the EU only has the competence conferred on it by the Treaties'.[15] The Treaty of Lisbon, which entered into force on 1 December 2009 and which amends the two treaties that establish the institutional framework and provide for the operation of the EU (the Treaty on European Union [TEU] and the Treaty on the Functioning of the European Union [TFEU]),[16] sets out the question of competence more clearly than had previously been the case. The EU may have exclusive competence, meaning that only the Union can take legislative action;[17] shared competence, under which both Union and Member States can legislate and adopt legally binding acts;[18] or competence only to take supporting, coordinating, or supplementary action without superseding Member State competence.[19]

---

11 Hervey and McHale (n 2), 333–334.
12 Lawrence Gostin and Lindsay Wiley, *Public Health Law: Power, Duty, Restraint* (3rd edn., Berkeley: University of California Press 2016) 73. Of course, the EU is not a 'government' in the usual sense, but as noted above, it may be seen as a 'system of governance'.
13 Torben Spaak, 'Norms that Confer Competence' (2003) 16 *Ratio Juris* 89, 91.
14 Loïc Azoulai, 'Introduction: The Question of Competence' in Loïc Azoulai (ed), *The Question of Competence in the European Union* (Oxford: Oxford University Press 2014) 2.
15 Craig and de Búrca (n 7), 73.
16 These have been described as 'like a constitution for the European Union': Hervey and McHale (n 9), 63.
17 Article 2(1) TFEU. Member States are able to legislate and adopt legally binding acts only if empowered to do so by the Union, or in order to implement Union acts domestically.
18 Article 2(2) TFEU.
19 Article 2(5) TFEU.

Article 4(2)(k) TFEU specifies that 'common safety concerns in public health matters, for the aspects defined in this Treaty' are issues of shared competence. Additionally, Article 6(a) TFEU lists 'protection and improvement of human health' as an area in which the Union has competence to support, coordinate, or take supplementary action. It is thus clear that public health is not a matter of exclusive competence for the Union but rather an area in which action takes place at both EU and Member State level. In the absence of exclusive competence, the principle of 'subsidiarity', set out in Article 5(3) TEU, applies. This provides that

> the Union shall act only if and insofar as the objectives of the proposed action cannot be sufficiently achieved by the Member States, either at central level or at regional and local level, but can rather, by reason of the scale or effects of the proposed action, be better achieved at Union level.

Hence, the presumption is that legal activities within the public health field will fall to Member States, unless the 'scale or effects' of the action render the Union the more appropriate actor.

Article 9 TFEU 'mainstreams' protection of human health as a requirement of which account is to be taken by the Union in defining and implementing its policies and activities. This gives health protection a high status in EU activities and might be said to reflect a 'Health in All Policies' approach consistent with an NPH paradigm.[20] However, the primary substantive provision under which public health action is taken is Article 168 TFEU. Paragraph (1) of this Article sets out a comparable 'mainstreaming' of human health protection to that contained in Article 9, before proceeding as follows:

> Union action, which shall complement national policies, shall be directed towards improving public health, preventing physical and mental illness and diseases, and obviating sources of danger to physical and mental health. Such action shall cover the fight against the major health scourges, by promoting research into their causes, their transmission and their prevention, as well as health information and education, and monitoring, early warning of and combating serious cross-border threats to health. The Union shall complement the Member States' action in reducing drugs-related health damage, including information and prevention.

This provision makes clear that the competence of the EU is merely of a supporting ('complementary') character; the fundamental choices on public health measures are to be made by Member States in accordance with the principle of subsidiarity.[21] The health strategy adopted by the Union (at that time, the European Community [EC]) in 2007 expands upon this:

> Member States have the main responsibility for health policy and provision of healthcare to European citizens. The EC's role is not to mirror or duplicate their work. However, there are areas where Member States cannot act alone effectively and where

---

20 See further Hervey and McHale (n 9), 60–63; Mark Flear, *Governing Public Health: EU Law, Regulation and Biopolitics* (Oxford: Hart Publishing 2015) 54–68.

21 Note, however, that paragraph 2 specifies that Member States should coordinate their policies and programmes in these areas and that the EU Commission 'may take any useful initiative to promote such coordination, in particular initiatives aiming at the establishment of guidelines and indicators, the organisation of exchange of best practice, and the preparation of the necessary elements for periodic monitoring and evaluation'. Paragraph 3 obliges Member States and the Union to foster cooperation in public health with other countries and international institutions.

cooperative action at Community level is indispensable. These include major health threats and issues with a cross-border or international impact, such as pandemics and bioterrorism, as well as those relating to free movement of goods, services and people.[22]

Further reinforcement of this position is afforded by Article 168(7) TFEU, which states that

Union action shall respect the responsibilities of the Member States for the definition of their health policy and for the organisation and delivery of health services and medical care. The responsibilities of the Member States shall include the management of health services and medical care and the allocation of the resources assigned to them.

It is therefore apparent that the organisation, functioning, and financing of health systems remain matters for the Member States, although the recent EU Directive on Patients' Rights in Cross-Border Healthcare impacts to some degree in this regard.[23]

Within specific fields, however, there exists shared competence between EU and Member States. Article 168(4) TFEU authorises the European Parliament and the Council of the EU to adopt legislative measures[24] that set standards of high quality and safety of organs and substances of human origin, blood, and blood derivatives;[25] in the veterinary and phytosanitary field, 'which have as their direct objective the protection of public health';[26] and for medicines and medical devices. Still more pertinent to the public health context is Article 168(5) TFEU, which authorises the same institutions, utilising the same process as under paragraph (4), to adopt:

incentive measures designed to protect and improve human health and in particular to combat the major cross-border health scourges, measures concerning monitoring, early warning of and combating serious cross-border threats to health, and measures which have as their direct objective the protection of public health regarding tobacco and the abuse of alcohol.

Such 'incentive measures' are explicitly stated to fall short of harmonisation of national laws, but they nonetheless amount to legally binding acts.[27]

---

22 European Commission, *White Paper: Together for Health: A Strategic Approach for the EU 2008–13*, COM (2007) 630 final, 2.

23 Directive 2011/24/EU on the application of patients' rights in cross-border healthcare, [2011] OJ L 88/45. For discussion, see Hervey and McHale (n 9), chapter 4; Kenneth Veitch, 'Juridification, Medicalisation and the Impact of EU Law: Patient Mobility and the Allocation of Scarce NHS Resources' (2012) 20 *Medical Law Review* 362.

24 By means of the 'ordinary legislative procedure', through which the European Commission submits a proposal to the Parliament and Council, which carry equal weight in approving it. See further Hervey and McHale (n 9), 63–69. Under both paragraphs (4) and (5), legislative action should only take place following consultation with two committees established for this purpose, the European Economic and Social Committee and the Committee of the Regions, for discussion of whose role see Christoph Hönninge and Diana Panke, 'Is Anybody Listening? The Committee of the Regions and the European Economic and Social Committee and Their Quest for Awareness' (2016) 23 *Journal of European Public Policy* 624.

25 This was the legal basis of the 'Blood Safety' Directive: Directive 2002/98/EC, which set standards of quality and safety for the collection, testing, processing, storage, and distribution of human blood and blood components and which amended Directive 2001/83/EC, [2003] OJ L 33/30.

26 This provision, which appears to have been a response to the BSE crisis, 'transfers' veterinary and phytosanitary measures with a public health protection objective from the Common Agricultural Policy (see Articles 38 to 44 TFEU) to the public health field. See further Anne Pieter van der Mei and Lisa Waddington, 'Public Health and the Treaty of Amsterdam' (1998) 5 *European Journal of Health Law* 129.

27 See Craig and de Búrca (n 7), 87.

It is through this latter means that various public health programmes managed by the European Commission have been instituted.[28] Of particular importance have been three Health Programmes, operating from 2003–8 and 2008–13 and 2014–20, which provide funding for health initiatives in the EU. Funding acts as a form of 'regulation through "steering" rather than "command and control" in that it is used to stimulate the support and development of EU public health policy'.[29] For example, the current Third Programme is the main instrument through which the Commission seeks to implement the EU's health strategy.[30] The Programme provides a budget of €449.4 billion to support cooperation projects at EU level, actions jointly taken by Member State health authorities, the functioning of non-governmental bodies, and cooperation with international organisations in pursuit of a variety of general and specific objectives relating to health care and public health, including promotion of health, prevention of diseases, fostering of supportive environments for healthy lifestyles, and protection of citizens from serious cross-border health threats. Programming and implementation occurs on the basis of annual work programmes through calls for grants and tenders, and the Programme is monitored by means of annual implementation reports to the European Parliament and Council, with a full mid-term review in 2017.[31]

While Article 168 TFEU is by far and away the most significant Treaty provision governing public health at EU level, brief mention should also be made of Article 35 of the Charter of Fundamental Rights of the European Union. As noted in Chapter 7, this previously non-binding instrument now has the same legal value as the other Treaties, by virtue of Article 6(1) TEU. The Charter provides as follows:

> Everyone has the right of access to preventive healthcare and the right to benefit from medical treatment under the conditions established by national laws and practices. A high level of human health protection shall be ensured in the definition and implementation of all Union policies and activities.

This provision is based upon Article 168 TFEU[32] and is addressed to EU institutions and agencies as well as to Member States when implementing EU law. Since the organisation of health systems is a matter for the Member States, and since no EU institutions provide preventive health care or medical treatment, 'the field of application of this provision would . . . seem to be extremely limited'.[33] It will be noted, also, that the first sentence of the Article is oriented more towards health care, to the apparent exclusion of wider aspects of public

---

28 Martin McKee, Tamara Hervey and Anna Gilmore, 'Public Health Policies' in Elias Mossialos, Govin Permanand, Rita Baeten, and Tamara Hervey (eds), *Health Systems Governance in Europe: The Role of European Union Law and Policy* (Cambridge: Cambridge University Press 2010) 237.

29 Flear (n 20), 72.

30 The initial health strategy was articulated in European Commission (n 22). A mid-term evaluation in 2011 confirmed that the principles and strategies identified therein would remain valid for the next decade. Health is a component of the 'Europe 2020' strategy agreed in 2010: European Commission, *Europe 2020: A Strategy for Smart, Sustainable and Inclusive Growth*, COM (2010) 2020 final.

31 Regulation (EU) 282/2014 on the establishment of a third programme for the Union's action in the field of health (2014–2020) and repealing Decision 1350/2007/EC, [2014] OJ L 86/1. See further European Commission, <www.ec.europa.eu/health/programme/docs/factsheet_healthprogramme2014_2020_en.pdf> accessed 5 April 2016; Flear (n 20), 72–76.

32 See explanatory text to Article 35, [2007] OJ C 303/17.

33 Tamara Hervey and Jean McHale, 'Article 35' in Steve Peers, Tamara Hervey, Jeff Kenner, and Angela Ward (eds), *The EU Charter of Fundamental Rights: A Commentary* (Oxford: Hart Publishing 2014) 952.

health responsibility. The Article has been invoked in litigation very infrequently,[34] and it would not seem that it has yet made any difference to the substantive outcome of cases, although it may have an impact upon the 'discursive framing' of the legal issues,[35] rights claims generally being regarded as especially weighty in consequence of their frequent conceptualisation as 'trumps' (see further: section 7.3.1 above).

8.2.2 EU public health activity: case studies

8.2.2.1 Case study 1: Pandemics

The legal basis for the EU's response to pandemics is to be found in Decision 1082/2013/ EU.[36] This legislative act of the Parliament and Council adopts an 'all-hazards' approach, as mandated by the International Health Regulations (discussed further below), applying to public health measures relating to threats of biological origin (including communicable diseases), threats of chemical origin, threats of environmental origin, threats of unknown origin, and events that may constitute public health emergencies under the International Health Regulations (provided that these fall within one of the four listed categories of threat).[37] It lays down rules on epidemiological surveillance, monitoring, early warning, and combating serious cross-border threats to health and provides a framework for preparedness and response planning.[38] The role of the EU is to 'support cooperation and coordination between Member States',[39] but the cross-border nature of the threats is such that it is envisaged that the objectives of intervention in this context can be better achieved at Union level, with the consequence that measures may be adopted by EU institutions in accordance with the principle of subsidiarity.[40] However, Member States 'retain the right to maintain or introduce additional arrangements, procedures and measures for their national systems' in the fields covered by the Decision.[41]

A Health Security Committee, consisting of representatives of the Commission, the European Centre for Disease Control, the European Medicines Agency, and Member State health ministries, was established in 2001 and given legal foundation by the Decision.[42] The Committee is tasked with supporting exchange and information between the Member States and the Commission and coordinating, in liaison with the Commission, preparedness and response planning by Member States and the risk and crisis communication of Member States to serious cross-border threats to health. Member States are required to provide updates on preparedness and response planning at a national level every three years;[43] as Flear observes, 'in this way, the gathering and production of knowledge on Member State preparedness planning and response is central to the EU's governance of preparedness'.[44]

---

34 In the public health context, see Case C-544/10 *Deutsches Weintor* (Judgment of 6 September 2012) (Regulation prohibiting health claims for beverages containing more than 1.2% alcohol by volume valid to ensure a high level of health protection); Case C-459/13 *Široka* (Judgment of 14 July 2014)(no jurisdiction to hear challenge to compulsory immunisation legislation as Member State legislation was not implementing EU law).

35 See Hervey and McHale (n 33), 960–961.

36 Decision 1082/2013/EU on serious cross-border threats to health and repealing Decision 2119/98/EC, [2013] OJ L 293/1.

37 ibid, Article 2.

38 ibid, Article 1(1).

39 ibid, Article 1(2).

40 ibid, Recital 28.

41 ibid, Article 2(6).

42 ibid, Article 17.

43 ibid, Article 4(2).

44 Flear (n 20), 152.

This having been said, the Union does have its own framework for responding to influenza pandemics, produced as a consequence of the work of the Committee, which allocates tasks between Member States, the Commission, and other EU agencies.[45] There is also a framework for cooperation in generic preparedness planning, whose 'overall goal is to assist Member States in developing their plans and factoring in the EU dimension, with its body of laws in various sectors with a bearing on public health emergency plans'.[46] This provides the 'backbone for developing core elements in national plans, addressing generically different types of health threats, whether anticipated (such as pandemic influenza) or unexpected (e.g. a SARS – like epidemic)'.[47]

8.2.2.3 Case study 2: Alcohol

An inherent tension exists in EU law and regulation between the pursuit of public health goals and preservation of the principles of the free market. This is well demonstrated in the context of regulation of the marketing and consumption of alcohol. Seminal cases of the Court of Justice have explored the lawfulness of national measures that sought to impose certain restrictions on alcoholic products on public health grounds,[48] and it has been concluded that 'the extent to which the EU Courts' growing role in alcohol policy defers to health interests is mixed'.[49] This having been said, Hervey and McHale detect a recent shift from the framing of alcohol as a matter for agriculture and trade (which would point to limited restrictions on marketing and availability) to conceptualisation of it as a health and social concern, which would point to a more interventionist approach being taken in future.[50]

Much of EU intervention on alcohol is of a complementary, 'soft law' character (see further: Chapter 9). Arguably, the most significant measure is the EU Alcohol Strategy adopted in 2006, which 'presents a comprehensive strategy to reduce alcohol-related harm in Europe until the end of 2012'.[51] It focuses on five areas: protecting young people, children, and the unborn child; reducing injuries and deaths from alcohol-related road traffic accidents; preventing alcohol-related harm among young adults and reducing the negative impact on the workplace; informing, educating, and raising awareness on the impact of harmful and hazardous alcohol consumption and on appropriate consumption patterns; and developing, supporting, and maintaining a common evidence base. The Strategy explicitly states that the Commission's 'main contribution . . . should be based upon the existing approach of complementing national actions and strategies in this area and therefore [the Commission] does not intend to implement the strategy through specific new legislative proposals'.[52] Instead, an Alcohol and Health Forum provides 'a common platform for all interested stakeholders at EU level that pledge to step up actions relevant to reducing alcohol-related harm',[53] while a Committee on National Alcohol Policy and Action, consisting of delegates of Member States, encourages cooperation and coordination between Member States and contributes to further

---

45 European Commission, *Pandemic Influenza Preparedness and Response Planning in the European Community*, COM (2005) 607 final.
46 European Commission, *Strengthening Coordination on Generic Preparedness Planning for Public Health Emergencies at EU Level*, COM (2005) 605 final, 4.
47 ibid.
48 See e.g. *Rewe-Zentral AG v Bundesmonopolverwaltung für Branntwein* ('Cassis de Dijon'), Case C-120/78, [1979] ECR 649; *Commission v Germany* ('Beer Purity'), Case C-178/84, [1987] ECR 1227.
49 Ben Baumberg and Peter Anderson, 'Health, Alcohol and EU Law: Understanding the Impact of European Single Market Law on Alcohol Policies' (2008) 18 *European Journal of Public Health* 392, 396.
50 Hervey and McHale (n 9), 422.
51 European Commission, *An EU Strategy to Support Member States in Reducing Alcohol-Related Harm*, COM (2006) 625 final.
52 ibid, 17.
53 European Commission, *Charter Establishing the European Alcohol and Health Forum* (Brussels: European Commission 2007) 2.

policy development.[54] It has been argued that 'there were significant shortcomings in how the Strategy operated'.[55] It has not yet been renewed notwithstanding a Resolution of the European Parliament calling for this to happen,[56] and there have been indications that any new approach to the issue may merely form an element of a broader, new Framework on Non-Communicable Diseases.[57]

This might lead one to question whether the 'cautious optimism' expressed by Hervey and McHale in this context might be somewhat misplaced.[58] However, an important pointer towards the likely trajectory of future EU responses in this area has been afforded by the Court of Justice ruling on the legality of minimum alcohol pricing in Scotland.[59] The Court ruled that a minimum price per unit, while acting as a quantitative restriction on the importation of goods contrary to Article 34 TFEU, could be justified under Article 36 as a measure aimed at 'the protection of health and life of humans'. For the measure to be lawful, it must be appropriate to securing the attainment of this objective, and must not go beyond what was necessary to attain it; thus, if life and health could be protected by a measure less restrictive of free movement of goods, minimum unit pricing would be unlawful. The Court stated that these questions – of appropriateness and proportionality – were for the Member State to determine in light of the evidence submitted. The Court of Session in Scotland ruled that the measure was lawful in these respects, thereby clearing the path for implementation of the Alcohol (Minimum Pricing) (Scotland) Act 2012.[60]

8.2.2.3 Case study 3: Food law and obesity

Legislation relating to labelling on food dates from the late 1970s,[61] and significant action was taken on food at EU level following the BSE scare, including the establishment of a European Food Safety Authority by way of the Food Safety Regulation.[62] However, these measures were concerned primarily with provision of accurate information to the consumer and with safety, rather than with encouraging healthy nutritional choices. The latter might be considered to be a matter warranting continuing and increasing attention, given rising rates of obesity in the EU (as elsewhere in the developed world), but there is an inevitable tension with commercial interests invoking the fundamental EU principle of the free movement of goods.[63]

Nonetheless, as Hervey and McHale note, EU law has, in recent years, developed beyond considerations of safety towards obesity as a proper subject of regulatory intervention, although its impact in this regard is, as yet, at best unproven.[64] Instructive here

---

54 See e.g. *Action Plan on Youth Drinking and Heavy Episodic Drinking (Binge Drinking) 2014–2016*, 16 September 2014.
55 European Union Committee, *A New EU Alcohol Strategy?* (HL 2014–15, 123) [110].
56 European Parliament Resolution on Alcohol Strategy, 2015/2543(RSP), 22 April 2015.
57 See Department of Health, *Government Response to the House of Lords European Union Committee's 8th Report of Session 2014–15: A New EU Alcohol Strategy?* (Cm 9092 2015) 10.
58 Hervey and McHale (n 9), 422.
59 *Scotch Whisky Association v Lord Advocate*, Case C-333/14, [2016] 1 WLR 2283.
60 [2016] CSIH 77.
61 Directive 79/112/EEC on the approximation of the laws of the Member States relating to the labelling, presentation, and advertising of foodstuffs for sale to the ultimate consumer, [1979] OJ L 33/1.
62 Regulation (EC) 178/2002 laying down the general principles of food law, establishing the European Food Safety Authority and laying down procedures in matters of food safety, [2002] OJ L 31/1.
63 See Paulette Kurzer, 'Non-Communicable Diseases: The EU Declares War on "Fat"' in Scott Greer and Paulette Kurzer (eds), *European Public Health Policy: Regional and Global Trends* (Abingdon: Routledge 2013) 155–167.
64 Hervey and McHale (n 9), 414–418; see also Kurzer, ibid.

is the Food Information for Consumers Regulation of 2011,[65] which now sets out the EU rules on food labelling. As Kurzer observes,[66] powerful industry lobbying served to dilute the original Commission proposal in this instance, as had also been the case with an earlier Regulation on nutrition and health claims.[67] Uniform rules on nutritional labelling are established:[68] these specify that calories, total fat, saturated fat, carbohydrates, protein, sugars, and salt per 100g/ml and per portion must be indicated on the packaging, with a minimum font size of 1.2mm, 'in the same field of vision' and 'in a clear format'.[69] By contrast, the original proposal had specified that information should appear on the front of the packaging, in a minimum font size of 3mm on a contrasting background. Furthermore, 'traffic light' labelling, of the type used on a voluntary basis in the UK, had not been part of the original proposal, and an attempt to reintroduce it during debate on the Regulation in the European Parliament was heavily defeated.[70] However, it remains possible for Member States to recommend 'additional forms of expression and presentation' in relation to nutritional information, provided that a number of requirements are met.[71] UK Health Ministers have recommended the continued use of 'traffic light' coding on a voluntary basis on the front of packaging, in addition to the back of packaging information mandated by the Regulation.[72]

In addition to legislative measures, the Commission has established an Obesity Strategy,[73] which seeks to address the root causes of health-related risks, working 'across government policy areas and at different levels of government using a range of instruments including legislation, networking, public-private approaches, and to engage the private sector and civil society', requiring actions from a wide range of private actors and underpinned by effective monitoring.[74] The Strategy encompasses a variety of Commission policies for which various Directorate-Generals have responsibility, such as fruit for schoolchildren, advertising,[75] clean urban transport, and the EU Work Plan for Sport.[76] In addition, a High Level Group on Nutrition and Physical Activity has been established, consisting of government representatives from all member states plus Norway and Switzerland. This has published an EU Action Plan on Childhood Obesity (2014) and has agreed a Framework for National Initiatives on Selected Nutrients. It holds regular meetings with the EU Platform for action on diet, physical activity, and health, which acts as a forum for industry, consumer protection, and public health NGOs to discuss and share actions and initiatives, with a view to entering into voluntary commitments.

---

65 Regulation (EU) No 1169/2011 on the provision of food information to consumers, [2011] OJ L 304/18. See Food Information Regulations 2014, SI 2014/1855, which provide for enforcement of certain aspects of the Regulation in England.
66 Kurzer (n 63), 162–165.
67 Regulation (EC) No 1924/2006 on nutrition and health claims made on foods, [2006] OJ L 404/9.
68 Alcoholic beverages containing more than 1.2% alcohol by volume are excluded from mandatory nutrition labelling: Regulation (EU) No 1169/2011, Article 16(4). Member States are not precluded from applying stricter national rules.
69 ibid, Articles 29–35.
70 Kurzer (n 63), 164.
71 Regulation (EU) No 1169/2011, Article 35.
72 See Department of Health/Food Standards Agency/Welsh Government/The Scottish Government, *Guide to Creating a Front of Pack Nutrition Label for Pre-Packed Products Sold through Retail Outlets* (London: Department of Health 2013).
73 European Commission, *A Strategy for Europe on Nutrition, Overweight and Obesity-Related Health Issues*, COM (2007) 279 final.
74 ibid, 3–4.
75 See Directive 2010/13/EU Audiovisual Services Directive, [2010] OJ L 95/1.
76 Resolution of the Council and of the Representatives of the Governments of the Member States of 21 May 2014 on the European Union Work Plan for Sport 2014–17, [2014] OJ C 183/12.

One unresolved question is whether a 'fat tax', of the type mooted in several countries, including the UK,[77] and introduced – but later abandoned – in Denmark, would be lawful under EU law. It would appear that any such law 'must ensure to tax foodstuffs that are similar and foodstuffs that are in competition so as to avoid any claim of discrimination or protectionism' under Article 110 TFEU.[78] In light of the energetic (and effective) oppositional role played by industry interests in this field over the past few years, it seems highly likely that any such measures would be subjected to challenge through the free market provisions of EU law. Indeed, the Commission itself launched an investigation into the legality of the Danish measures under the provisions precluding state aid[79] in February 2015.

8.3 Introduction to international law

The United Kingdom joined what was then the European Economic Community from 1 January 1973. It did so by entering into a treaty with the six members of the Community, under which it became a party to the existing treaties, most importantly the Treaty of Rome 1957.[80] This was an act of international law: the UK government, exercising its prerogative powers,[81] entered into a legally binding agreement with other states. What is distinctive about this example, as outlined in section 8.1, is that directly applicable laws of the European Union, that is Treaty provisions and Regulations, automatically became part of the law of the Member State (as the Court of Justice indicated in the *Costa* case)[82] and could be enforced by individual applicants in national courts (as the Court held in the *Van Gend en Loos* case).[83] It is not clear that this outcome had been anticipated by states.[84]

The novelty of the EU legal order in this regard becomes apparent when juxtaposed to the form of law discussed in this part of the chapter. 'According to the traditional definition, international law is a complex of norms regulating the mutual behaviour of states, the specific subjects of international law';[85] thus, 'the principal subjects of international law are nation-states, not individual citizens'.[86] This reflects the origin of international law – and the modern international political system – in the Peace of Westphalia 1648, from which emerged notions of state sovereignty (and, correspondingly, a decline in the role of religion in the international order):[87] a 'law of nations' theorised by the 'father of international law',[88] Hugo Grotius.[89] While this position has altered significantly over recent years – particularly, since 1945 – as international organisations and individuals (especially in the context of human rights) have emerged as subjects of this form of law, 'international law . . . is still very much state-centric. States still hold the keys to the international system'.[90]

---

77 See 'UK Could Introduce "Fat Tax" Says David Cameron', *The Guardian* (4 October 2011).
78 Alberto Allemanno and Ignacio Carreño, '"Fat Taxes" in Europe – A Legal and Policy Analysis under EU and WTO Law' (2013) 2 *European Food and Feed Law Review* 97, 104.
79 Articles 107–109 TFEU. On possible challenges to the 'sugar tax' announced in the Budget of March 2016 (see Chapter 7), see 'Drinks Makers Consider Legal Action against Sugar Tax', *The Guardian* (20 March 2016).
80 Treaty of Accession of Denmark, Ireland and the United Kingdom [1972] OJ L 73/1.
81 For discussion of these, see Keith Syrett, *The Foundations of Public Law* (2nd edn., Basingstoke: Palgrave Macmillan 2014) 136–152.
82 (n 4).
83 (n 6).
84 Craig and de Búrca (n 7), 189.
85 Hans Kelsen, *Pure Theory of Law* (Berkeley: University of California Press 1967) 320.
86 Malcolm Shaw, *International Law* (7th edn., Cambridge: Cambridge University Press 2014) 1.
87 Gideon Boas, *Public International Law: Contemporary Principles and Perspectives* (Cheltenham: Edward Elgar 2012) 8–9.
88 Shaw (n 86), 17.
89 Stephen Neff, 'A Short History of International Law' in Malcolm Evans (ed), *International Law* (Oxford: Oxford University Press 2010) 9.
90 Boas (n 87), 207.

Article 38(1) of the Statute of the International Court of Justice, the 'principal judicial organ of the United Nations',[91] 'is widely recognised as the most authoritative and complete statement as to the sources of international law'.[92] This lists the following sources: international conventions; international custom, as evidence of a general practice accepted as law; the general principles of law recognised by civilised nations; and, as subsidiary means for the determination of rules of law, judicial decisions and 'teachings of the most highly qualified publicists of the various nations'. Of these, it is the first – conventions or treaties – which are now the most important source of international law.[93] Since these are by far the most germane source to the public health context, they will form the focus of discussion here.

'Treaties are express agreements and are a form of substitute legislation undertaken by states. They bear a close resemblance to contracts in a superficial sense in that the parties create binding obligations for themselves'.[94] They are binding as a consequence of acceptance of the principle *pacta sunt servanda*, that is, 'that which has been agreed to must be respected':[95] in this sense, consent is the foundation of international law.[96] Treaties may be classified under two broad headings: contractual treaties, which are concluded between small numbers of states (often, only two) on limited topics – such as extradition treaties and bilateral investment treaties, and law-making treaties, agreed to by large numbers of states, 'whereby states elaborate their perception of international law upon any given topic or establish new rules which are to guide them for the future in their international conduct'.[97]

Globalisation and the growing scope of international law have resulted in an increasing interpenetration of legal systems; this book is itself testament to the multilevel character of regulation, ranging from the local, through subnational (in light of devolution) to national, regional (EU) and, here, international. Such penetration makes it especially important to understand the nature of the relationship between systems of law. The two best-known approaches to this relationship are the monist and dualist theories. 'Monists view international and national law as part of a single legal order. Thus, international law is directly applicable in the national legal orders. There is no need for any domestic implementing legislation; international law is immediately applicable within national legal systems'.[98] By contrast, dualists 'view international and national law as distinct legal orders. For international law to be applicable in the national legal order, it must be received through domestic legislative measures, the effect of which is to transform the international rule into a national one'.[99]

On this analysis, which might be regarded as somewhat simplistic,[100] and taking account of the particular nature of EU law as outlined above, the UK is a dualist state.[101] It adopts a transformative approach to treaties,[102] meaning that enactment of legislation is necessary for implementation of the obligations in domestic law: for example, the Human Rights Act 1998 gave domestic effect to the UK's treaty obligations under the European Convention on

---

91 United Nations, *Charter of the United Nations*, 26 June 1945, entered into force 24 October 1945, 1 UNTS 16, Article 92.
92 Shaw (n 86), 50.
93 Martin Dixon, Robert McCorquodale and Sarah Williams, *Cases and Materials on International Law* (5th edn., Oxford: Oxford University Press 2011) 22.
94 Shaw (n 86), 67.
95 Hugh Thirlway, 'The Sources of International Law', in Evans (ed) (n 89), 97.
96 See Matthew Lister, 'The Legitimating Role of Consent in International Law' (2011) 11 *Chicago Journal of International Law* 663.
97 Shaw (n 86), 67.
98 Richard Oppong, 'Re-Imagining International Law: An Examination of Recent Trends in the Reception of International Law into National Legal Systems in Africa' (2006) 30 *Fordham International Law Journal* 296, 297.
99 ibid, 297–298.
100 See Shaw (n 86), 94–95.
101 See European Scrutiny Committee, *The EU Bill and Parliamentary Sovereignty* (HC 2010–12, 633-I) [10].
102 See Boas (n 87), 147.

Human Rights, thus 'bringing rights home' insofar as they could henceforward be invoked directly in UK courts. As Shaw notes, this approach is more closely consonant with the separation of powers, in view of the fact that ratification of treaties in the UK is a matter for the executive branch alone:[103]

> Were treaties to be rendered applicable directly within the state without any intermediate stage after signature and ratification and before domestic operation, the executive would be able to legislate without the legislature. Because of this, any incorporation theory approach to treaty law has been rejected. Indeed, so far as this topic is concerned, it seems to turn more on the particular relationship between the executive and legislative branches of government than upon any preconceived notions of international law.[104]

Where legislation has not been enacted to give domestic effect to treaties to which the UK government has agreed, the obligations exist only as matters of international law. However, courts do apply a presumption when interpreting statutes that Parliament intends to legislate in accordance with the UK's international obligations;[105] similarly, they may choose to develop common law in a manner that complies with those obligations.[106] In this manner, such treaties may be said to have 'indirect' legal effect: they may impact upon judicial reasoning in a case, but the provisions cannot in themselves be used as bases for bringing a case in a UK court.

8.4 International law and public health

International law has an increasingly broad reach, but *international public health law* is a relatively new area of activity. Fidler has stated that:

> in the decades since the Second World War, international activities concerning public health carried out by intergovernmental organizations and nongovernmental organizations made little use of international law. During a period in which the field of international law expanded dramatically, the potential for international law to contribute to global public health remained unexplored.[107]

Largely as a consequence of globalisation, which has necessitated international cooperation in order to ensure control of transboundary threats to population health, which has presented opportunities to address health problems (e.g. through dissemination of scientific knowledge), and which has enhanced understanding of the interconnectedness of health with other global concerns (such as poverty or climate change), this position has significantly changed in recent years.[108] Writing in 2008, Gostin and Taylor argue that 'the need for a coherent system

---

103 The Constitutional Reform and Governance Act 2010, s. 20, provides that a treaty must be 'laid before Parliament' and may only be ratified if a period of 21 days has elapsed without the House of Commons resolving that it should not be ratified. There are no requirements for a parliamentary debate or vote to take place, although of course any enacting legislation would provide opportunity for such debate.
104 Shaw (n 86), 106.
105 See R v Secretary of State for the Home Department, ex parte Brind [1991] 1 AC 696, 748 (Lord Bridge), noting that this 'mere canon of construction . . . involves no importation of international law into the domestic field'.
106 See Assange v The Swedish Prosecution Authority [2012] UKSC 22, [10] (Lord Phillips), referring to 'the presumption that our domestic law will accord with our international obligations'.
107 David Fidler, 'International Law and Global Public Health' (1999) 48 University of Kansas Law Review 1, 1.
108 See Allyn Taylor, 'Global Governance, International Health Law and the WHO: Looking towards the Future' (2002) 80 Bulletin of the World Health Organization 975.

of international health law and governance has never been greater',[109] but conclude that the 'state-centricity' of existing international law presents a significant obstacle to amelioration of population health and reduction of health inequalities worldwide. They therefore propose a new model of 'global health law', which seeks to 'move beyond its traditional confines of formal sources and subjects of international law . . . [to] foster more effective global health action among governments, businesses, civil society and other actors'.[110] Gostin has significantly expanded upon this idea in more recent work, considering also (as do we in this book) a variety of more or less formal forms of law and governance, and expanding the reach of global health law to encompass 'regimes that are not specifically designed to alter health outcomes [but which] nonetheless have profound effects on the public's health and safety' (such as trade, food, and the environment).[111] We return to his analysis briefly in Chapter 10.

This is a complex, diverse, and rapidly evolving field, and full exploration of it would go well beyond the primary focus of this book on public health law in the UK. Instead, as with EU law in the first part of this chapter, three areas will be briefly outlined as illustrations of the subject-matter and functioning of this form of law.

8.4.1 Case study 4: Communicable disease (and beyond): the international health regulations[112]

Measures to respond to the threat posed by infectious diseases originating from beyond a state's borders have a lengthy history; the modern international legal framework has its origins in the international sanitary conferences that took place from the mid-nineteenth century onward.[113] The World Health Assembly, the principal decision-making organ of the World Health Organization (WHO) – and the body that is accorded authority by the WHO Constitution (which is itself a treaty) to adopt binding regulations concerning 'sanitary and quarantine requirements and other procedures designed to prevent the international spread of disease'[114] – retitled the International Sanitary Regulations as the International Health Regulations in 1969.[115] By the time of their replacement, these Regulations applied to only three diseases – cholera, plague, and yellow fever[116] – while compliance was patchy and monitoring ineffective.[117] However, it was the outbreak of SARS in 2003 that really provided impetus to the process of revision that had commenced in 1995[118] and that led to the adoption of new Regulations, 'among the world's most widely-adopted treaties',[119] in 2005.

The new Regulations are much broader in scope than their predecessor. Most significantly, they adopt an 'all hazards' approach rather than being limited to specific diseases. Instead, 'disease' is defined widely as 'an illness or medical condition, irrespective of origin or source, that presents or could present significant harm to humans',[120] thus covering

109 Lawrence Gostin and Allyn Taylor, 'Global Health Law: A Definition and Grand Challenges' (2008) 1 *Public Health Ethics* 53, 53.
110 ibid, 55.
111 Gostin (n 1), 60.
112 WHA Res 58.3, 23 May 2005, entered into force 15 June 2005.
113 See David Fidler, *International Law and Infectious Diseases* (Oxford: Oxford University Press 1999), chapter 2.
114 United Nations, *Constitution of the World Health Organization*, 22 July 1946, entered into force 7 April 1948, 14 UNTS 185, Article 21(a).
115 25 July 1969, entered into force 1 January 1971, 764 UNTS 3.
116 Smallpox was removed from the list of applicable diseases in 1981.
117 See David Fidler, 'From International Sanitary Conventions to Global Health Security: The New International Health Regulations' (2005) 4 *Chinese Journal of International Law* 325.
118 See David Fidler, *SARS, Governance and the Globalization of Disease* (Basingstoke: Palgrave Macmillan 2004).
119 Gostin (n 1), 181.
120 Article 1(1).

biological, chemical, and radiological threats and extending to non-communicable diseases. Additionally, the Regulations require states to develop surveillance capacity;[121] to notify WHO of events that may constitute a 'public health emergency of international concern',[122] in such case, providing it with public health information;[123] and to develop capacity to respond to such situations.[124] If a public health emergency of international concern is notified, WHO determines whether it exists[125] and, if so, may issue temporary recommendations to the state in question 'regarding persons, baggage, cargo, containers, conveyances, goods and/or postal parcels to prevent or reduce the international spread of disease and avoid unnecessary interference with international traffic'.[126] WHO also has power to issue standing recommendations of appropriate health measures, for routine or periodic application.[127]

The purpose of the Regulations is expressed as 'to prevent, protect against, control and provide a public health response to the international spread of disease in ways that are commensurate with and restricted to public health risks, and which avoid unnecessary interference with international traffic and trade'.[128] This represents an attempt to balance health and trade concerns, but Gostin detects a 'conceptual shift', with trade risks determining the scope of the old Regulations and health risks defining the new version.[129] The Regulations also seek to strike a balance between public health measures and human rights: they are to be implemented 'with full respect for the dignity, human rights and fundamental freedoms of persons',[130] and measures are to be applied in a transparent and non-discriminatory manner.[131]

The Regulations have been welcomed by commentators: Fidler argues, perhaps somewhat portentously, that they might 'contribute to the elevation of public health as a marker for the quality of twenty-first century governance pursued by states, intergovernmental organisations and non-governmental organisations'.[132] However, the same author notes that the Regulations are rooted in global health security, which is

> essentially a defensive, reactive strategy because it seeks to ensure that states are prepared to detect and respond to public health threats and emergencies of international concern. The strategy does not require states go on the offensive against the factors that lead to disease emergence and spread.[133]

He also cautions that compliance cannot be guaranteed, given weak mechanisms of enforcement.[134] The two major communicable disease outbreaks since the adoption of the Regulations – the H1N1 pandemic in 2009 and Ebola in 2014 – tend to reinforce the latter concern. Gostin notes that 'many states disregarded WHO advice' during the first episode;[135]

---

121 Article 5.
122 Article 6. This is defined as an 'extraordinary event which is determined . . . (i) to constitute a public health risk to other States through the international spread of disease and (ii) to potentially require a coordinated international response': Article 1(1).
123 Article 7. WHO may take account of information produced by parties other than state actors: Article 9.
124 Article 13.
125 Article 12.
126 Article 15.
127 Article 16. Examples of recommendations (whether temporary or standing) are provided in Article 18.
128 Article 2.
129 (n 1), 185.
130 Article 3(1).
131 Article 42.
132 Fidler (n 117), 387.
133 ibid, 389.
134 ibid, 389–390.
135 Gostin (n 1), 202.

it has also been claimed that WHO overreacted to the pandemic.[136] In respect of Ebola, 'nearly a quarter of WHO's Member States instituted travel bans and other additional measures not called for by WHO, which significantly interfered with international travel, causing negative political, economic and social consequences for the affected countries'.[137] It has also been argued that countries have failed to develop the necessary public health capacities and that WHO's response was insufficiently timely and that it lacked the organisational culture to effectively respond. There has therefore been a call for further strengthening of the Regulations and development of a notion of 'shared sovereignty' in the interests of protecting global public health.[138]

Compliance with, and implementation of, the Regulations necessitates 'an adequate legal framework to support and enable implementation of all of their obligations and rights'.[139] Enactment or revision of legislation is not obligatory, but the WHO has observed that doing so can institutionalise and strengthen the role of the Regulations and facilitate coordination among the various bodies concerned with implementation.[140] In the UK, various pieces of primary and secondary legislation give effect to the commitment to implement the Regulations.[141] Most notably, the amendments to the Public Health (Control of Disease) Act 1984 effected by Part 3 of the Health and Social Care Act 2008, and enactment of the Public Health etc (Scotland) Act 2008, give effect to an 'all hazards' approach in England and Wales, and Scotland, respectively. Northern Irish legislation seems likely shortly to follow suit.[142]

8.4.2 Case Study 5: Tobacco – the Framework Convention on Tobacco Control[143]

This Convention, 'one of the most widely and rapidly embraced treaties in United Nations history'[144] and the first global health treaty negotiated under the auspices of the WHO,[145] entered into force in February 2005. As of March 2015, 180 countries had ratified the treaty, including the UK but not the US.[146] The treaty had a difficult gestation: the WHO lacked experience in the process of negotiation and none of the representatives of civil society who participated in the creation of the Convention had familiarity with international law-making.[147] However, Taylor and Dhillon note that the novelty of the situation was also advantageous in that 'those interests opposed to effective regulation did not take the international legislative process seriously until it was essentially too late to stop'.[148]

---

136 See WHO, *Implementation of the International Health Regulations (2005): Report of the Review Committee on the Functioning of the International Health Regulations (2005) in Relation to Pandemic (H1N1) 2009*, A64/10 (Geneva: WHO 2011) 17.
137 World Health Organization, *Report of the Ebola Interim Assessment Panel* (Geneva: WHO 2015) 5.
138 ibid, 10.
139 World Health Organization, *IHR Core Capacity Monitoring Framework: Checklist and Indicators for Monitoring Progress in the Development of IHR Core Capacities in States Parties* (Geneva: WHO 2011) 17.
140 ibid.
141 See e.g. Health Protection Agency (Amendment) Regulations 2007, SI 2007/1624; Public Health (Ships)(Scotland) Amendment Regulations 2007, SSI 2007/515.
142 See Department of Health, Social Services and Public Safety, *Review of the Public Health (Northern Ireland) Act 1967: A Consultation Document* (Belfast: DHSSPS 2015).
143 21 May 2003, entered into force 27 February 2005, 2302 UNTS 166.
144 Gostin (n 1), 214.
145 World Health Organization, <www.who.int/tobacco/framework/background/en/> accessed 5 April 2016.
146 See Framework Convention Alliance, <www.fctc.org/about-fca/tobacco-control-treaty/latest-ratifications/parties-ratifications-accessions> accessed 5 April 2016.
147 See Allyn Taylor and Ibadat Dhillon, 'An International Legal Strategy for Alcohol Control: Not a Framework Convention – At Least Not Yet' (2012) 108 *Addiction* 450, 451.
148 ibid.

The *Framework Convention* mechanism was selected as the best means of building consensus and overcoming industry opposition.[149] One of the chief architects of the treaty, Allyn Taylor, took the view that a treaty laying down 'clear, detailed and specific rules' would be unlikely to be effective, as states would resist enactment of detailed legislation.[150] Instead, an approach was adopted that did 'not attempt to resolve all significant issues in a single instrument. Rather, states first adopt a Framework Convention that calls for international cooperation in realising broadly stated goals. Ideally, the parties to the Convention will then conclude separate protocols containing specific measures designed to implement these goals'.[151] This makes for a 'continuous and dynamic process of law-making that can gradually and incrementally build support to reduce tobacco use'.[152] However, it lengthens the international law-making process – insofar as both the initial Convention and the Protocols require negotiation; and, still more problematically, the 'broad format of the Framework Convention enables states to relieve public pressure for action without resolving to take concrete steps to control tobacco production and consumption'.[153]

The objective of the Convention is 'to protect present and future generations from the devastating health, social, environmental and economic consequences of tobacco consumption and exposure to tobacco smoke'.[154] Parties have general obligations to develop, implement, update, and review national tobacco control strategies, plans, and programmes,[155] to which end, they should provide and finance a national coordinating mechanism for tobacco control and to 'adopt and implement effective legislative, executive, administrative and/or other measures and cooperate, as appropriate, with other parties in developing appropriate policies for preventing and reducing tobacco consumption, nicotine addiction and exposure to tobacco smoke'.[156] More specifically, the Convention contains a range of measures aimed at reducing demand (including regulation of the contents of tobacco products; of packaging and labelling, and of advertising, promotion and sponsorship);[157] reducing supply (e.g. illicit trade in tobacco products and sales to and by minors);[158] research, surveillance, reporting, and exchange of information;[159] and cooperation in the scientific, technical, and legal spheres.[160] Several of the broadly worded provisions in the Convention are fleshed out by guidelines for implementation that are intended to assist parties in meeting their obligations and to propose measures that might be adopted to fulfil them.[161] In addition, the Convention has been supplemented by a further treaty, the Protocol to Eliminate Illicit Trade in Tobacco Products.[162] This Protocol has yet to achieve the necessary number of ratifications to enter into force.

Article 21 requires state parties to make periodic reports on their implementation of the Convention; such reports are now required every two years. Based upon these, the Convention's

---

149 Another example of this model is the Framework Convention on Climate Change, 9 May 1992, entered into force 21 March 1994, 1771 UNTS 107.

150 Allyn Taylor, 'An International Regulatory Strategy for Global Tobacco Control' (1996) 21 *Yale Journal of International Law* 257, 294.

151 ibid.

152 ibid.

153 ibid, 295; Gostin (n 1), 215.

154 Article 3.

155 Article 5(1).

156 Article 5(2).

157 Articles 6–14.

158 Articles 15–17.

159 Articles 20–21.

160 Article 22.

161 See e.g. WHO, *Guidelines for Implementation of Article 11: Packaging and Labelling of Tobacco Products*, FCTC/COP3 10 (Geneva: WHO 2008).

162 12 November 2012.

Secretariat is able to measure progress in implementation. Its most recent report notes that '80% of the parties have strengthened their existing or adopted new tobacco control legislation after ratifying the Convention, but one third of the parties have still not put in place legislative measures in line with the requirements of the Convention'; the average implementation rate of the Articles is stated to approach 60%, but there are identifiable weaknesses in national coordination and capacity.[163] Some commentators have therefore seen the Convention as merely a 'qualified' or 'perceived' success,[164] while others evaluate it more positively.[165]

The EU is a party to the Convention and has also signed the additional Protocol. Accordingly, certain EU legal measures,[166] notably the revised Tobacco Products Directive of 2014,[167] are intended to give effect to the obligations under the Convention, but the Union has sought to go further than the provisions of the Convention in taking regulatory action in respect of tobacco.[168] Elements of this Directive are transposed into UK domestic law by secondary legislation providing for standardised packaging;[169] other provisions were implemented in May 2016.[170] However, as is the case with the EU, legal and regulatory intervention in respect of tobacco in the UK, while in some instances influenced by the Convention,[171] is not solely driven by it and extends well beyond its requirements.

8.4.3 Case study 6: International law versus public health? International trade agreements

As was noted above in respect of the European Union, a difficult tension exists between international agreements that seek to enhance trade between nations and measures that seek to protect or advance the health of populations. The linkage between trade and public health is centuries old: the quarantine measures outlined briefly in Chapter 3 were early examples of restrictions on free trade imposed in the interests of health, while the International Sanitary Regulations, and later the International Health Regulations, also sought to limit the impact of the spread of contagious disease upon trade. More recently, attention has turned to the impact of trade upon the incidence of non-communicable disease, for example, through encouragement of demand for tobacco, alcohol, and/or obesogenic products. Thus, it is now recognised that

> the general benefits of liberal trade policies, such as greater competition and lower prices, can translate into negative health consequences. In particular, where increased

---

163 WHO, 2014 Global Progress Report on Implementation of the WHO Framework Convention on Tobacco Control (Geneva: WHO 2014) vii.

164 See e.g. Taylor and Dhillon (n 147), 450; Thomas Bollyky and David Fidler, 'Has a Global Tobacco Treaty Made a Difference?', The Atlantic (28 February 2015).

165 See e.g. Arthur Wilson and Abdallah Daar, 'A Survey of International Legal Instruments to Examine their Effectiveness in Improving Global Health and in Realizing Health Rights' (2013) 41 Journal of Law, Medicine and Ethics 89, 94; Oscar Cabrera and Juan Carballo, 'Tobacco Control Litigation: Broader Impacts on Health Rights Adjudication' (2013) 41 Journal of Law, Medicine and Ethics 147, 149.

166 See also Directive 2011/64/EU on the structure and rates of excise duty applied to manufactured tobacco, [2011] OJ L 176/24, recital (2).

167 Directive 2014/40/EU on the approximation of the laws, regulations, and administrative provisions of the Member States concerning the manufacture, presentation, and sale of tobacco and related products and repealing Directive 2001/37/EC, [2014] OJ L 127/1. See especially recital (7): 'legislative action at Union level is also necessary in order to implement the WHO Framework Convention on Tobacco Control ('FCTC') of May 2003, the provisions of which are binding on the Union and its Member States'.

168 See Alberto Alemanno, 'Out of Sight, Out of Mind: Towards a New EU Tobacco Products Directive' (2012) 18 Columbia Journal of European Law 197, 202.

169 Standardised Packaging of Tobacco Products Regulations 2015, SI 2015/829.

170 Tobacco and Related Products Regulations 2016, SI 2016/507.

171 See e.g. Government Response to the House of Commons Health Committee's First Report of Session 2005–06: Smoking in Public Places, Cm 6769 (Norwich: TSO 2006) [10]–[11] referring to the Convention in respect of proposals that were enacted as Part 1 of the Health Act 2006.

competition and lower prices stimulate consumption of harmful products, there is likely
to be a correlative increase in associated morbidity and mortality.[172]

The linkages may also be more indirect: for example, trade may affect macroeconomic conditions, which might impact upon employment levels, which may in turn increase inequalities in health status between particular population groups.

The World Trade Organization (WTO), established in 1995, is the 'centre of authority
for the governance of trade',[173] and Fidler argues that its 'existence has done more to increase
the political profile of public health globally than almost anything else in the history of
international health cooperation'.[174] There is a basic principle of non-discrimination underpinning the WTO agreements, but there are exceptions that enable WTO members to adopt
restrictive measures in order to protect health,[175] provided that such measures are no more
restrictive on trade than necessary.[176] However, it has been argued that the manner in which
the exceptions are specified

> puts the onus on the Member State arguing public health interests to provide scientific
> justification for deviation from its general obligations. This burden will make it very
> difficult for poor countries to ensure that the multilateral trade agreements do not
> adversely impact on the health status of their populations.[177]

The operation of these principles is illustrated by the 1989 dispute between Thailand
and the United States;[178] the former prohibited the importation of cigarettes, but authorised
the sale of those which were domestically produced. The argument that these measures were
permissible on the basis of Article XX(b) was rejected. No scientific evidence was found to
support the Thai government's claim that chemicals and other additives contained in US-
produced cigarettes made them more harmful than those manufactured in Thailand; and
restrictions on importation were not 'necessary to protect human . . . life or health' since
other, less trade-restrictive, methods could have been selected that would not discriminate
in favour of domestic producers (such as bans on advertising). In view of this decision, the
ban on imported cigarettes was lifted in 1990, although smoking prevalence in Thailand did
subsequently decline as stronger tobacco control measures were introduced in response to
the opening up of the marketplace.[179]

Perhaps the best-known area in which public health and international trade agreements
have intersected is in respect of the impact that WTO's Trade-Related Aspects of Intellectual
Property Rights agreement (TRIPS) has had upon access to pharmaceuticals in developing

---

172 Benn McGrady, Trade and Public Health: The WTO, Tobacco, Alcohol and Diet (Cambridge: Cambridge University Press 2011) 2.
173 David Fidler, Nick Drager and Kelley Lee, 'Managing the Pursuit of Health and Wealth: The Key Challenges' (2009)
       373 Lancet 325, 327.
174 Fidler (n 117), 389.
175 See e.g. General Agreement on Tariffs and Trade (GATT), 5 April 1994, entered into force 1 January 1995, 1867 UNTS
       187, Article XX(b).
176 See World Health Organization/World Trade Organization, WTO Agreements and Public Health: A Joint Study by the WHO and
       WTO Secretariat (Geneva: WHO/WTO 2002) 31.
177 Kent Ranson, Robert Beaglehole, Carlos Correa, Zafar Mirza, Kent Buse and Nick Drager, 'The Public Health
       Implications of Multilateral Trade Agreements' in Kelley Lee, Kent Buse, and Suzanne Fustukian (eds), Health Policy in a
       Globalising World (Cambridge: Cambridge University Press 2002) 35.
178 GATT Panel Report, Thailand – Restrictions on Importation of and Internal Taxes on Cigarettes, DS10/R, adopted 7 November 1990,
       BISD 37S/200.
179 World Health Organization/World Trade Organization (n 176), 73.

nations.[180] Article 27 of the agreement requires Member States to provide patent protection for 'any invention, whether products or processes, in all fields of technology', including pharmaceuticals: this is therefore likely to act as 'a barrier to affordability',[181] and various United Nations bodies have expressed concern in this regard.[182] In response, a WTO ministerial statement, the Doha Declaration on the TRIPS Agreement and Public Health, emphasises that the

> TRIPS Agreement does not and should not prevent Members from taking measures to protect public health . . . [and] that the Agreement can and should be interpreted and implemented in a manner supportive of WTO Members' right to protect public health and, in particular, to promote access to medicines for all'.[183]

The Declaration underlines the importance of using the 'flexibilities' embedded in TRIPS to protect public health, such as rights to grant compulsory licences (e.g. for generic medicines) and to engage in parallel importation. The Secretariats of the WHO and WTO proclaimed that the Declaration 'demonstrates that a rules-based trading system is compatible with public health interests'.[184] However, others have been more critical – for example, Smith, Correa, and Oh argue that developing countries have not made full use of the TRIPS flexibilities[185] because of lack of capacity and resources; vulnerability to political and economic pressure from developed nations (with many such nations negotiating 'TRIPS-plus' bilateral agreements that subvert the flexibilities);[186] and misunderstanding of the conditions under which the flexibilities can be deployed.

This particular issue is unlikely to impact upon public health law and regulation in the UK, although the value of the pharmaceuticals sector to the British economy means that government has a significant interest in the operation of TRIPS. However, it is plausible that international trade agreements could serve to restrict the forms of intervention that can lawfully (that is, as a matter of *international* law) be adopted to address particular public health problems. For example, taxes on fat or salt in foods might amount to discrimination under the General Agreement on Tariffs and Trade, unless the taxes pertained equally to all 'like' domestic and imported products: it is not clear that the health exception in Article XX(b) would apply, since it may prove difficult to establish that the measure is *necessary* to protect human health.[187] Similar difficulties may arise in respect of policies of minimum pricing on alcohol:[188] indeed, opposition to the Alcohol (Minimum Pricing) (Scotland) Act 2012 has been expressed on this ground.[189]

---

180 See Kennet Shadlen, Samira Guennif, Alenka Guzmán, and N. Lalitha (eds), *Intellectual Property, Pharmaceuticals and Public Health: Access to Drugs in Developing Countries* (Cheltenham: Edward Elgar 2011).
181 Richard Smith, Carlos Correa and Cecilia Oh, 'Trade, TRIPS and Pharmaceuticals' (2009) 373 *Lancet* 684, 686.
182 See e.g. World Health Assembly, *WHO Medicines Strategy*, WHA Res. 54.11, 21 May 2001; UN General Assembly, *Declaration of Commitment on HIV/AIDS*, A/RES/S-26/2, 2 August 2001.
183 14 November 2001, WT/MIN(01)/DEC/2, [4].
184 World Health Organization/World Trade Organization (n 176), 111.
185 Smith et al (n 181), 690.
186 See Carlos Correa, 'Implications of Bilateral Free Trade Agreements on Access to Medicines' (2006) 84 *Bulletin of the World Health Organization* 399.
187 See Allemanno and Carreño (n 78), 106–111.
188 See GATT Panel Report, *Canada – Import, Distribution and Sale of Certain Alcoholic Drinks by Provincial Marketing Agencies*, DS17/R, adopted 18 February 1992, BISD 39S/27, [5.27]–[5.32].
189 See Position of Poland on Notification 2012/0394/UK on the draft Alcohol (minimum price per unit) (Scotland) Order, reported by the BBC, <www.bbc.co.uk/news/uk-scotland-scotland-politics-22186762> accessed 5 April 2016; Scottish Parliament, *Passage of the Alcohol (Minimum Pricing) (Scotland) Bill 2011*, SPPB 173 (Edinburgh: Scottish Parliamentary Corporate Body 2013), evidence by Scotch Whisky Association, MIN65, [15].

Chapter 8: Summary

- While the UK remains a Member State, the law of the European Union takes precedence over the law of England and Wales. However, while protection of human health is 'mainstreamed' into all Union policies and activities, its competence to act in this field is of a complementary character; primary responsibility for public health lies with Member States, including the UK.
- Nonetheless, the Union legislative institutions play an important function in developing measures to address public health threats in areas where Member States cannot act effectively on their own, including those relating to communicable diseases, tobacco, and alcohol. In other areas, such as obesity, an initially narrow sphere of competence (here, relating to consumer protection) has broadened into a wider public health role and is likely to continue to develop.
- Beyond the European Union, international treaties relating to matters of public health will have domestic legal effect if their provisions are incorporated into legislation by the UK Parliament; if not, the legal obligations for the UK are solely matters of international law.
- Recent years have witnessed growing activity on matters of public health at international level, with two major treaties – the Framework Convention on Tobacco Control and the revised International Health Regulations – being concluded under the auspices of the World Health Organization. This area of law continues to evolve, and we shall return to it in Chapter 10. However, in other areas, notably trade, international agreements may sometimes hinder the pursuit of public health goals.

8.5 Further readings

Alberto Alemanno and Amandine Garde (eds), *Regulating Lifestyle Risks: The EU, Alcohol, Tobacco and Unhealthy Diets* (Cambridge: Cambridge University Press 2014).

David Fidler, *SARS, Governance and the Globalization of Disease* (Basingstoke: Palgrave Macmillan 2004).

Mark Flear, *Governing Public Health: EU Law, Regulation and Biopolitics* (Oxford: Hart Publishing 2015).

Lawrence Gostin, *Global Health Law* (Cambridge, MA: Harvard University Press 2014).

Tamara Hervey and Jean McHale, *European Union Health Law: Themes and Implications* (Cambridge: Cambridge University Press 2015).

Benn McGrady, *Trade and Public Health: The WTO, Tobacco, Alcohol and Diet* (Cambridge: Cambridge University Press 2011).

Andrew Mitchell and Tania Voon (eds), *The Global Tobacco Epidemic and the Law* (Cheltenham: Edward Elgar 2014).

Chapter 9

Policy, self-regulation, and governance for public health

9.1 Beyond legal approaches and public health

The previous four chapters have provided an overview of different areas and approaches within, or that bear on, the English legal system, explaining both their foundations and how they might serve or constrain public health agendas. We have sought to present an understanding of the breadth of laws that are relevant to the study and practice of public health and to provide the foundations for critical and practical reflections on the strengths and limits of different branches of law in the context of public health. Prior to those chapters, in Part I of this book, we explained in our presentation of the idea of public health itself the importance of *social coordination*. That discussion raised the importance of laws in providing social coordination but also noted the wider concept of *governance*: in looking to social and governmental 'machinery', public health activity is not regulated solely by rules found in statutes and case law. The Faculty of Public Health (FPH) has a role in informing and educating the public in matters concerning health, for example, and local authorities (LAs) have considerable discretion in establishing how to prioritise and discharge their public health responsibilities (albeit, as explained in Chapter 7, that such discretion is provided and constrained by law).

The value of recognising the broad social coordination function in public health practice is underscored by our discussion in Chapter 3 of the way that, on its face at least, law has lagged behind contemporary understandings of public health approaches and how a superficial reflection on 'public health law' misses the breadth and reach of public health agendas. Public health law properly understood is an extremely broad field, much wider than is suggested by definitions that are limited to questions such as notifiable diseases. In Chapter 4, therefore, in presenting our characterisation of public health law as an area of study and practice, we advanced reasons to look across the legal spectrum and also to incorporate wider measures of *governance*. Within the concept of governance, we include regulatory devices such as government policies, professional guidelines, self-regulation, and 'private' means of coordinating activity. In short, we aim to capture forms of achieving social control that are real and effective but not formally laws. The purpose of this chapter is to introduce and explore the relationship between such regulatory approaches and public health.

The next section will present some foundational ideas about regulation. We explore the idea of being a 'regulator', outline different modes of intervention, and highlight some of the tensions both in relation to 'public' and 'private' actors and in terms of public health ethics. Section 9.3 then considers questions of individual responsibility and self-regulation. Here, we first consider the scope and limits of individuals' public health responsibilities, before reflecting on questions of corporate social responsibility. Having identified both strengths and shortcomings in regard to these matters, and in the light of concerns about 'hard law' sometimes providing too blunt a tool, in section 9.4, we examine a broad concept of public policy and public health. This involves discussion of government policy and regulations in light of discourses of the influential (if questionable) idea of 'nudge theory', moving to publicly formulated social controls that rely on soft law measures of intervention.

9.2 Governance for public health

9.2.1 Regulating and regulators

This book is entitled *Public Health Law*. Yet, like authors of cognate textbooks, we are taking 'public health law' – or at least the subject of our analysis under that heading – to connote something broader than just formally instituted and recognised legal provisions.[1] Strictly, *legal* measures may be identified as rules or principles that are recognised as laws because they derive from a particular source in a particular way (in English law, we recognise these as emanating both from judge-made law and statute); they apply to actors within a defined jurisdiction (say England and Wales); and they may be enforced through recognised institutions (the courts).[2] However, many rules that we are compelled to follow, or find ourselves obeying, are not laws in this sense: think, for example, of doctors' obligations to follow the General Medical Council's rules and guidance, or patients' obligations to respect NHS non-smoking policies such as the one referred to in Chapter 5. Many aspects of social coordination are based on rules, principles, or norms whose source is not the basic political and legal authority that we associate with statutory and common law rules. And, just as is the case with hard legal measures, in practice we find that analysis of other modes of coordination requires consideration of how and why some rules, principles, and norms are more stringently followed and enforced than others.[3] Such considerations bring us into the sphere of regulatory theory and practice.

Regulation is an area of academic inquiry that is arguably separate to legal studies.[4] Nevertheless, at base, a book on public health law is about social coordination mechanisms that impact population health and that require us to consider non-law based social controls. 'Nudge theory', for example, which we consider in section 9.4, looks to achieve good policy ends through softer styles of governance: i.e. modes of intervention that are indirect, minimally invasive, non-binding, and so on. Nudge has been cast as revolutionary because it apparently avoids the controversies of coercive control mechanisms whilst still producing better outcomes at the individual and the population level.[5] Yet, amongst the observations

---

1 Consider, for example, Jonathan Montgomery's definition of health care law in his leading textbook: 'the subject of health care law is wider than medical law. It embraces not only the practice of medicine, but also that of the non-medical health care professions, the administration of health services and the law's role in maintaining public health. It also means that the concept of "law" in this context must be examined carefully. Legal rules in a strict sense, as developed by Parliament and the courts, are not the only type of binding norm that is relevant to health care law'. See Jonathan Montgomery, *Health Care Law* (2nd edn., Oxford: Oxford University Press 2002) 4.
2 For an influential theoretical account on how, conceptually, we identify law, see H.L.A. Hart, *The Concept of Law* (2nd edn., Oxford: Clarendon Press 1997).
3 Such questions have not been a central theme of this book, but it is important when considering the normative and practical force of laws and regulations to consider, not just what they say, but also what effect they have: e.g. do people choose to follow them, are they policed, and are sanctions applied when they are breached?
4 Bronwen Morgan and Karen Yeung, *An Introduction to Law and Regulation: Text and Materials* (Cambridge: Cambridge University Press 2003).
5 Richard Thaler and Cass Sunstein, *Nudge: Improving Decisions about Health, Wealth, and Happiness* (London: Penguin 2009). See also Richard Thaler and Cass Sunstein, 'Libertarian Paternalism Is Not An Oxymoron' (2003) 70 *University of Chicago Law Review* 1159.

advanced from within public health is that non-legal regulatory techniques have for a long time formed a part of public governance of health-related (and other) strategies.[6] Regardless of critical appraisals of different modes of governance, or their novelty, it is important to understand the place for these in the overall social coordination functions pertinent to public health theory and activity. We would provide an incomplete picture of the foundations of public health law if we limited our analysis just to hard law.

Christopher Hood and colleagues identify three components that are common to regulatory systems: first, they *set standards*; second, they *gather information* or *monitor* the system; and third, they have a role in *modifying behaviour*.[7] Working from this observation, Bronwen Morgan and Karen Yeung, in their leading textbook on regulation, say:

> At their narrowest, definitions of regulation tend to centre on deliberate attempts by the state to influence socially valuable behaviour which may have adverse side-effects by establishing, monitoring and enforcing legal rules. At its broadest, regulation is seen as encompassing all forms of social control, whether intentional or not, and whether imposed by the state or other social institutions.[8]

Like Morgan and Yeung, we recognise the importance of broader understandings of regulation. Importantly, therefore, where we take an interest in modes of governance regarding public health, we will be concerned with the regulatory roles and social impacts of (and on) public agencies such as Public Health England (PHE). Furthermore, our focus reaches beyond the functions of governmental bodies. Many other actors and agencies can impact on our behaviour, with consequent implications for population health. Supermarkets, for example, whilst not being accountable or motivated in the same way as public bodies, have a role in setting standards, monitoring activity, and indeed modifying behaviour.[9] They are private actors, yet their activities impact populations. In this sense, the governance activity of supermarkets and other organisations will be of interest to the public health lawyer, just as much as guidance issued by PHE or laws enacted by Parliament. Governance is a phenomenon that, as is widely observed, is not limited to legislators and governments.

Morgan and Yeung's introduction to regulatory theory explains this point about the need to look to broader understandings of who may be conceived as regulators. Lawyers (and others), when considering how society is governed, understandably look to controls that emanate from a sovereign legal power. Sometimes this includes also *delegated* powers of public authorities, such as those considered in Chapter 7. But looking just to these means missing alternative sources of governance that impact heavily on how society is coordinated. In their characterisation of regulatory theory, Morgan and Yeung express how a fuller analysis of governance challenges the underlying assumptions of approaches to social coordination that only consider measures rooted in law:

> The first assumption is that the state is the primary locus for articulating the collective goals of a community. Recent scholarship challenges this assumption by highlighting

6   Chris Bonell, Martin McKee, Adam Fletcher, Paul Wilkinson, and Andy Haines, 'One Nudge Forward, Two Steps Back' (2011) 342 *British Medical Journal* d401.
7   Christopher Hood, Henry Rothstein and Robert Baldwin, *The Government of Risk – Understanding Risk Regulation Regimes* (Oxford: Oxford University Press 2001) 23.
8   Morgan and Yeung (n 4), 3–4.
9   Recall also Gostin and Wiley's definition of public health law, which refers to the state in collaboration with its partners, including business: Lawrence Gostin and Lindsay Wiley, *Public Health Law: Power Duty Restraint* (3rd edn., Berkeley: University of California Press 2008) 4.

the emergence of non-state institutions, including commercial enterprise and non-governmental organisations, that operate as both a source of social influence and a forum in which public deliberation may occur. The second assumption is the hierarchical nature of the state's role: the idea that the state has final authority is increasingly challenged by the emergence of multiple levels and sites of governance that operate concurrently or in overlapping ways, rather than being vertically arranged. The third assumption is the centrality of rules as 'command' as the primary mode of shaping behaviour: the challenge here is twofold, not only encompassing empirically observed limitations to the effectiveness of legal rules, but also increasing recognition of the potential for alternative techniques of policy implementation.[10]

Given these observations and responses to more law-centric modes of analysis, the following sections of this chapter open up a range of pertinent discussions regarding the ways in which different modes of regulation can facilitate public health ends and raise questions about when and why non-legal governance approaches might be the only or best means available to advance a public health agenda. The discussions map onto ongoing contemporary political discourse, which we might trace back to the previous Conservative–Liberal Democrat Coalition's programme for government, in the foreword of which then Prime Minister David Cameron and Deputy Prime Minister Nick Clegg wrote:

> [T]here has been the assumption that central government can only change people's behaviour through rules and regulations. Our government will be a much smarter one, shunning the bureaucratic levers of the past and finding intelligent ways to encourage, support and enable people to make better choices for themselves.[11]

This position endures into the current Conservative Government's approach, and thus, it is essential to look to the governance functions of central and local governmental actors, harder and softer modes of regulation, and to the roles of non-public actors and the sorts of regulatory interventions they might deploy. Scholars and practitioners in public health and public health law need to consider too, not just whether people are supported and enabled in making better choices, but also whether they actually do so.[12] We will also consider governance by private organisations. Overarching an understanding of regulation as entailing a fragmented network of regulators opens up questions about potentially competing interests and agendas: if, for example, we accept that supermarkets' governance can impact population health, it will not necessarily follow that their regulatory choices will – still less, should – be designed to serve public health ends. We will raise some questions about tensions both within public and private governance below but, first, will present an overview of the range of measures available in regulation: defined in Hood and colleagues' framing, as the means available to public and private actors to *set standards, gather information* or *monitor the system,* and have a role in *modifying behaviour.* In considering the following discussion, it is useful to keep in mind the difference that regulatory theorists draw between *process* and *outcome.* Although we do not elaborate on this in any depth, when looking at questions of process, the focus

---

10 Morgan and Yeung (n 4), 4.

11 Cabinet Office, *The Coalition: Our Programme for Government* (London: Cabinet Office 2010) 7–8.

12 Theresa Marteau, David Ogilvie, Martin Roland, Marc Suhrcke, and Michael Kelly, 'Judging Nudging: Can Nudging Improve Population Health?' (2011) 342 *British Medical Journal* d228.

is on coordination. When studying outcome, the interest is in the norms, institutions, and cultures that arise in a system.[13]

9.2.2 Regulatory interventions

As would be expected given the previous discussion, there are various ways of conceiving different modes of regulation.[14] One influential and widely used account in the area under analysis in this book, which we have also outlined above, is found in the Nuffield Council on Bioethics' report on public health ethics.[15] In this section, we reproduce in fuller detail the Nuffield Council's 'intervention ladder', which provides a scheme for understanding softer and harder modes of governance. We note at the outset that the report's presentation of the 'intervention ladder' has invited criticism. In particular, it has been attacked by scholars including Angus Dawson and Marcel Verweij for placing too high a value on liberty.[16] As we will presently see, the Nuffield Council stipulates that regulators bear a higher burden of justification whenever positive governance measures are advanced, and the 'heavier' the intervention, the greater the justification, they suggest, is required. Although the report holds that regulators are responsible for omissions as well as positive interventions, it says that regulators should always start at the minimum possible level of intervention: it presents a (rebuttable) presumption that liberty is the highest value.[17]

We explicitly acknowledge criticisms such as Dawson and Verweij's not to accept or reject them. Rather, we mean to be clear that ethical critiques of the Nuffield Council's proposed framework do not of themselves undermine the practical benefits of the metaphor of the intervention ladder. Dawson and Verweij and others invite us to question the stewardship model that Nuffield employs in its analysis of regulatory interventions.[18] When we suggest that the intervention ladder be used as a framework for understanding different modes of governance, we do so on the basis that it is possible to use it to help understanding without having to apply it as the Nuffield Council urges. It is a concise representation of the spread of different possible regulatory approaches available. Whilst it suffers some problems of simplification, it also affords good explanatory potential and is prevalent in academic and policy materials regarding public health practice.

With the above in mind, consider the intervention ladder, presented again here for completeness (see also Chapter 2) with the Nuffield Council's own framing of it:

> Our proposed 'intervention ladder' suggests a way of thinking about the acceptability
> and justification of different public health policies. The least intrusive step is gener-
> ally 'to do nothing', or at most monitor the situation. The most intrusive is to legislate
> in such a way as to restrict the liberties of individuals, the population as a whole, or

---

13 See further Julia Black, 'Decentring Regulation: Understanding the Role of Regulation and Self-Regulation in a "Post-Regulatory" World' (2001) 54 *Current Legal Problems* 103.

14 See Morgan and Yeung (n 4).

15 Nuffield Council on Bioethics, *Public Health: Ethical Issues* (London: Nuffield 2007). The ladder is used, for example, in Local Government Association, *Changing Behaviours in Public Health – To Nudge or to Shove?* (London: LGA 2013); HM Government, *Healthy Lives, Healthy People: Our Strategy for Public Health in England* (CM 7985 2010).

16 Angus Dawson and Marcel Verweij, 'The Steward of the Millian State' (2008) 1 *Public Health Ethics* 193; Angus Dawson, 'Snakes and ladders: state interventions and the place of liberty in public health policy' (2016) 42 *Journal of Medical Ethics* 510.

17 Such a position is consistent with various approaches in public health ethics: however, the view that political systems privilege liberty rather than the good is challenged in the field: see John Coggon, *What Makes Health Public? A Critical Evaluation of Moral, Legal, and Political Claims in Public Health* (Cambridge: Cambridge University Press 2012).

18 Dawson and Verweij (n 16). See also, e.g. John Coggon, 'Harmful Rights-Doing? The Perceived Problem of Liberal Paradigms and Public Health' (2008) 34 *Journal of Medical Ethics* 798; John Coggon, 'What Help Is a Steward? Stewardship, Political Theory, and Public Health Law and Ethics' (2012) 62 *Northern Ireland Legal Quarterly* 599.

specific industries. In general, the higher the rung on the ladder at which the policy maker intervenes, the stronger the justification has to be. A more intrusive policy initiative is likely to be publicly acceptable only if there is a clear indication that it will produce the desired effect, and that this can be weighed favourably against any loss of liberty that may result.

The intervention ladder

The ladder of possible government actions is as follows:

- Eliminate choice. Regulate in such a way as to entirely eliminate choice, for example through compulsory isolation of patients with infectious diseases.
- Restrict choice. Regulate in such a way as to restrict the options available to people with the aim of protecting them, for example removing unhealthy ingredients from foods, or unhealthy foods from shops or restaurants.
- Guide choice through disincentives. Fiscal and other disincentives can be put in place to influence people not to pursue certain activities, for example through taxes on cigarettes, or by discouraging the use of cars in inner cities through charging schemes or limitations of parking spaces.
- Guide choices through incentives. Regulations can be offered that guide choices by fiscal and other incentives, for example offering tax-breaks for the purchase of bicycles that are used as a means of travelling to work.
- Guide choices through changing the default policy. For example, in a restaurant, instead of providing chips as a standard side dish (with healthier options available), menus could be changed to provide a more healthy option as standard (with chips as an option available).
- Enable choice. Enable individuals to change their behaviours, for example by offering participation in a NHS 'stop smoking' programme, building cycle lanes, or providing free fruit in schools.
- Provide information. Inform and educate the public, for example as part of campaigns to encourage people to walk more or eat five portions of fruit and vegetables per day.
- Do nothing or simply monitor the current situation.[19]

In some senses, as explained in Chapter 3, the Nuffield Council's breakdown of interventions suffers potential conceptual simplifications. For example, providing information can represent more than a minor intervention. And, depending on how an agency informs and educates, further questions may be raised about how ethically and politically 'heavy' an intervention is: consider, for example, stigmatisation being employed as a means of advancing a public health campaign.[20]

Overall, however, the intervention ladder neatly encapsulates the range of governance approaches that might be used in the context of public health law. As we progress through the current chapter, and in wider evaluation of potential and actual public health policy, consider how different measures on different rungs of the ladder might be used, not only

---

19 Nuffield Council on Bioethics (n 15), xviii–xix (cross-references within the report omitted).
20 cf Ronald Bayer and Jennifer Stuber, 'Tobacco Control, Stigma, and Public Health: Rethinking the Relations' (2006) 96 *American Journal of Public Health* 47; contrast also the concerns and analysis in Martin McKee and Pascal Diethelm, 'How the Growth of Denialism Undermines Public Health' (2010) 341 *British Medical Journal* c6950.

by state actors, but also by private bodies and agencies. Recall too that whilst here such measures are presented in regard to serving public health ends, regulators may act to achieve alternative agendas. We will now note how some of these tensions are framed and understood, before considering in greater depth three case studies from contemporary debates in public health theory and practice.

9.2.3 Tensions in governance for public health

In introducing different critical approaches to understanding regulation, Morgan and Yeung highlight three clusters of analytical perspectives.[21] These indicate the distinct kinds of regulator that we might find and the potential for contrasting – and conflicting – motivations and effects in their achieving social coordination. First, we have theories that present regulators as serving common goals: the legislator and public policy-makers, aiming to serve the common good. Second, there are approaches that seek to explain regulatory interests by reference to competing private interests: governance here is understood as a phenomenon that can be understood as the result of the 'gaming' of competing self-interested actors. Third, scholarly approaches to regulation might look to systems: this can include looking at different sectors within different systems, such as, for example, public health. The overarching analytical tensions implicit in the existence of these different critical perspectives find parallels in tensions inherent to public health policy-making and practice. When approaching questions regarding the advancing or limiting of public health agendas, we need to consider the potential role and impact of different actors, be they private or public.

Public health practitioners will be all too familiar with the political realities of attempts to protect and promote population health. Even if, in a broad sense, law and public policy may be born of a commitment to serve the common good, in reality, there are clashes within government about where priorities should lie. In the context of public health law, this is perhaps particularly so. With public health governance roles delegated to local authorities (LAs) in England (see also Chapters 3 and 7), political battles will vary in their form and outcome across the country. According to the statutory position outlined below, LAs have a broad discretion, given their assessments of 'local need and other factors', to determine how best to approach wide-ranging issues, such as governance of tobacco, alcohol, nutrition and exercise, workplace health and safety, child health, and behaviour and lifestyle.[22] Different voices will be raised around the policy-making tables, and their respective strengths will be relative both to dominant (party) political perspectives and to the relative power of different stakeholders. Within the public health literature, we find a great deal of purchase in the call for a 'Health in All Policies' approach: a mantra that demands that, across sectors, health impacts be considered and properly attended to (see also Chapters 3, 4, and 7).[23] However, just as health advocacy may feature in policy discussions, so will advocacy in support of other, sometimes contradictory, interests. Public health theory and practice are both well informed by concerns for public health ethics and the mission advanced by pioneers such as Winslow (see Chapter 1). But they require also an acceptance of political realism.[24]

---

21 Morgan and Yeung (n 4), chapter 2.
22 National Health Service Act 2006, s. 2B. See also NHS, *Public Health Supplement to the NHS Constitution* (2015) 7, <www.gov.uk/government/uploads/system/uploads/attachment_data/file/473475/NHS_Constitution-PublicHealthSupp.pdf> accessed 5 April 2016.
23 See World Health Organization, *Health in All Policies: Training Manual* (Geneva: WHO 2015).
24 Coggon (n 17); Though not directly about public health, see also Raymond Geuss, *Philosophy and Real Politics* (Princeton: Princeton University Press 2008).

When considering governance – whether at the level of hard law, as the upshot of privately instituted measures that have population health impacts (e.g. where a supermarket sells very cheap alcohol), or somewhere in between these two sorts of activity – we need to be alive to tensions between the matters that drive different actors, be they public or private. We also, from legal, political, and ethical perspectives, need to keep an eye on questions of justification, accountability, and the potential (or otherwise) for restraint. For example, can we hold fast food franchises to the same standards of accountability as public bodies or have the same expectations of what interests they serve? If not, what follows in terms of public health and governance? Nationally and locally, the place of public health alongside other concerns requires consideration. Of necessity, tensions will arise. These will relate to questions such as the mandate different governance actors have (are they acting rightfully?), their responsibilities (what obligations do they owe and to whom?), value judgments regarding substantive questions (what should be the priority in a given situation?), and questions of how to achieve given ends (is a potential intervention actually a viable mode of regulation in a particular instance?). In critiquing private actors, observers will also look to the validity of strategies that might be employed: for example, if manufacturers of 'unhealthy' products for consumption sponsor health-promoting activities, such as sporting events, does their support represent a positive health intervention or one that leads to population-level harms to health?[25]

As well as these sorts of tensions, we need to approach the ideas explored below remembering that, in regard to English public health law, rightly or wrongly, a great deal of primacy is given to concerns for individual liberty and the capacity of private actors to serve common goals. The dominant political ideology puts a strong premium on individual choice and responsibility,[26] and the current economic context offers less fiscal support to public health agendas.[27] Through its 'cutting red tape programme', furthermore, the Government aims to promote economic growth by reducing constraints on business.[28] Trust, furthermore, is placed in commercial and other private actors to serve the common good.[29] As such, it is necessary to consider how public policy measures might be conceived to advance public health ends but also to question whether and how these are adequate as responses to the challenges of twenty-first-century public health. In any system, soft law measures will be used. Students of, and actors in, public health law need to understand practically when such measures are most appropriate and do well to consider, too, when and why politically such measures may be suboptimal but the only viable form of governance. We thus move in the next section to consider the political freedoms and obligations of individuals and corporate actors and what might be viewed as their governance roles. Section 9.4 goes on to look at regulatory approaches that public agencies might take where public health ends are considered desirable but where hard legal interventions are unavailable or inadequate to serve them and where self-regulation alone, at least from a public health perspective, seems not to be working.

---

25 Consider, for example, the analysis in Jonathan Gornall, 'World Cup 2014: Festival of Football or Alcohol' (2014) 348 British Medical Journal g3772.

26 Jesse Norman, The Big Society (Buckingham: University of Buckingham Press 2010).

27 A £200 million cut was made to the public health budget in 2015/16: see Department of Health, Local Authority Public Health Allocations 2015/16: In-Year Savings (London: DoH 2015).

28 See Cabinet Office, <https://cutting-red-tape.cabinetoffice.gov.uk/> accessed 5 April 2016.

29 See HM Government (n 15) and further the discussion below.

9.3 Individual responsibility, self-regulation, and public health

This section looks to non-governmentally exercised public health responsibilities. Our first case study here relates to private individuals. This allows us to examine further (see also Chapter 5) the tensions between paternalistic, collectivist public health goals of improved population health and individual freedoms to make decisions, including ones that are unhealthy. Dominant norms in English law and political ideology represent concerns for safeguarding welfare but also a strong commitment to personal liberty as a highly prized value.[30] Within political and philosophical literatures, as in public debates (consider e.g. the debates on smoking legislation), paternalistic interventions are treated as especially controversial (see also chapter 6): adults, it is argued, know their own best interests and should be free to live as they choose. In regard to public health, we find commitments to personal liberty and personal responsibility to be particularly strongly voiced, with allusions to nanny-statism arising in the face of proposed agendas and policies.[31]

The big-picture political discourses alluded to in the previous paragraph should also be contextualised alongside the extensive bioethical literature on the idea of individual responsibility for health. A general theme within this discourse holds that whilst we might find, for a range of reasons, that people have *moral* obligations to protect their own health, it is hard to justify the imposition of hard legal obligations to do so.[32] In short, even if we wished that people would take better care of their health, it does not follow that we could find justification to compel them to do so (see Chapter 2). The Nuffield Council accordingly claims to espouse the principle that law and policy-makers should 'not attempt to coerce adults to lead healthy lives'.[33] As the preceding chapters have shown, there are in reality many instances where law forces healthy choices. Furthermore, we would suggest that, at least in principle, it must be acceptable in some instances for hard legal measures to be used to advance public health ends (including on the terms of the Nuffield Council). However, we would also accept the subtler claim that *generally* it will be wrong, according to dominant political ideologies, for the state to coerce adults to lead healthy lives. Does this mean that generally adults bear no political responsibility to safeguard their health? In other words, is there no political aspect to an individual responsibility for health?

Taking the case study of individuals' responsibilities as expressed in the NHS *Constitution for England*, these questions can be explored in the Government's representations of our responsibilities for health. The Constitution provides an example of a political measure designed to encourage individuals to behave in a way that is conducive to better population health outcomes. But, simultaneously, it betrays the relative weakness of the obligations that are asserted: whilst the Constitution purports to make individuals responsible for their health, it also assumes a general social responsibility for health that reflects equal rights to all, regardless of their health-affecting choices.[34]

---

30 Although reasonable disagreement exists over what might be considered the predominant political morality, consider in particular the influence and relevance of John Stuart Mill, *On Liberty* (Edward Alexander (ed), first published 1859, Peterborough, Ontario: Broadview 1999).

31 For example, whilst we saw above (n 16) that the Nuffield Council's report was seen as too 'liberty friendly' by Dawson and Verweij, it got a contrasting reception in *The Times*: David Rose, 'No to the Nanny State, but Yes to Telling Us All What to Do through "Stewardship"', *The Times* (13 November 2007); David Rose, 'Higher Alcohol Tax and No Smoking at Home – Beware of the New Nanny State', *The Times* (13 November 2007).

32 Margaret Brazier, 'Do No Harm – Do Patients Have Responsibilities Too?' (2006) 65 *Cambridge Law Journal* 397.

33 Nuffield Council on Bioethics (n 16), 26.

34 See also Harald Schmidt, 'Patients' Charters and Health Responsibilities' (2007) 335 *British Medical Journal* 1187.

9.3.1 Case study 1: Individuals' public health responsibilities

Within medical and health care law, analysis of individuals' responsibilities for health can generally be seen as constructed around narrowly conceived bioethical conceptions of autonomy.[35] Although such paradigms have been challenged,[36] the idea of the *patient* as a person who should be free from unwanted interference is explicable: the fields of biomedical ethics[37] and medical law[38] were established in response to a health care system wherein deference to professionals predominated and protections of patients' rights were limited. Developments in these areas of study and practice may therefore be characterised as founded on liberal concerns to allow adults with decision-making capacity to decide for themselves how they should live their lives: in John Harris's phrase, medico-legal protections of patients' autonomy 'enables the individual "to make her life her own"'.[39] As we have seen in Chapter 5, patients' rights in the law of battery afford general protection against interference. And, as suggested in the previous paragraph, from ethical perspectives, it is often hard to find politically acceptable justifications for paternalistic interventions on persons who do not consent.

The pre-eminence of rules and norms protecting people's right to live as they choose presents challenges within, but also beyond, the health care system, extending into the other spheres of public health activity. One of the foundational concerns for the field of public health ethics has been to question and potentially reset the paradigms that we use to analyse health-related responsibilities:[40] whilst self-regarding decisions of adults in a doctor–patient relationship might be best governed by reference to more ostensibly libertarian ideals regarding individual rights and freedom, in the context of health policy and population approaches, responsibilities for health might be more stringent. If we move beyond mere *health care* law and the dominant paradigms that inform it from medical ethics,[41] it is less obviously controversial to suggest that individual freedom will not always be the easiest value to justify protecting.[42] Indeed, as noted above, much of the discussion in this book has demonstrated areas where the law compels individuals and private actors to act in a way that serves public health ends regardless of individual choice.

Whilst a study in public health law therefore allows us to displace overly simplistic claims about the blanket illegitimacy of paternalistic regulation,[43] considerable challenges nevertheless arise in relation to this. As we saw in Chapter 2, it is relatively straightforward to justify regulating for safeguards against unreasonable harms to third parties. In some instances too – e.g. in relation to legislation compelling the use of seatbelts – laws have been generally accepted as legitimately safeguarding the individual's own health.[44] However, as explained in Chapter 1 and exemplified throughout this text, the contemporary public health agenda does not just aim to promote health through eradication of harm and disease; it also looks to do so by eradicating or minimising *risks* or *indicators* of *potential* disease. A person who

---

35 See e.g. Brazier (n 32).
36 See John Coggon, 'Would Responsible Medical Lawyers Lose Their Patients?' (2010) 18 *Medical Law Review* 541.
37 E.g. John Harris, *The Value of Life* (London: Routledge 1985).
38 E.g. Ian Kennedy, *Treat Me Right: Essays in Medical Law and Ethics* (Oxford: Clarendon Press 1991).
39 John Harris, 'Consent and End of Life Decisions' (2003) 29 *Journal of Medical Ethics* 10. The philosophical bedrock of this position is contestable but can be well traced to ideas expressed in Mill (n 30).
40 Angus Dawson and Marcel Verweij, 'Public Health Ethics: A Manifesto' (2008) 1 *Public Health Ethics* 1.
41 See Kenneth Veitch, *The Jurisdiction of Medical Law* (Aldershot: Ashgate 2007).
42 Coggon (n 17).
43 Lawrence Gostin and Kieran Gostin, 'A Broader Liberty: J.S. Mill, Paternalism and the Public's Health' (2009) 123 *Public Health* 214.
44 See also Coggon (n 17), chapter 10.

is obese, for example, is at higher risk of suffering conditions including heart disease and type-2 diabetes. Yet obesity itself is not a disease. Thus, whilst there may be both individual and population-level reasons to reduce levels of obesity, interfering with a person's freedom to a live as she chooses, in response to her obesity (or indeed her risk of becoming obese), is controversial: we are seeking to direct people to guard against a risk of being at risk.

In light of these ethical and political considerations, we therefore consider a flagship policy document – the NHS Constitution for England[45] – that purports to direct individuals' health-affecting lifestyle choices, with a view to achieving better individual and population health. Notably, this Constitution addresses individuals, health professionals (both within the NHS and LAs), and the government. When considering these different audiences, consider how individuals in their private capacity are possessed of different sorts of obligations as compared with professional and public actors. How, if at all, can the Constitution serve as a document that regulates population-level problems by impacting individual risk factors? Let us begin by seeing how the document itself presents its scope and authority:

> **This Constitution** establishes the **principles** and **values** of the NHS in England. It sets out **rights** to which patients, public and staff are entitled, and **pledges** which the NHS is committed to achieve, together with **responsibilities**, which the public, patients and staff owe to one another to ensure that the NHS operates fairly and effectively. The Secretary of State for Health, all NHS bodies, private and voluntary sector providers supplying NHS services, and local authorities in the exercise of their public health functions are required by law to take account of this Constitution in their decisions and actions.[46]

The first two sentences apply to all 'stakeholders': the rights and responsibilities of patients, public, and staff are all mentioned. Note immediately, however, how the final sentence, in referring to a legal obligation 'to take account of this Constitution in their decisions and actions', only applies to public authorities and actors (private or public) providing health services. Patients, and the public generally, do not fall within this ambit: as the NHS Constitution is, in essence, public law, the legal obligations within it do not fall upon individuals (see further: Chapter 7). Accordingly, whilst individuals are addressed by the Constitution, they do not have any legal reason to be aware of it, less still to respect it. Given this already relatively weak beginning, let us consider how it addresses questions that are relevant in the context of public health.[47]

Section 3 of the Constitution addresses 'patients and the public'. It begins by spelling out rights: these refer to hard legal rights, such as rights to access health care that is free at the point of delivery, rights not to suffer unlawful discrimination, and the right:

> [T]o expect your NHS to assess the health requirements of your community and to commission and put in place the services to meet those needs as considered necessary, and in the case of public health services commissioned by local authorities, to take steps to improve the health of the local community.[48]

---

45 Department of Health, The NHS Constitution (London: DoH 2015).
46 ibid, 2 (emphases in original).
47 The Constitution also spells out the 'principles that guide the NHS' and 'NHS values'.
48 Department of Health (n 45), 7.

Following five pages outlining these and a great array of further legally supported rights, there is a single page entitled 'Patients and the public – your responsibilities'. The title is followed by the statement that: 'The NHS belongs to all of us. There are things that we can all do for ourselves and for one another to help it work effectively, and to ensure resources are used responsibly'.[49] Unlike the rights, which can be traced back to sources of legal authority, these responsibilities are simply stipulated, each one following a polite 'please'. (This contrasts too with the section on 'staff responsibilities', which also in fact present legal duties.)[50] The unenforceable responsibilities that are listed cover questions in relation to responsibilities within the health care system (e.g. 'Please keep appointments, or cancel within reasonable time')[51] but also present two in particular that are drafted with public health considerations in mind: first, 'Please recognise that you can make a significant contribution to your own, and your family's, good health and wellbeing, and take personal responsibility for it' and, second, 'Please participate in important public health programmes such as vaccination'.

The British Medical Association, and scholars involved in health policy, have supported the idea that the NHS Constitution should include people's health responsibilities.[52] And there may be important value in expressing responsibilities that people, in the ideal, would hold and honour. However, we might question what effect, if any, the Constitution has on people's decision-making: remember that the characterisation of regulation given above included the criterion that behaviour is modified by the governance tool. The contrast in the weight of patients' and the public's responsibilities with the weight of the patient rights or the staff and government responsibilities is striking. Whilst the legally supported rights and duties have a clear normative force, and offer redress where they are breached, it is not clear how 'real' the patient and public responsibilities are: will people who do not already consider the responsibilities to exist start to do so given their place in the NHS Constitution? It is hard to imagine how they will, given the lack of enforcement mechanisms – even ones that fall short of coercion – that go alongside the listed responsibilities. In other words, whilst the personal responsibilities are also somehow presented as political responsibilities, they are responsibilities that are backed up by no form of threat or sanction.

As such, when considering personal responsibilities for health, we might find that there is force in arguments in public health ethics for the mere existence of particular duties to safeguard our health. Equally, we may find force in arguments from public health and politics that people have social responsibilities to protect and promote their own health. However, there are questions that will be raised in relation to individuals' making health-promoting decisions for themselves on the basis of legally and politically toothless responsibilities that are expressed in documents such as the NHS Constitution, but which find little to underpin them beyond that. Inevitably, perhaps, we might conclude, when considering individuals' responsibility for public health ends, that in public health law there is limited mileage in considering either basic lists of personal responsibilities even where these are published in formal governmental instruments. Certainly, research into the effect (or otherwise) of

---

49 ibid, 11.
50 For a presentation and analysis explaining the relationships between existing legal rights and the NHS Constitution, see Judith Laing and Jean McHale (eds), Principles of Medical Law (4th edn., Oxford: Oxford University Press 2016) [1.73]–[1.83].
51 Department of Health (n 45), 12.
52 See Schmidt (n 34).

measures such as the NHS Constitution would be of value.[53] It is, we would suggest, emblematic of the status of individuals' political responsibilities for health.

From a practical perspective, the lack of a legal basis for individuals' public health responsibilities seems to present problems in a way that does not apply to (some) public actors and private organisations. Arguably, if public health problems are recognised and to be successfully addressed, a more or less radical decision has to be made at the state level: either a legal underpinning is given to more individual health responsibilities (but consider the political sensitivities that speak against this), or public policy-makers need to implement more and further regulatory interventions to steer people towards healthy decisions, perhaps in line with nudge theory (or something similar, but consider also the limitations that speak against that).[54] These matters are explored further in section 9.4, following a brief consideration of corporate responsibility and self-regulation.

9.3.2 Case study 2: Critical questions concerning corporate responsibility and public health

Corporations can have legal personality just as people do: in other words, they can be holders of legal rights and duties. Their activities will be motivated towards particular ends, for example, maximising profits or promoting a particular agenda. And, depending on their nature and size, they clearly can have significant social impacts, including on population health. Our *moral* concerns for corporations, and our political justifications for interfering with their decision-making, will differ from how these matters relate to people. But, as with people, there is fierce (and effective) political resistance from many quarters to state regulation of private actors, particularly within industry. Whilst a functioning free market requires enforceable rules and regulations (note e.g. the discussion of contract law in Chapter 5 and controls on trade through EU and international law, discussed in Chapter 8), the dominant – though not universally espoused – consensus in jurisdictions such as England and Wales is that, where it works, self-regulation is best. What is meant by 'works', of course, is the source of considerable controversy: as various commentators note, what works well for a business may not, for example, serve public health or even the common interest more generally understood.[55]

We raised above in this chapter and, in Chapter 3, how the previous and current governmental agendas represent an espousal of the regulatory roles and capacities of private actors. Founded on the proposals for reform of the health care system and public health governance, the current regulatory system has been developed on the basis of the proposals of then Secretary of State for Health, Andrew Lansley, outlined in the 2010 White Paper *Healthy Lives, Healthy People*.[56] As well as leading to the statutory reforms that led to public health responsibilities being transferred to LAs in England, this provided the foundations for the 'Responsibility Deal'.[57] The Responsibility Deal is premised on the idea that: 'Businesses must

---

53 Existing evidence suggests that public awareness of the NHS Constitution is low. See Department of Health, *Report on the Effect of the NHS Constitution* (London: Department of Health 2012), chapter 2; Patients Association, *Patient and Public Awareness of the NHS Constitution* (London: Patients Association 2014).

54 See also Robert Baldwin, 'From Regulation to Behaviour Change: Giving Nudge the Third Degree' (2014) 77 *Modern Law Review* 831.

55 Note that, whilst many works exist criticising private interests in the context of public health, there are also prominent defences of public health regulation in accordance with economic libertarianism: see especially Richard Epstein, 'In Defense of the "Old" Public Health' (2004) 69 *Brooklyn Law Review* 1421.

56 HM Government (n 15).

57 See Department of Health, *The Public Health Responsibility Deal* (London: Department of Health 2011).

take more responsibility for the impact of their practices on people's health and wellbeing'.[58] It was designed to include 'five networks on food, alcohol, physical activity, health at work and behaviour change'.[59] Although the future of the Responsibility Deal is, at the time of writing, still unclear, following the change of government in May 2015, it is instructive to outline its approach. It should be noted too that that Responsibility Deal, and similar policy approaches, share foundations with *corporate social responsibility*: a phenomenon defined by the European Commission as 'a concept whereby companies integrate social and environmental concerns in their business operations and in their interaction with their stakeholders on a voluntary basis'.[60] The Commission says on its website that:

> Companies can become socially responsible by:
>
> - following the law;
> - integrating social, environmental, ethical, consumer, and human rights concerns into their business strategy and operations.[61]

In presenting detail of its stance on how the Responsibility Deal would be approached, it becomes quickly evident that government places considerable trust in industry to assume a role in advancing health policy goals. The White Paper refers directly to the Nuffield Council's intervention ladder and indicates, furthermore, only a cautious commitment to hard measures by government to assure health promotion where industry fails:

> Working through our new Public Health Responsibility Deal, the Government will aim to base these approaches on voluntary agreements with business and other partners, rather than resorting to regulation or top-down lectures. However, if these partnership approaches fail to work, the Government will *consider the case* for 'moving up' the intervention ladder where necessary. For example, if voluntary commitments from business are not met after an agreed time period, we will *consider the case* for introducing change through regulation in the interests of people's health.[62]

In accordance with this approach, a large variety of partners signed up to the Responsibility Deal,[63] each committing to at least one pledge. The pledges are clustered under each of the five different networks of activity. Under Food, for example, they include pledges in relation to non-use of artificial trans fat, calorie reduction, and front-of-pack nutrition labelling.[64]

Non-industry partners signed up to the Responsibility Deal, including FPH. However, having already expressed concerns about the alcohol pledges,[65] FPH eventually withdrew from the Deal, based on concerns that government prioritised industry interests over population

---

58 HM Government (n 15), 25.
59 ibid, 8.
60 This definition emanates from the European Commission Green Paper, *Promoting a European Framework for Corporate Social Responsibility* (COM 2001) 366 final.
61 See European Commission, <www.ec.europa.eu/growth/industry/corporate-social-responsibility/index_en.htm> accessed 5 April 2016.
62 HM Government (n 15), 31 (emphases added). The presentation of ideas here is reflective of Ian Ayres and John Braithwaite's 'regulatory pyramid': see Ian Ayres and John Braithwaite, *Responsive Regulation: Transcending the Deregulation Debate* (Oxford: Oxford University Press 1992).
63 At the time of writing, there were 776 partners: see Department of Health, <https://responsibilitydeal.dh.gov.uk/partners/> accessed 5 April.
64 See Department of Health, <https://responsibilitydeal.dh.gov.uk/pledges/> accessed 5 April.
65 Faculty of Public Health, <www.fph.org.uk/uk_faculty_of_public_health_rejects_alcohol_pledges> accessed 5 April.

health improvement.[66] It is perhaps pertinent, therefore, to consider an example from pledges under the Responsibility Deal in relation to alcohol. Rather than subject signatories to legislation or directive public policy forcing them to act in particular ways, eleven alcohol pledges were agreed to.[67] Amongst these, retailers agreed in July 2014 to contribute to efforts to reduce alcohol-related harms by 'committing to the responsible display and promotion of alcohol in shops and supermarkets', and producers of alcoholic drinks pledged to stop selling 'super-strength' drinks in large cans.[68]

For groups such as FPH, measures such as those spelled out here do not go far enough. More burdensome interventions, such as the imposition of minimum pricing (see also the discussion in Chapter 8) are considered necessary if public health ends are to be served in relation to drinking. The Institute of Alcohol Studies, a charity whose 'core aim is to serve the public interest on public policy issues linked to alcohol' and which receives no funding from government or industry,[69] released a report in November 2015 entitled *Dead on Arrival? Evaluating the Public Health Responsibility Deal for Alcohol*.[70] The report is scathing of the effectiveness of the Responsibility Deal as a governance approach, suggesting that evidence in support of it is scant, support from public health bodies and academe is absent and that more effective measures have been overlooked. In its conclusion, it states:

> The Responsibility Deal has never been a genuine partnership, having been boycotted by almost every independent public health group. Many of their objections have been vindicated in the four years since. The RD has systematically focused on relatively ineffective interventions that are unlikely to reduce alcohol consumption. It has set up its pledges in ambiguous terms that resist assessment. The alcohol industry has obstructed rigorous evaluation of the RD, through the unreliability of its progress reports, and more damningly through its misconduct in the official evaluation process. Where independent evaluation has occurred . . . the industry has generally failed to show it has met its targets. And even when the industry has lived up to the letter of its pledges, it has sought to circumvent the spirit of the endeavour. All of this would be forgivable if the RD were a harmless sideshow. Yet it appears to have been the main element of the UK's alcohol strategy in recent years.

The Government, of course, presents the achievements under the Responsibility Deal in a contrastingly positive light.[71] In terms of public health outcomes, there are empirical questions to be addressed here, both on the effect of the voluntary arrangements and the comparable effect that would obtain in counterfactual situations (e.g. if minimum pricing were implemented or the Responsibility Deal itself had not been).[72] As a focal point in our study of soft measures in public health law, it opens up the need to analyse questions concerning the interests and good faith of industry actors who are entrusted with public health governance roles. It also raises issues regarding the political acceptability of avoiding harder forms

---

66 Faculty of Public Health, <www.fph.org.uk/fph_withdraws_from_responsibility_deals> accessed 5 April.
67 (n 64).
68 See UK Government, <www.gov.uk/government/news/alcohol-industry-takes-action-to-tackle-irresponsible-drinking> accessed 5 April.
69 Institute of Alcohol Studies, <www.ias.org.uk/> accessed 5 April.
70 Available at <www.ias.org.uk/What-we-do/IAS-reports.aspx> accessed 5 April.
71 Department of Health, <https://responsibilitydeal.dh.gov.uk/category/alcohol-network/> accessed 5 April 2016.
72 See Cécile Knai, Mark Petticrew, Mary Alison Durand, Courtney Scott, Lesley James, Anushka Mehrotra, Elizabeth Eastmure, and Nicholas Mays, 'The Public Health Responsibility Deal: Has a Public-Private Partnership Brought about Action on Alcohol Reduction?' (2015) 110 *Addiction* 1217.

of regulatory control. However, before reaching conclusions on this, it is important also to consider how such measures might sit alongside alternative, complementary governmental interventions.

9.4 Public policy and public health

As seen above, the lowest rung on the Nuffield Council's intervention ladder asks public agencies with public health responsibilities simply to do nothing or monitor the situation. For reasons already explored, born of both real politics and more philosophical concerns about protecting individual and commercial freedom, sometimes all that a public authority can do is nothing, even if this is in some sense regrettable. People have rights to make unwise decisions, and societies are governed according to concerns beyond public health: for example, an optimally healthy economy may be a political end that is pursued even it is not fully compatible with an optimally healthy populace. However, as the intervention ladder reminds us, just because hard legal measures are inappropriate or otherwise unfeasible, it does not follow that governmental interventions cannot be directed to altering the social conditions: where public health ends are sought, softer means are available to provide conditions in which people can be healthy. In this final substantive section of the chapter, we therefore consider public modes of governance that are found beyond, albeit that sometimes they derive their authority from, hard law.

As with the different legal measures and approaches explored elsewhere in this book, a great range of case studies could be chosen under the heading of public policy and public health. As we have seen, in England, responsibility for a wide divergence of public health problems has been delegated to the governance of LAs to address at their discretion (see also Chapter 7). Section 2B(1) of the National Health Service Act 2006 provides that 'Each local authority must take such steps as it considers appropriate for improving the health of the people in its area'. As well as affording scope for prioritising locally, the Act also invites LAs to address problems using a range of measures that sit below coercion on the intervention ladder. Section 2B(3) states that the steps that LAs might use include:

(a) providing information and advice;

(b) providing services or facilities designed to promote healthy living (whether by helping individuals to address behaviour that is detrimental to health or in any other way);

(c) providing services or facilities for the prevention, diagnosis, or treatment of illness;

(d) providing financial incentives to encourage individuals to adopt healthier lifestyles;

(e) providing assistance (including financial assistance) to help individuals to minimise any risks to health arising from their accommodation or environment;

(f) providing or participating in the provision of training for persons working or seeking to work in the field of health improvement;

(g) making available the services of any person or any facilities.

Considering these public health responsibilities and the above discussion of potential regulatory approaches, this section looks at how LAs might consider policy-making in public health. Given its centrality to public discourse on public health ethics and law, we do so with particular reference to nudge theory and the way it has impacted on how LAs are encouraged to engage in public health regulation. At the end of this discussion, we highlight a practical example of a nudge technique that has been employed by LAs, but we first provide a general overview.

9.4.1 Case Study 3: Nudges (and hugs, shoves, and smacks . . .)

Richard Thaler and Cass Sunstein's book Nudge[73] builds on their earlier work explicating the idea of 'libertarian paternalism'[74] and presents what they characterise as 'a real Third Way – one that can break through some of the least tractable debates in contemporary democracies'.[75] The essence of libertarian paternalism is that, while governments (and private actors, such as employers and restaurants) have good reason to promote people's wellbeing, they also should be respectful of individual liberty. The argument goes that there is much to recommend an approach to paternalistic government interventions that advances the individual and collective good without denying freedom of choice. Through this idea, a mode of interventionism is advanced that purportedly achieves the ends of a welfare-directed state in a way that is compatible with neo-liberal ideals. Readers of Nudge, including policy-makers, are accordingly entreated to explore regulatory techniques that promote (say) public health ends, but without the need for coercive legislation.

To explain how this might be done, Thaler and Sunstein combine expertise in law, economics, behavioural science, and regulation to argue in favour of modes of governance that are developed in light of empirical understandings derived from behavioural economics. If, for example, we have evidence that people will tend simply to accept the default side dish when they order a steak, we could make the standard accompaniment be salad, whilst leaving open the option that it may come instead with chips. This way, the 'choice architecture' is conducive to better health outcomes, without infringing people's right to choose less healthy options. To be successful, therefore, a nudge approach relies (at least in theory) on scientific knowledge of how people react to their environment, so that regulators can develop the choice architecture so that the best choice is the easiest one made. Depending on the desired behaviour or outcome, nudge involves the use of a range of potential regulatory strategies. As a general characterisation of the concept, Thaler and Sunstein say that any given nudge:

> Alters people's behaviour in a predictable way without forbidding any options or significantly changing their economic incentives. To count as a mere nudge, the intervention must be easy and cheap to avoid. Nudges are not mandates. Putting the fruit at eye level counts as a nudge. Banning junk food does not.[76]

In addition to stimulating a vast industry in academic literature,[77] the idea of nudging has had a large effect politically and in the popular imagination.[78] In Jesse Norman's presentation of former Prime Minister David Cameron's government's political ideology, The Big Society, it is claimed that, philosophically, nudge theory is not an approach favoured by the government: whilst Nudge rests on a presumption that people are (at least in economic terms) flawed decision-makers, advocates for the big society suppose that persons are 'high energy bundles of capability

---

73 Thaler and Sunstein, Nudge (n 5).
74 Thaler and Sunstein, 'Libertarian Paternalism' (n 5).
75 Thaler and Sunstein, Nudge (n 5), 253–254.
76 ibid, 6.
77 For whatever its representative value, a Google Scholar search for "libertarian paternalism" in quotation marks, on 5 April 2016, produced 4,170 results. Google Scholar, on 5 April 2016, also suggested that the essay 'Libertarian Paternalism Is Not an Oxymoron' has been cited by 1,419 pieces.
78 See for example The BBC Radio 4 Programme, 'Nudge Theory in Practice', <www.bbc.co.uk/programmes/b01rg1hb> accessed 5 April 2016 (first broadcast 31 December 2013); 'The Rise of Nudge – The Unit Helping Politicians to Fathom Human Behaviour', The Guardian (23 July 2015); 'Four Money "Nudges" the Government Recently Used on You', The Telegraph (24 July 2015).

and potential'.[79] Nevertheless, the previous Conservative-led Coalition Government and the current Conservative regime clearly find something resonant in libertarian paternalism: in 2010, the Behavioural Insights Team – known colloquially as the 'Nudge Unit' – was established within the Cabinet Office and privatised in 2014 (albeit still receiving some of its funding from government).[80] Reflective of the impact of *Nudge*, Richard Thaler has been involved with the Unit since its inception and is currently on its Academic Advisory Panel. And, even since its privatisation, the Behavioural Insights Team continues to hold a high-profile advisory function in public policy.[81]

It is therefore pertinent to consider how LAs have been explicitly encouraged to adopt softer governance measures, framed by reference to nudges, in their public health regulation. A briefing document that captures this well, especially when read alongside section 2B of the NHS Act 2006, was produced by the Local Government Association (LGA) in 2013: *Changing behaviours in public health – to nudge or to shove?*[82] This was directed at councillors and officers and aimed to demonstrate how nudges might be used to advance public health agendas. Building both on the work of Thaler and Sunstein and on the Nuffield Council's intervention ladder, the document outlines different governance approaches that might be taken. It does so by underscoring the desirability of taking less invasive measures and, interestingly, advances a further regulatory taxonomy to those that we have already seen:

> Techniques like direct incentives, such as vouchers in return for healthy behaviour are being labelled hugs, while the tougher measures that restrict choice, like restricting takeaways from schools, are shoves. Bans, such as the restriction on smoking in public places, are simply known as smacks.[83]

The briefing goes on to say:

> In terms of behavioural change, it could be said local authorities have two roles: taking a strategic lead for their area, such as setting policy and evaluating schemes, as well as playing a part in organising the interventions along with other partners from the private, public and voluntary sectors.[84]

While the document acknowledges that much remains to be proven in terms of the efficacy of specific nudges, it casts them in favourable light.[85] This favour can also be found in analysis of recent public health reports. For example, in October 2015, Public Health England produced a report on the need for population-level action to reduce the intake of sugar.[86] The term 'nudging' is used in this only to characterise industry practices that encourage overconsumption, but the recommendations for governmental responses include measures that fit the definition of nudges, for example, raising public awareness in regard to diet.

---

79 Norman (n 26), 188.
80 For general information, see Behavioural Insights Team, <www.behaviouralinsights.co.uk> accessed 5 April 2016; see also Cabinet Office, *Applying Behavioural Insight to Health* (London: Cabinet Office 2010).
81 See Behavioural Insights Team, <www.behaviouralinsights.co.uk/about-us/> accessed 5 April 2016.
82 LGA (n 15).
83 ibid, 2.
84 ibid, 4.
85 ibid, 6.
86 Public Health England, *Sugar Reduction: The Evidence for Action* (London: Public Health England 2015).

To exemplify what the LGA advocates in terms of nudging, consider one of the case studies that it uses.[87] In 2005, Gateshead Council conducted research that showed that people's intake of salt was particularly high when buying fish and chips: a problem attributed to salt being delivered through flour shakers, which have many more holes than salt shakers do. In response, the Council paid for and distributed smaller salt shakers free of charge, so that people would add it in more moderated quantities. The intervention is triumphed by the LGA as 'demonstrating how a low-cost nudge can have an impact'. We might note that, in terms of population health, this impact will likely have been quite limited: taken on its own, the intervention would probably do little to improve population health significantly. This brief example both allows us, though, to capture the essence of the nudge and, through its limitations in terms of probable health impacts, to be clear how nudges can often only be effective if they are part of a wider scheme of interventions – to include, in the LGA's terms, 'shoves' as well as nudges.[88]

The high-profile presentation of nudges, and other regulatory mechanisms, demonstrates a sense of how LAs are being encouraged to respond to the public health problems that fall within their remit through varied means of governance. As well as seeking evidence bases for the efficacy of nudge approaches, questions may be asked from a public health perspective about the strength of a commitment to public health ends when measures such as the salt shaker example are given such prominence: on the one hand, it provides an illustration of an inventive governance approach; on the other hand, it arguably overemphasises relatively limited approaches at the cost of more effective ones.

In conclusion, from a public policy perspective, the use of governance measures beyond hard law is actively encouraged by existing statutory frameworks and the outputs of influential bodies including the LGA and PHE. When confronted with concerns about 'nanny state' interventions, within nudge, we potentially find a means of promoting health that enjoys political viability. We would stress, however, that neither the authors of *Nudge*, nor government, nor agencies such as PHE, suggest that soft regulatory approaches can exhaust governance for public health. For practical and political reasons, it is important to understand the scope for policy-making that uses less invasive interventions. Whilst public policy-makers will also need to rely on coercive measures, much activity will be more pragmatically achieved, and less politically contentious, when implementation encourages, rather than demands, healthier choices.

Dissenting voices within (and beyond) public health advance concerns that the efficacy of nudges is greatly limited: if we wish to address significant public health problems facing society – such as ill population health linked to poor diet – it is inadequate simply to be employing soft measures of governance. It is important therefore to consider both where it is proper to use a nudge and to consider whether the power or political attraction of nudges risks unacceptably weak overall responses to public health concerns: the prominence of nudges might overshadow the need, too, for harder intervention. Measures such as the salt shaker example form a part of an analysis in public health law. Conceptually, this sort of intervention must be understood, and for legal and political reasons, LAs and public health bodies do well to explore the potential of inventive and innovative modes of governance. But it is arguable that in the current political climate this potential is overstated. There is a risk that public health law as approached in this chapter will lead regulators to ignore the harder faces of public health law presented in the preceding four chapters. Of necessity, a

---

87 ibid, 8.
88 See also Karen Jochelson, *Nanny or Steward? The Role of Government in Public Health* (London: King's Fund 2005).

firm answer to this point is dependent on political perspectives and priorities. But, when making the assessment, recall the need to consider Hood and colleagues' three measures of a regulatory system: setting standards; gathering information or monitoring; and, crucially to the current discussion, modifying behaviour.

Chapter 9: Summary

- The study of public health law requires an understanding of non-legal forms of social coordination.
- Such analysis, consistently with analysis of hard laws that bear on public health, has to be undertaken in the context of political and social realities, e.g. accounting for a dominant political commitment to individual responsibility for health.
- The idea of *regulation* is not limited to legal measures and also reflects the function of public and private actors. As Christopher Hood, Henry Rothstein, and Robert Baldwin suggest, regulatory systems set standards, gather information or monitor the system, and have a role in modifying behaviours.
- Discussions of public health governance often refer to the Nuffield Council on Bioethics' 'Intervention Ladder', which distinguishes different modes of regulation by reference to the level of pressure that they apply: for example, it contrasts policies that might discourage 'unhealthy behaviours' (e.g. by raising taxes on cigarettes) and policies that compel or prohibit particular behaviours (e.g. a ban on smoking inside enclosed and substantially enclosed public spaces).
- Official policy puts a great emphasis on individual responsibility for health but provides less by way of political or legal means of forcing people to follow 'healthy lifestyles'.
- Official policy embraces corporate social responsibility and formally provides governance roles to private actors.
- Key public health actors, such as local authorities, are encouraged to develop policy in accordance with the 'nudge agenda'.

9.5 Further readings

Robert Baldwin, 'From Regulation to Behaviour Change: Giving Nudge the Third Degree' (2014) 77 *Modern Law Review* 831.

Julia Black, 'Decentring Regulation: Understanding the Role of Regulation and Self-Regulation in a "Post-Regulatory" World' (2001) 54 *Current Legal Problems* 103.

Bronwen Morgan and Karen Yeung, *An Introduction to Law and Regulation: Text and Materials* (Cambridge: Cambridge University Press 2003).

Nuffield Council on Bioethics, *Public Health: Ethical Issues* (London: Nuffield 2007), chapter 3.

Richard Thaler and Cass Sunstein, *Nudge: Improving Decisions about Health, Wealth, and Happiness* (London: Penguin 2009).

Part III

Concluding reflections

Chapter 10

Law and public health: Future directions

10.1 Introduction

This book has sought to delineate and explain the nature and scope of public health law, a field that Robyn Martin and Richard Coker described a decade ago as 'obscure and unbounded'.[1] As an area of inquiry, public health law perhaps continues to be a 'field without boundaries';[2] however, we hope that we have succeeded, through this book, to make it somewhat less obscure. To develop a clear map of the terrain, we sought, in Part I, first to explain our understanding of public health itself and then to outline related ethical questions and the history of law and public health. In Part II, we presented relevant legal approaches and their relationships to pertinent practical points regarding health and governance and exemplified their operation through a selection of specific examples. Of course, a book even several times the length of this one could not offer an exhaustive presentation of law, governance, and public health activities. Therefore, we have attempted to bring coherence to the field by advancing a definition of public health law and by describing the importance of its various features and implications (see especially Chapter 4).

The purpose of this final chapter is to present ideas about the future directions of study and practice in the field. Given the unruliness of public health law's domain, there is much uncharted territory left to explore. However, it is possible to perceive factors that will bear on the development of the field: that is, how the subject might continue to emerge and grow (or indeed narrow itself) as an area of specialisation. The following three sections consider both practical and academic influences that will impact on how matters develop. First, we look at how public health will have to adapt to changes in social and political norms. Second, we consider the impact of globalisation on the field. And, finally, we close with reflections on public health law as a field of academic inquiry, considering scholarly approaches that might arise, and the contributions that studies in public health law can bring to policy and practice.

---

1 Robyn Martin and Richard Coker, 'Conclusion: Where Next?' (2006) 120 (Supplement 1) *Public Health* 81, 81.
2 John Coggon, *What Makes Health Public? A Critical Evaluation of Moral, Legal, and Political Claims in Public Health* (Cambridge: Cambridge University Press 2012), chapter 5.

10.2 Changing norms: how public health law must adapt in its wider contexts

This book is framed around a particular understanding of public health law (see Chapter 4), but there are two key points of focus in any legal study in public health. First, there are measures specifically designed to address public health concerns, such as those contained in the Health and Social Care Act 2012 (see especially Chapters 7 and 9). Second, and consistently with the 'Health in All Policies' approach outlined in Chapters 3 and 4, regulatory interventions that are not purposely designed or designated as 'public health laws', may nonetheless comprise governance measures that might serve or constrain public health agendas and practice.[3] As the historical analysis in Chapter 3 demonstrates, the development of public health law is necessarily contingent. Of course, contingency is a phenomenon familiar across legal studies: this is why scholars so frequently examine laws in their wider social, economic, professional, and political contexts. Nevertheless, public health law seems, perhaps, particularly susceptible to the broader context within which it exists. Theory and practice are circumscribed by questions concerning:

- *Public acceptability*: does a measure enjoy popular support, or does it represent a step too far, for example, because it is perceived as 'nannying'? (See especially Chapters 2, 6, and 9.)
- *Ethical acceptability*: would a policy or practice be consistent with professional and/or moral standards within public health ethics? (See Chapters 1 and 2.)
- *Political prioritisation*: does a specific public health concern 'trump' other governmental priorities, such as securing economic growth? (For different perspectives that might be brought to such questions, see Chapters 2, 3, and 7.)
- *Legal support and legal constraints*: do legal rules, principles, and practices provide a basis for a public health activity or constrain its implementation? (See Chapters 5–9.)
- *Political, legal, and professional willingness*: even if a law mandates a particular practice, such as vaccination, will the law be followed or enforced in practice? (See e.g. the discussion of this matter in Chapter 3.)
- *Economic viability*: are there adequate resources to promote specific public health agendas? (Consider matters raised about public decision-making in Chapters 7 and 9.)
- *Appropriate governance approaches*: given different public, ethical, political, legal, professional, and economic concerns, what is an appropriate governance approach in any given instance? Building on the other points in the current list (and see also Chapter 4), this includes exploration of questions such as:

  o Should harder or softer modes of governance be employed? There will be considerations here of efficacy, political and social acceptability, and practicality (e.g. is it feasible to legislate in a timely way, or is a 'softer' regulatory measure easier to devise?).
  o Should measures be devised locally, regionally, nationally, or supranationally?
  o Are private or non-governmental stakeholders better positioned to act than public authorities?
  o What, if any, resources, and resource constraints, are there?

---

3 cf Martin and Coker (n 1); see also John Harrington, 'Commentary on "Legal Foundations of Public Health Law and Its Role in Meeting Future Challenges"' (2006) 120 (Supplement 1) *Public Health* 14.

o   What, if any, legal mandates or constraints are there?

o   What scientific evidence and standards of evidence support the approach?

In this book, we have sought to offer a framework that will assist in attempts to respond to these crucial, broad-ranging questions and concerns. Both the study and the practice of public health law require a capacity satisfactorily to address challenges that are not limited to pure legal analysis: social, political, economic, ethical, and professional understandings are essential. Only then is it possible to engage fully in debates on, and advance agendas concerning, specific matters such as alcohol regulation, pandemic planning, and/or sound occupational health.

It follows that there is a need to sharpen the focus on multi- and interdisciplinarity. Chapter 1 explains how inherently multidisciplinary the field of public health itself is. And, in practice, the variety of disciplinary approaches is reflected in a cross-sectoral approach to governance, most starkly represented in the idea of 'Health in All Policies' (see Chapters 3 and 4). With a concern, too, for non-legal forms of governance – including the regulatory roles of private and non-governmental actors – advances in public health law will require a participative agenda that reflects this wider approach (see Chapter 9). Those with legal expertise should be prepared to share their specialist knowledge and understanding, but in a multilateral process that entails that they also learn from experts and practitioners within other disciplines and sectors. Equally, and following Martin and Coker,[4] we have suggested that the field of public health law requires scholars and practitioners to draw from across different legal subjects: a public health lawyer cannot limit her approach just to one of the 'core' areas represented, respectively, in Chapters 5–8. Indeed, as explained in Chapter 9, the area cannot even limit itself to 'hard' legal approaches; questions of public policy and regulation, and even more diffuse aspects of governance such as the regulatory functions of private actors, are crucial to public health law's contribution to wider discourses on public health. These points will be further developed in section 10.4 below.

10.3 Public health and globalisation

A perhaps striking omission from the discussion in the previous section is the *global* context – not least because, as explained in Chapter 8, there are significant regional and international influences on public health law. However, given its discrete importance, the global context requires its own analysis. As is widely recognised, the impacts of economic globalisation have significant social repercussions within any given jurisdiction.[5] Nor should it be forgotten that the UK has substantial global influence, influence that extends to the legal domain. And, from a scholarly perspective, considerations of public health law and globalisation must be viewed against the backdrop of the emergence of the important, related subject of *global* (as opposed to *international*) health law.[6]

The impacts of globalisation are recognised in many areas of legal study, but public health law is particularly amenable to being shaped by this phenomenon. Within a national setting, we might consider how studies of globalisation and health expose inward-facing concerns, for example, how modern trends in migration and global travel affect disease transmission,[7] how the tobacco industry might exploit international laws to challenge domestic anti-smoking

---

4 Martin and Coker (n 1).
5 Lawrence Gostin, *Global Health Law* (Cambridge, MA: Harvard University Press 2014), chapter 2.
6 ibid, chapter 3.
7 ibid, chapter 12.

agendas,[8] or how globalisation facilitates trade in 'unhealthy products' that were previously difficult to access.[9] Equally, an outward-facing perspective can examine the UK's influence on global health[10] and scrutinise the responsibilities that it ought to assume, for example, in relation to contributing economic and other support to global health efforts;[11] how the UK impacts other nations' health infrastructure and population health outcomes by stimulating emigration of health care workers;[12] or how its consumption of natural resources contributes to global environmental harms, both directly (e.g. through carbon emissions) and indirectly (e.g. by enabling its participation in a global economic order whose imperatives make an international regulatory system that might lead to greater sustainability more difficult to achieve).[13] As before, much of the analysis here may require us to move beyond the state, for example, to explore the effect that UK-based (and regulated) corporations, such as those involved in manufacturing pharmaceuticals, foodstuffs, or alcohol products, might have upon the health of populations in various countries.[14]

With such issues in mind, it is interesting to examine further the role of law. Given the variety of profound impacts on broad populations – and, ultimately, one overall global population – one might wish for law to assist in assuring the capacity for social coordination to assure conditions for good health. This could be based on concerns for safeguarding national population health but also upon a desire to create a more equitable world, where avoidable disease and suffering are forestalled.[15] However, global health gives rise to distinctive concerns from a public health law perspective. Lawrence Gostin and Allyn Taylor characterise global health law as follows:

> Global health law is a field that encompasses the legal norms, processes, and institutions needed to create the conditions for people throughout the world to attain the highest possible level of physical and mental health. The field seeks to facilitate health-promoting behaviour among the key actors that significantly influence the public's health, including international organizations, governments, businesses, foundations, the media, and civil society. The mechanisms of global health law should stimulate investment in research and development, mobilize resources, set priorities, coordinate activities, monitor progress, create incentives, and enforce standards. Study and practice of the field should be guided by the overarching value of social justice, which requires equitable distribution of health services, particularly to benefit the world's poorest populations.[16]

---

8 ibid, chapter 7.
9 ibid, chapter 13.
10 For discussion of development of a methodology to evaluate such impacts, see Modi Mwatsama, Sidney Wong, Dena Ettehad, and Nicola Watt, 'Global Health Impacts of Policies: Lessons from the UK' (2014) 10 Globalization and Health 13.
11 See especially the remit and work of the Department for International Development, <www.gov.uk/government/ organisations/department-for-international-development/about> accessed 5 April 2016.
12 See Gostin (n 5), chapter 11; Department of Health, Code of Practice for the International Recruitment of Healthcare Professionals (London: Department of Health 2004).
13 For a collection of essays on climate change and public health, considered from ethical and policy perspectives, see Cheryl Cox MacPherson (ed), Climate Change and Health: Bioethical Insights into Values and Policy (New York: Springer 2016).
14 For a positive evaluation of the contribution made by the UK pharmaceutical sector, see All-Party Parliamentary Group on Global Health, The UK's Contribution to Health Globally – Benefiting the Country and the World (APPG on Global Health 2015), chapter 4. For a more negative analysis in a particular field, see e.g. Chris Holden, Kelley Lee, Anna Gilmore, Gary Fooks, and Nathaniel Wander, 'Trade Policy, Health and Corporate Influence: British American Tobacco and China's Accession to the World Health Organization' (2010) 40 International Journal of Health Services 421.
15 For analysis of these points, see John Coggon, 'Global Health, Law, and Ethics: Fragmented Sovereignty and the Limits of Universal Theory' in Michael Freeman, Sarah Hawkes and Belinda Bennett (eds), Law and Global Health (Oxford: Oxford University Press 2014) 369–385.
16 Lawrence Gostin and Allyn Taylor, 'Global Health Law: A Definition and Grand Challenges' (2008) 1 Public Health Ethics 53, 55. For a slightly different definition, see Gostin (n 5), 59–60.

While the relevant legal sources (especially, treaties) and subjects (especially, states) are pri-marily those that we analysed in Chapter 8, the pioneers of this emerging domain are at pains to emphasise that the existing framework of international law is likely to prove inef-fective in realising the value of social justice, which 'infuses the field'.[17] Gostin observes that the state-centredness of international law renders it inadequate to capture the 'creativity and resources' of other actors, including individuals, civil society organisations, and private corporations.[18] Further, he identifies weak enforceability and vague standards – factors that he acknowledges as 'endemic to international law' as a whole[19] – as being particularly prob-lematic in the health context, as witnessed by the contested nature and scope of the human right to health.[20]

As a nascent area of study and practice, global health law possesses both descriptive and normative dimensions. Descriptively, it seeks to capture developments that amount to 'chipping away at the classical notion of sovereignty' in the international arena,[21] such as the increasing emphasis on human rights, the growing involvement of non-state actors as 'partners' in global health funding and policies, and the enhanced coordinating role of the World Health Organization (evident in the two treaty regimes discussed in Chapter 8).[22] Normatively, it signals a concern that 'new models will be required to channel more con-structive and cooperative action to address one of the defining issues of our time – the health of the world's population'.[23] Consideration of possible forms that such 'new models' might take – as well as the impact (if any) that they might have upon domestic legal frameworks, including those in the UK – is a matter that seems likely to sit right at the forefront of the scholarly agenda in public health for some considerable time to come.[24]

10.4 Public health law: towards an established field of academic inquiry

Defining the nature and scope of the field of public health law remains an ongoing pro-cess. Debates about its foundational assumptions, rationales, methods, and approaches will continue.[25] Nevertheless, the area is now clearly recognised as an important field of study. Although Martin and Coker lamented in 2006 that 'British "Health Law" programmes at undergraduate and postgraduate level have addressed almost exclusively issues pertaining to the treatment of the individual patient',[26] and Syrett and Quick noted in 2009 that 'public

---

17 ibid, 60.

18 ibid, 62.

19 ibid, 64.

20 For discussion, see e.g. Brigit Toebes, The Right to Health as a Human Right in International Law (Antwerp: Intersentia 1999); Jonathan Wolff, The Human Right to Health (New York: W.W. Norton & Co. 2012); John Tobin, The Human Right to Health in International Law (Oxford: Oxford University Press 2012).

21 Gostin and Taylor (n 16), 61.

22 This should not be taken to imply an uncritical appraisal of the existing role, structure, or financing of the WHO: see e.g. Gostin (n 5), chapter 4.

23 Gostin and Taylor (n 16), 61.

24 One possibility that has been canvassed is a Framework Convention on Global Health, drawing upon the approach taken in the tobacco context (discussed in Chapter 8). See e.g. Gostin (n 5), 437–439; Michel Sidibé and Kent Buse, 'A Framework Convention on Global Health: A Catalyst for Justice' (2012) 90 Bulletin of the World Health Organization 870; Lawrence Gostin and Eric Friedman, 'Towards a Framework Convention on Global Health: A Transformative Agenda for Global Health Justice' (2013) 13 Yale Journal of Health Policy, Law and Ethics 1.

25 See e.g. Wendy Parmet, Populations, Public Health, and the Law (Washington: Georgetown University Press 2009); Coggon (n 2); Lawrence Gostin and Lindsay Wiley, Public Health Law: Power, Duty, Restraint (3rd edn., Berkeley: University of California Press 2016).

26 Martin and Coker (n 1), 81.

health law remains substantially neglected as a subject of academic study',[27] increasingly, university curricula now address public health ethics and law for students in law, public health, and other disciplines. This is thanks in no small part to the pioneering work and collaborations of scholars such as Martin and Coker in this country and the wider influence of international scholars including Gostin and others discussed in Chapter 4.

As public health law continues to mature, it will remain crucial to consider the questions of boundary, scope, and influence outlined in the previous sections and chapters. But it is also important to think about the field as a basis for teaching and research. What methods and approaches are appropriate? What should be covered in curricula and research agendas? How ought legal studies be placed in relation to other disciplines? In addressing such matters, it is useful to keep in mind the points of emphasis that we presented in Chapter 4 as fundamental to public health law. In that chapter, we advanced the idea that:

> Public health law is a field of study and practice that concerns those aspects of law, policy, and regulation that advance or place constraints upon the protection and promotion of health (howsoever understood) of within, between, and across populations

In explaining our rationale for this characterisation of the field, we highlighted some key characteristics, which have guided our approach to understanding public health law and which bear equally on ideas about the development of curricula and research agendas. To reiterate these briefly, those teaching public health law should take as their starting points that public health is itself a very broad field and that the intersections of law and governance span across a very wide spectrum of legal approaches and governmental sectors. Furthermore, as the focus lies with the stimulation of social coordination, rather than the development of a 'purist' account of the concept of law merely as a series of rules issued by authoritative institutions, analysis of the relative merits and effect of law in a public health context must embrace a diverse variety of regulatory measures, and the roles of private and non-governmental bodies, as well as of the state.

Of course, this presents a significant challenge for the future pedagogical evolution of the field. As Syrett and Quick have observed, teaching public health law demands a degree of polymathism that does not sit comfortably with the specialised nature of much contemporary academic practice, especially (though not exclusively) in law.[28] Practical measures, such as the development of physical and virtual networks for exchange and sharing of materials and curricula,[29] leveraging institutional support for establishment of cross-disciplinary courses, and the publication of texts (such as the present book) or online materials (such as blogs and working papers) with an interdisciplinary orientation, can alleviate some difficulties in this regard. However, the most crucial element is likely to be attitudinal: a willingness on the part of those who work in the field to cross disciplinary boundaries and a receptiveness to unfamiliar methodologies and forms of knowledge. In short, we need to recognise, as did J.S. Mill, that 'it is hardly possible to overestimate the value . . . of placing human beings

---

27 Keith Syrett and Oliver Quick, 'Pedagogical Promise and Problems: Teaching Public Health Law' (2009) 123 *Public Health* 222, 223.

28 ibid, 227.

29 For an example of such a network (connecting education in the geosciences with societal issues), see Carleton College, <http://serc.carleton.edu/integrate/index.html> accessed 5 April 2016. There is a US-based network on public health law, The Network for Public Health Law, <www.networkforphl.org/> accessed 5 April 2016: however, this focuses on connecting *practitioners* in public health and law, as distinct from education. The O'Neill Institute for National and Global Health Law, based at Georgetown University and directed by Lawrence Gostin <www.law.georgetown.edu/oneillinstitute/> accessed 5 April 2016, houses many useful resources but is not a network.

in contact with persons dissimilar to themselves, and with modes of thought and action unlike those with which they are familiar',[30] or as did the American jurist Oliver Wendell Holmes, that 'to be master of any branch of knowledge, you must master those which lie next to it; and thus to know anything you must know all'.[31]

Similar observations might be made about the development of a future interdisciplinary research agenda in public health that encompasses, but moves beyond, the legal approaches explored in this book. Transcending disciplinary (or even subdisciplinary) silos is not only demanding from an epistemological standpoint: it can also create internal institutional tensions. For example, it has been argued that this form of research is not always valued highly within the 'home' discipline, perhaps because other scholars do not fully comprehend it or because engagement with those working in other disciplines may necessitate some degree of simplification of ideas and methodologies that results in diminution of credibility for the scholar vis-a-vis her departmental peers.[32] There is also quantitative evidence that citation rates for interdisciplinary research are lower, which would seem to substantiate the existence of negative perceptions of this type.[33]

Whilst we acknowledge these challenges, our view is that they are significantly outweighed by the rewards that may be reaped by those willing to work across disciplinary borders. There are practical benefits for the individual researcher who chooses to do so: notably, support from research councils for this type of work, enhancing opportunities for obtaining funding.[34] There are intellectual benefits for her too, arising from a broadened and enriched understanding of concepts, theories, and methods[35] and more straightforwardly – but crucially, given the approach that we have taken in this book – in respect of the mere capacity to *comprehend* a field that is intrinsically situated within a social, economic, political, cultural, historical, and scientific context. There is also significant potential value to society. First, interdisciplinary research is acknowledged to be particularly effective in stimulating innovatory thinking.[36] And, second (but relatedly), problems of population health – perhaps especially those of a global nature to which allusion was made in the preceding section of this chapter – are inherently complex: indeed, they may be seen as 'wicked problems':[37] that is, those that are particularly resistant to resolution, at least in part because they are linked to other problems (for example, poor health status connects to social disadvantage). It is this

---

30 John Stuart Mill, *Principles of Political Economy with Some of Their Applications to Social Philosophy* (London: John W. Parker 1848), Book III, chapter 17: 14.

31 Oliver Wendell Holmes, Jr., *Speeches* (Boston: Little Brown & Co. 1934) 23.

32 For discussion of these and other barriers, see National Academies, *Facilitating Interdisciplinary Research* (Washington: National Academy Press 2005) 88–93; and further, Garry Brewer, 'The Challenges of Interdisciplinarity' (1999) 32 *Policy Sciences* 327.

33 Elsevier, *A Review of the UK's Interdisciplinary Research Using a Citation-Based Approach* (Bristol: HEFCE 2015) 3.

34 See e.g. Research Councils UK, *Memorandum from Research Councils UK in Response to the British Academy Call for Evidence on Interdisciplinarity* (2015), <www.rcuk.ac.uk/RCUK-prod/assets/documents/submissions/BAInterdiscipilinarity RCUKsubmission.pdf> accessed 5 April 2016.

35 See Diana Rhoten, 'Interdisciplinary Research: Trend or Transition' (2004) 5 *Items & Issues* 6, 9.

36 See e.g. National Academies (n 32), 35–39; Jorge Alves, Maria José Marques, Irina Saur, and Pedro Marques, 'Creativity and Innovation through Multidisciplinary and Multisectoral Cooperation' (2007) 16 *Creativity and Innovation Management* 27; Alan Blackwell, Lee Wilson, Charles Boulton, and John Knell, *Creating Value Across Boundaries: Maximising the Return from Interdisciplinary Innovation* (London: NESTA 2010).

37 See Horst Ritter and Melvin Webber, 'Dilemmas in a General Theory of Planning' (1973) 4 *Policy Sciences* 155. For a brief general discussion of the concept of 'wicked problems' in the context of health, see Ilona Kickbusch, 'Health in All Policies: The Evolution of the Concept of Horizontal Health Governance' in Ilona Kickbusch and John Buckett (eds), *Implementing Health in All Policies: Adelaide 2010* (Adelaide: Department of Health, Government of South Australia 2010) 11; and for a specific illustration, see Diane Finegood, 'The Complex Science of Obesity' in John Cawley (ed), *The Oxford Handbook of the Social Science of Obesity* (Oxford: Oxford University Press 2011) 208–236.

interconnectedness that creates the need and space for an interdisciplinary response of the type that we advocate here.[38] As Popper has argued:

> Disciplines are distinguished partly for historical reasons and reasons of administrative convenience (such as the organisation of teaching and appointments) and partly because the theories we construct to solve our problems have a tendency to grow into unified systems. But all this classification and distinction is a comparatively unimportant and superficial affair. *We are not students of some subject-matter but students of problems.* And problems may cut right across the borders of any subject-matter or discipline.[39]

10.5 Conclusion

We see law as an integral component of the holistic approach that is needed for those seeking to understand and respond to issues of population health in the twenty-first century, whether they are educators, researchers, practitioners, or policy-makers and whether in the UK or beyond. We indicated in Chapter 1 that one of the crucial components of understandings of public health is a concentration on social coordination, and the design and provision of organised community efforts that provide the conditions where people can be healthy.[40] Law and governance are crucial, if sometimes undervalued, tools in this regard, and there is a clear and essential contribution to be made by people with the sorts of critical and practical knowledge and understanding that this book has sought to advance. In short, public health policy and practice will be bolstered by a voice for public health ethics and law. It is our hope and ambition that this book will assist in significantly strengthening that voice.

---

38 See National Academies (n 32), 34–35; Roderick Lawrence, 'Beyond Disciplinary Confinement to Imaginative Transdiciplinarity' in Valerie Brown, John Harris and Jacqueline Russell (eds), *Tackling Wicked Problems: Through the Transdisciplinary Imagination* (London: Earthscan 2010) 16–30.

39 Karl Popper, *Conjectures and Refutations: The Growth of Scientific Knowledge* (London: Routledge Classics 2002) 88 (emphasis in original).

40 Charles-Edward Winslow, 'The Untilled Fields of Public Health' (1920) 51 (1306) *Science* 23.

Index

accountability of government 120
Ackerknecht, Erwin 38
actors, public health 56–9, 71, 73
administrative law 118–19
advocacy ethics 28–9
aide-mémoire 30
alcohol consumption 8, 147–8
Alcohol (Minimum Pricing) (Scotland) Act 2012 159; Responsibility Deal and 174–5
allocation of resources, public law as framework for 125–7
anthrax 115
Anti-Compulsory Vaccination League 42
Anti-Vaccination League 42
applied ethics 28
approach-led versus issue-focussed analysis of public health law 73–4
asbestos and mesothelioma 84–6
Asbestos Industry Regulations 1931 49
Atkin, Lord 83
autonomy 106, 130, 131
A v National Blood Authority 82

bacteriology 44
battery 81
Bayley, Thomas 43
behavioural economics 177
Bennett, Belinda 68–70
Bentham, Jeremy 39
Big Society, The 177
Bingham, Lord 85
bioterrorism 115–16
Brincat v Malta 136
British Medical Association 172
bubonic plague 37

Cameron, David 164, 177
Campbell, John 24

capacity-building 60, 121–5
Cecil, William 38
Chadwick, Edwin 39–40, 46, 51
Children Act 1989 87, 96
Children and Families Act 2014 52
Children and Young Persons (Protection from Tobacco Act) 1991 49
Children and Young Person's Act 1933 48
Children's Act 1908 48
choice architecture 177
Civil Contingencies Act 2004 108, 130
civil liberties 119
civil obligations: common law developments of negligence rules 81–6; private law as 78–81
Clarke MR, Lord 93
Clegg, Nick 164
clinical negligence 81
Coker, Richard 46–7, 67–8, 79, 80, 183, 187–8
common law 70–1; developments of negligence rules 81–6
communicable disease legislation 127–30; international regulations 153–5
Compensation Act 2006 86
Condliff 134
constitutional law 118
Consumer Protection Act 1987 82
consumer protection and public health 82–4
Consumer Rights Act 2015 78
contagion, criminalising of 108–10
contract and tort 78–81
Control of Asbestos Regulations 1969 49
corporate responsibility and public health 173–6
corporate social responsibility 174
Correa, Carlos 159
criminalisation 105–6

criminal justice system 104; public health
    as tool for 115–16
criminal law: aims, agendas, and
    relationship with public health 103–8;
    as competing or shared agenda with
    public health 101–3; criminalising
    behaviours that harm the public's health
    106–8; criminalising contagion 108–10;
    criminal sanctions in support of disease
    control measures 110–11; ensuring
    responsibility for one's own health
    and 112–14; liability for wrongful and
    harmful behaviour 103–5; road safety
    laws and 113–14
Crown Prosecution Service (CPS) 115

Dawson, Angus 32, 73, 165
Dead on Arrival? Evaluating the Public Health
    Responsibility Deal for Alcohol 175
decision making: child welfare and 88;
    private rights in the home and 90–4;
    regarding vaccinations 95–8; trivial
    versus more deeply held personal choices
    and 88–9
definition of public health law 17–18,
    65–6, 72
definitions of public health 9–13; shared
    themes and emphases 12–13
deliberation, ethical 30
Denning MR, Lord 126
deontic aspect to normativity 21–4
deontology 21–4
Department for Environment, Food and
    Rural Affairs (DEFRA) 115
descriptive claims 21
descriptive concepts in public health 8–9
Dhillon, Ibadat 155
Dicey, Albert Venn 128
Di Sarno v Italy 135
disease, states of 66
Diseases Prevention Act 1855 41
Doll, Richard 90
Donoghue v Stevenson 82–4
dualist theory 151
Duff, Antony 103

Ebola 15, 51, 154–5
Elefteriadis v Romania 135

Elizabeth I, Queen 38
Enhorn v Sweden 132, 133
Environmental Protection Act 1990 49, 80
epidemiology, forensic 115–16
Epstein, Richard 14–15, 17, 71
Equalities Act 2010 127
equality 23–4
ethical action guidance 30
ethical awareness 30
ethical deliberation 30
ethical justification 30, 31–2
ethics, public health 27–9; differences
    between theories, frameworks, and
    models in 33–5; frameworks 32–3;
    guidance and regulation 29–35; models
    33; normative theories in 31–2
European Centre for Disease Control 146
European Communities Act 1972 141
European Convention on Human Rights
    (ECHR) 89–90, 94, 111, 119, 132–3,
    151–2
European Court of Human Rights 133, 134,
    135
European Court of Justice 140
European Medicines Agency 146
European Social Charter 136
European Union law: alcohol regulation
    and 147–8; introduction to 139–41;
    obesity and 148–50; pandemics and
    146–7; public health activity 146–50;
    public health and 142–50; public health
    competence 142–6
European Union "Television without
    Frontiers" Directive 1991 49
evaluative aspect to normativity 21–4

Factory and Workshop Act 1901 49, 66
Faculty of Public Health (FPH) 5, 10–11,
    17, 161
Fairchild v Glenhaven Funeral Services Ltd 82, 84–6
family law, private law as 86–90
fault-based offences 104
Feinberg, Joel 113
Fidler, David 152, 154
Food and Drug Administration, US 134
Food Information for Consumers
    Regulation of 2011 149
forensic epidemiology 115–16

Framework Convention on Tobacco Control 155–7
frameworks, ethical 32–5; stewardship 34

Garrett, Jeremy 26
General Agreement on Tariffs and Trade 159
General Medical Council 81, 162
germ theory 44
globalisation 151, 152, 185–7
Goldberg, Daniel 21
Gostin, Lawrence 9, 28, 56, 60, 73, 78, 124; on conceptual shift 154; definition of public health law 69–70; on global health law 153, 186–7; on human rights law 130; on normative concepts 71–2; on public health governance 68–70
governance, public health 68–70, 162–8; by private organizations 164–5; regulatory interventions 165–7; tensions in 167–8
Grill, Kalle 32, 112
Grotius, Hugo 150

Hamlin, Christopher 44
hard law 70–1, 162
Harlow, Carol 120
harm principle 106, 114, 131
Health Act 2006 52, 71, 91–2
Health and Social Care Act 2008 52, 53, 128, 155
Health and Social Care Act 2012 184
Healthy Lives, Healthy People 173
helmet laws 89
herd immunity 95
Hervey, Tamara 148
history of public health legislation 37–56; origins 37–8; role of private and non-government actors in 55–6; twentieth century 43–50; twenty-first century revitalisation of 51–5; Victorian era 39–43
HIV/AIDS 50; criminalising transmission of 108–10
H1N1 pandemic 154
Hoffmann, Lord 85
Holland, Walter 48
Holmes, Oliver Wendell 189
Hood, Christopher 163

Human Rights Act 1998 92, 118, 119, 133, 134
human rights law 119, 130–6
Hume-Rothery, William 42

ideal theories 31–2
indicators of potential disease 170–1
individual responsibility and public health 169–76
individual rights 68, 134
inequality 23–4
infrastructure, public health 4, 9
International Court of Justice 151
International Health Regulations 54, 128, 133, 153–5
international law: communicable diseases and 153–5; international trade agreements and 157–9; introduction to 150–2; public health and 152–9; tobacco control and 155–7
intervention ladder 34–5, 165–7

Jehovah's Witness 87
Jenner, Edward 95
Jennings, Bruce 25, 26–7, 29
junk food 25
jurisdictional critique of public health 14, 16
justification, ethical 30, 31–2

Kaul, Inge 59
Keene LJ 93
Kurzer, Paulette 149

Lansley, Andrew 11, 173
Lewis, Jane 47
libertarian critique of public health 14–15
libertarian paternalism 177–80
liberty 106
lifestyle diseases 58
Local Government Act 1929 45, 46
Local Government and Public Involvement in Health Act 2007 123
Local Government Association 2013 178–9
Local Government Board Act 1871 45

Magnusson, Roger 55, 60; on public health governance 68–70
Marangopoulos Foundation for Human Rights v Greece 136

Marmot, Michael 7
Martin, Robyn 46–7, 49, 67–8, 73, 79,
    183; influence on public health law as
    academic field 187–8; on nuisances 80;
    on public health governance 68–70
McHale, Jean 149
Mental Capacity Act 2005 87
mesothelioma 84–6
miasmatism 39
Mill, John Stuart 33, 106, 114, 131
Ministry of Health Act 1919 45
models, ethics 33
monist theory 151
Morgan, Bronwen 163, 167
Moses LJ 93
motorcycle helmets 89

National Blood Authority 82
National Health Service (NHS) 44, 47,
    56; capacity-building function 122–3;
    as executive branch 57; individual
    responsibility and 171–3
National Health Service, A 47
National Health Service Act 1977 126
National Health Service Act 2006 123, 176
negligence: clinical 81; rules, common law
    developments of 81–6
"neighbour principle" 83
new public health (NPH) paradigm 51, 53
New Zealand Bill of Rights Act 1990 134
Nicholls, Lord 85
non-ideal theories 31–2
Norman, Jesse 177
normative claims 21
normative concepts in public health 8–9,
    21, 71–2; ethics and 31–2, 33–5;
    libertarian critique and 15
normativity 21–4
Nudge 177–80
nudge theory 162, 177–80
Nuffield Council on Bioethics 14, 33–4, 61,
    165–6, 169, 174, 178
nuisances, statutory 80
Nuisances Removal and Diseases Prevention
    Acts 1848 and 1849 41

obesity 15, 24, 58–9; food law and 148–50
objective of public health law 71–2

obligations, positive 135–6
Offences Against the Person Act 1861
    107, 108
Oh, Cecilia 159
Ottawa Charter of 1986 51

pandemics 146–7, 154
Parliamentary Sovereignty 92
paternalism: hard 112–13; libertarian
    177–80
Peace of Westphalia 150
personal choice and public health 90–4
philosophy: normativity 21–4; and public
    health 20–7; significance in public health
    law and practice 19–20; values and the
    task of 24–7
police powers 38, 39, 66, 110
Poor Law 45
Popper, Karl 190
population health and individual choice
    95–8
populations and institutions in public
    health approaches 5–7
positive obligations 135–6
Prevention of Damage by Pests Act 1949 48
prevention paradox 5, 95
privacy 89–90
private and non-government actors role in
    public health 55–6
private law 77–8; as civil obligations
    78–81; common law developments of
    negligence rules 81–6; as family law
    86–90; population health and individual
    choice 95–8; rights in the home and
    90–4
private rights in the home 90–4
Privy Council, England 38, 41
Product Liability Directive (EEC) 82
Protection of Children (Tobacco) Act
    1986 49
Protocol to Eliminate Illicit Trade in Tobacco
    Products 156–7
public health: actors 56–9, 71, 73;
    approaches 5–7; beyond legal
    approaches and 161–2; common law
    developments of negligence rules
    81–6; consumer protection and 82–4;
    corporate responsibility and 173–6;

criminal law and 101–16; definition and understanding the field 66–72; definition of public health law and 17–18; descriptive and normative in 8–9; ethics of, in, and for 27–9; European Union law, international law, and 139–59; globalisation and 151, 152, 185–7; governance 68–70, 162–8; hard paternalism and 112–13; human rights law and 119, 130–6; individual responsibility, self-regulation, and 169–76; information assets 60; infrastructure 4, 9; intervention ladder 34–5; key definitions of 9–13; personal choice and 90–4; philosophy and 20–7; prevention paradox 5; private law and 77–98; private rights in the home and 90–4; private sphere law and 77–8; public law and 117–36; public policy and 176–80; regulators 162–5; regulatory approaches and 59–61; safety at work and 84–6; scope of 13–16; social determinants of health and 4, 7; systems of 4; as tool for criminal justice 115–16
Public Health Act 1848 117
Public Health Act 1872 41
Public Health Act 1875 41
Public Health Act 1896 111
Public Health Act 1936 46, 48, 49
Public Health Act 1961 48
Public Health Act 1984 133
Public Health (Control of Disease) Act 1984 49–50, 108, 127, 155
Public Health (Recurring Nuisances) Act 1969 48
Public Health England (PHE) 5, 10, 13, 17, 53, 66, 179; jurisdictional critique and 16; mission statement 27–8
public health law 3–5; adapting in wider contexts 184–5; approach-led versus issue-focussed analysis of 73–4; definition of 17–18, 65–6, 72; as field of academic inquiry 187–90; framings of 67–72; hard versus soft 70–1, 162; history of 37–56; imposing constraints on public health activity 67–8; imposing duties on public officials 67; marginalisation of 43–50; origins of

37–8; prime objective of 71–2; public health actors and 56–9; public health governance and 68–70; significance of philosophy in 19–20; twenty-first century revitalisation of 51–5; Victorian era 39–43
Public Health Law: Power, Duty, Restraint 69
Public Health (Infectious Diseases) Regulations 1988 50
public law: capacity-building and 121–5; communicable disease legislation 127–30; defined 118; as framework for allocation of resources 125–7; functions of 120–1; human rights law as 119, 130–6; introduction to 117–21; nature and forms of 117–20; positive obligations 135–6; public health and constitutional and administrative 121–30
public policy and public health 176–80
public wrongs 103

Quick, Oliver 187–8
quid pro quo 78

Rawlings, Rick 120
regulatory approaches and public health 59–61
responsibility, individual 169–76
"Rethinking the Meaning of Public Health" 16
retribution 104
Reynolds, Christopher 60
road safety laws 113–14
Road Traffic Act 1988 89
Rose, Geoffrey 5, 6–7, 95
Rothstein, Mark 16
R v Konzani 109
R v Nottinghamshire Healthcare NHS Trust 93
R v Secretary of State for Social Services 126

safety at work and public health 84–6
Sanitary Acts 1866 and 1868 41
Sanitary Condition of the Labouring Population of Great Britain, The 40
sanitary movement 39–40
scope of public health 13–16
secondary legislation 71, 92
self-regulation and public health 169–76

sewers 37
sexually transmitted diseases,
    criminalisation of transmission of
    108–10
Shaw, Malcolm 152
"Sick Individuals and Sick Populations" 6
smallpox 50, 95
Smith, Richard 159
Smith, Thomas Southwood 39
smoking *see* tobacco use
social coordination through law 163–4
social determinants of health 4, 7
social security 79
soft law 70–1, 147–8
stewardship framework 34
Stewart, Susie 48
strict liability offences 104
sugar tax 125, 178
Sunstein, Cass 177
swine flu 51
Syrett, Keith 187–8

Tătar v Romania 135
Taylor, Allyn 155, 186
Television Act 1964 49
Thaler, Richard 177, 178
tobacco use 6, 24; bans 91–2; by children
    48–9; international law and 155–7;
    private rights in the home and 90–4;
    secondary regulations regarding 71,
    92–3
Tomkins, Adam 121
tort and contract 78–81
trade agreements, international 157–9
Trade-Related Aspects of Intellectual
    Property Rights (TRIPS) 158–9

Treaty of Lisbon 142
Treaty of Rome 150

UK Government 5, 11–12, 13
Unfair Contract Terms Act 1977 78
Upshur, Ross 32
upstream issues 9
utilitarianism 23

Vaccination Acts 1853, 1867, and 1871 41
vaccination programmes 41, 95–8
values: clarification 25; criminalisation,
    harm, and 105–6; integration 26;
    reassessment 26–7; and the task of
    philosophy 24–7
Verweij, Marcel 73, 165
Victorian era public health legislation
    39–43

Well-being of Future Generations (Wales)
    Act 2015 54, 124
Wiley, Lindsay 56, 60; definition of public
    health law 69–70
Winslow, Charles-Edward 9, 12, 16
World Health Assembly 153
World Health Organization (WHO) 5, 10,
    12, 13, 17, 66, 153, 187; International
    Health Regulations 54, 128, 133, 153–5;
    on smallpox eradication 50
World Trade Organization (WTO) 158–9
wrongful and harmful behaviour, liability
    for 103–5

Yeung, Karen 163, 167

Zika 51